Democracy's Midwife

Democracy's Midwife

An Education in Deliberation

Jack Crittenden

LEXINGTON BOOKS
Lanham • Boulder • New York • Oxford

LEXINGTON BOOKS

Published in the United States of America
by Lexington Books
4720 Boston Way, Lanham, Maryland 20706

12 Hid's Copse Road
Cumnor Hill, Oxford OX2 9JJ, England

British Library Cataloguing in Publication Information Available

Library of Congress Cataloging-in-Publication Data

Crittenden, Jack.
    Democracy's midwife : an education in deliberation / Jack Crittenden.
        p. cm.
    Includes bibliographical references and index.
    ISBN 0-7391-0328-8 (cloth : alk. paper) — ISBN 0-7391-0329-6 (pbk. : alk paper)
        1. Democracy 2. Autonomy. 3. Liberalism. I. Title.

    JC423 .C7486 2001
    321.8—dc21

                                                    2001038912

Printed in the United States of America

♾™ The paper used in this publication meets the minimum requirements of American
National Standard for Information Sciences—Permanence of Paper for Printed Library
Materials, ANSI/NISO Z39.48–1992.

To our sons, Jordan, Todd, and Devin:

Each came from Both and were different,
Yet beneath and above, All were the same;
For All, each is the future,
and for Both each is the greatest treasure.

Democracy has to be born anew every generation,

And education is its midwife.

—John Dewey

Contents

Acknowledgments   xi

Introduction   1

1 The Rise of Liberal Democracy   13

2 Liberalism and Autonomy   35

3 Autonomy and Deliberative Democracy   57

4 Civic Education   83

5 Critical Thinking: The Core across the Curriculum   119

6 Reform Schools: Implementing the Democratic Curriculum   157

Epilogue   207

Bibliography   223

Index   241

About the Author   249

Acknowledgments

In researching and writing this book I happily confess to "gilt" by association. Three institutions with which I am, or have been, associated provided gold in the form of financial assistance. The National Academy of Education provided a Spencer Postdoctoral Fellowship, enabling me to devote two consecutive spring semesters to research and writing; the Spencer Foundation provided a small grant that funded another semester of research; and Arizona State University, the College of Arts and Sciences, and the Department of Political Science granted me a sabbatical semester, also devoted to research and writing.

The remaining associations are personal rather than institutional, and the "gifts" provided by them, while never financial, despite my repeated requests, were always and in every case more than a simple gilding. Those who read the earliest drafts of this book and read it now will see the substantial changes in it, all due to their helpful suggestions. Among those subjected to such early readings, presumably against their wills, were students in some of my graduate seminars. I would especially like to thank Katherine Philippakis, Tara Lennon, Michael Morrell, David Thomason, Debi Campbell, Dan McDermott, Mary Sigler, and Jerry Duff for their various comments—scathing, sardonic, and even complimentary—on various chapters. I would also like to thank two undergraduates for their comments: David Purcell and Cindy Wasnesky.

My good fortune is to have two theory colleagues who are also friends. I thank Rich Dagger and Avital Simhony not only for their comments on the manuscript, which both read more than once, but also for their encouragement. Had I been wiser and more patient, I would have taken more of their suggestions. Gordon Wood graciously gave his time to a virtual stranger to read and comment on chapter 1, and John Geer read and commented on an early chapter on school choice, which, alas, failed to make the final cut. I would like to say that that was due to John's advice, but that would be to give him too much credit. The focus of the book began to take form in seemingly innocuous conversations with Sara Monoson and Al Damico, both of whom thought that we were meeting just to have coffee. To both I say thanks for leaving the tips, pecuniary and intellectual. My colleague Pat Kenney, who never read the text, offered advice anyway as well as sympathetic encouragement, while adroitly hiding his true feelings.

As always, two people deserve special thanks for their patient listening and careful reading. My great friend Ken Wilber wisely advised against some of my grandiose claims on behalf of autonomy. This was not the first, nor will it be the last, time that he has saved me from embarrassment. My wife, Pat, with whom I have the deepest association that two human beings can establish, remains the finest editor whom I have known and, to add to my good fortune, have experienced. Any flaws in the writing, grammar, syntax, and structure of this book are no fault of hers but lie solely in the depths of my intransigence.

Finally, since at the center of this book is a theory about democratic education, I kept in the back of my mind throughout the research and writing what is deep in my heart: my love for our three sons, Jordan, Todd, and Devin. I dedicate this book to them and, given that, now wish I had made it better by taking more of Pat's advice.

Introduction

In *Beyond Individualism* (1992) I discussed the importance of individual autonomy in the context of liberalism and communitarianism. I did not discuss, however, how individuals become autonomous. That was the initial focus of the research that makes up this book.

But as often occurs in research, that focus took an unexpected turn, for I soon realized that although public education is the most suitable locus for preparing persons for autonomy, the state through public schools does not have the right to impose autonomy on its students. Preparing students for autonomy means, as the reader will see, teaching the skills of critical thinking, which makes up the core of what I call "an education in deliberation." To require students to turn those skills onto their own rules, roles, values, standards, and beliefs, which I take to be the core of autonomy, jeopardizes ways of life in which autonomy is not honored; indeed, in which autonomy is considered pernicious.

Therefore, I am proposing an education *for* autonomy, which is an education *in* deliberation. The change of prepositions is crucial and represents the fine line that I am drawing between autonomy and deliberation. For while an education in deliberation immerses students in and requires them to use the skills of deliberation, an education for autonomy prepares them for autonomous decision making without requiring them to be self-reflective, the hallmark of autonomy, in making those decisions. Such an education most certainly rules out having public officials—such as public school teachers—require students to question their own ways of life, no matter how nonautonomous those ways of life might be.

The state does have a right and a duty, however, to prepare its future citizens through public education for participation in our democratic system. Pundits, politicians, and citizens agree that we all want citizens who can make well-informed, independent, and thoughtful political judgments. Politics, after all, as Aristotle reminds us, is a matter of judgment, not proof, and the kind of judgment we want in liberal democracy is informed, deliberative judgment. An education in deliberation can prepare citizens for that.

But is that really the kind of education we need? Or want? Our democratic system does not really require such judgments; they are not necessary for participation. The representative democratic system gives citizens too few opportunities to exercise deliberation publicly, in ways that count. Critical thinking is essential to decision making, but not necessarily for selecting among candidates marketed like consumer products and limited by the rosters configured through our two predominant political parties. The power to deliberate formally with others before deciding for oneself how to vote on an issue is largely denied all citizens but those elected to represent our views.

The Founding Fathers, the inventors of the republic as a representative democracy, devised our democratic system to exclude citizens from participating directly in decision making. Democratic participation today focuses citizen involvement on voting in nominating primaries and in elections where the level and kind of education, insight, and deliberation are minimized. The intentions of the Founding Fathers for doing so were noble: the United States was to be a country of voter egalitarianism where no single vote, regardless of the voter's education or position or occupation, would count for any more than any other vote. But to achieve this equality the Founding Fathers reduced citizens to the lowest common denominator. That meant that each vote would not directly count for much.[1]

So why do we need, or want, citizens who can make deliberative judgments, when the very training in critical thinking and deliberation may lead them to question the scope and structure of our representative democracy? Are we all— pundits, politicians, and citizens—merely paying lip service to a kind of education that we really want reserved for an elite while the vast majority of students receive something else, something less?

Persons educated in deliberation who are then willing and able to turn the skills of critical thinking onto themselves and their roles as citizens may well question why our system does not ask them to use their abilities in self-government. That, too, is the essence of autonomy, and autonomous citizens may well ask themselves—and I think will ask themselves—why their exercise of autonomy should stop at the political border. Why should autonomy really count only in private? Why can't we as autonomous citizens rule ourselves by governing ourselves? Why isn't our democracy direct or at least direct more often?

Perhaps our democracy should be, or so I shall argue in this book. Both *democracy* and *autonomy* are actually verbs masquerading as nouns; that is, they are not something we have as much as they are something we do. Both are more process than substance, processes for making self-reflective, deliberative decisions, where the self in one case is the individual, and in the other the collectivity. So, autonomy pertains to individual and private matters, while democracy pertains to collective and public concerns. Yet the intimacy of the relationship between the skills involved in these two processes enables us to say that democracy is the public exercise and expression of autonomy.

To be truly self-ruling, the literal definition of autonomy, autonomous persons must take part in making those decisions that are important to their lives. Thus, for many, to be truly self-ruling they must also be self-governing, since

[margin, handwritten:] isn't autonomous citizenship an oxymoron?

[margin, handwritten:] odd definitions

our very identities are often constructed within political contexts. The call, therefore, must be for more participatory and deliberative forums within democracy. Such forums would fulfill both the needs of autonomous persons and the essential definition of democracy—"people power" or "people rule."

Of course, my position on this is not the only possible conclusion. In "The Disharmony of Democracy" Amy Gutmann concludes differently.[2] Although she understands autonomy to be "self-determination through deliberation," an understanding that I accept, and while she states that "[d]eliberative democracy is committed to expressing and supporting the autonomy of all persons in collective decision-making" (128), also a view that I endorse, she and I have quite different notions about what collective decision making entails. Autonomy on her understanding means that we as citizens should hold accountable our elected public officials. But if autonomy is, as she says, "the ability to shape our lives in accordance with well-considered judgments," and deliberative democracy is a politics in which "people collectively shape their own politics through persuasive argument" (141), why is there not more discussion on her part of participatory or direct democracy?

Perhaps Gutmann does not see autonomy as self-government strictly understood. But she does: "Autonomy . . . as self-government [is] the willingness and ability to shape one's private or public life through deliberation, informed reflection, evaluation, and persuasion that allies rhetoric to reason" (140). Autonomy is also the "ability to deliberate together on matters of public concern and to abide by the results of this deliberation" (140).

Should autonomy as self-government be limited to certain kinds of matters of public concern? On the contrary, "self-government," she says, "requires people [to] engage in deliberation in shaping the many dimensions of their lives, personal and political" (140). Indeed, she goes on, "[m]any of the most important . . . of our life choices are influenced and constrained by social context, over which political authority has the greatest control. If we are excluded from that authority, then we lack autonomy in an important dimension of our lives" (142). We cannot, in other words, be truly self-ruling if we cannot be self-governing.

Clearly, all of this is in keeping with my position. Yet where I see autonomy leading us toward more deliberative forums of direct democratic decision making, Gutmann sees autonomy as necessitating that each citizen have an equal share "in electing one's representatives and in holding them and other officials accountable" (143). What happened to collective deliberations in shaping the many dimensions of our lives? When do members of the electorate deliberate politically, and why would they or should they deliberate in a representative system that elects officials to pass legislation and make political decisions? In this system what are citizens to deliberate about?

Gutmann's response is that accountability should be our democratic goal, because direct decision making requires "continual and direct involvement in politics" (143). What's wrong with that? As Gutmann suggests and as I shall

[margin notes, handwritten]

criticism/ fear of Gutmann's other cite not

The answer is to avoid political infantalization, and the use of more opinion for wicked or shortsighted eda.

argue in this book, continual involvement is not *continuous* involvement, nor is it involvement always by the same people.

I agree with Gutmann that the complexity of some issues and the number of issues on which political decisions must be made and made quickly require a representative democratic system at all levels. So I am not advocating the abandonment of representative democracy, but rather a widening of deliberation among both representatives and citizens. Likewise, I agree that we need to hold elected officials accountable; at a minimum that is what deliberative democracy requires, and where we should begin. But "where collective deliberation is the only legitimate basis for making controversial decisions that are binding on us all" (149), why restrict the deliberations and the decision making to elected representatives? Instead, as Gutmann herself says and I shall argue, we need to have power over the dimensions of our lives to make decisions about those lives (152). That requires the introduction of some deliberative democratic forums.

Thus my thesis is straightforward: many persons who are self-ruling, or autonomous, will also want to be self-governing, or directly and deliberatively democratic. Not all autonomous persons will want to participate politically, and certainly not all of the time; some may autonomously choose not to do so. But many, perhaps most, and possibly all, will want to make those political decisions that affect their lives; they will not simply want representatives, however deliberative and accountable they may be, making those decisions for them. Therefore, if we are serious about leading autonomous lives and about the education that prepares our future citizens to make autonomous public choices, then we must also be serious about the possibilities for, and plausibility of, increasing deliberative democratic opportunities and creating an education in deliberation.

Persons who want to be autonomous, who want to be the authors and directors of their own lives, must learn to be self-reflective. That is, they must learn to step back reflectively from their own activities, thoughts, and even identities to examine them critically or introspectively. Hence, this self-reflection requires the ability to think critically and to take up the perspectives of others so as to assume a position outside one's own positions. Central to autonomy, therefore, are the skills of critical thinking and dialogue—both of which are encompassed by the term "deliberation." An education in deliberation would be to develop those skills without requiring the students to use them self-reflectively; that is, without requiring them to call into question, as part of the mandatory curriculum, their own ways of life or deeply held beliefs.

To effect such deliberation at all levels of public schooling, the curriculum would consist of teaching the skills of critical thinking through writing and exercising those skills through democratic decision making within the schools. Each school would represent a community of students, teachers, administrators, and staff, and each would be operated democratically, to the extent that that is feasible. Each school would be a microdemocracy, not simply teaching the lessons of democratic participation, cooperation, and deliberation, but also putting those lessons into practice. In short, the community would deliberate about and decide real issues, those that affect some of the quotidian operations of the schools.

Ironically, if our schools did offer a real education in deliberation, the effect might well be to encourage protest: our students, our future citizens, armed with the skills of deliberation and schooled in the practice of democratic decision making, might then demand a political system in which, more and more, they could put those skills to use; in which, that is, they could be both self-ruled and self-governing. Such a political act would also be an autonomous act, as citizens would turn their skills of reflection onto their own public lives and would examine their roles as democratic citizens. This is precisely why I advocate an education in deliberation; such an education is both a propaedeutic to, and a form of, political activism to engender greater and greater deliberative democratic opportunities.

Could an education in deliberation be subversive, as citizens armed with this education come to challenge our representative democratic system? They might well want, and demand, to change the system so to better project their autonomy into the political sphere where decisions are made that affect their lives but that are currently beyond their power or influence.

But an education in deliberation need not be democracy's executioner, as if subversion required representative democracy's demise. Deliberative democracy is not just rule by the people, but deliberative rule by the people. The preliminary step, to reprise Gutmann's position, is to push for more deliberation within representative democracy. The argument behind this is that those in decision-making positions would make those decisions deliberatively—that is, thoughtfully. Thus, the idea behind deliberative democracy—some direct deliberative decision making by citizens, which I advocate—is that citizens will make decisions thoughtfully, and those decisions will reflect the thoughtfulness that went into making them.

Education in deliberation, therefore, to paraphrase John Dewey, is deliberative democracy's midwife, helping to bring forth new, but ancient, democratic forms. I am not arguing for populism, for a direct deliberative democracy over a representative system. Instead, I am arguing for more formal deliberative opportunities for our citizens, so that we have a mixed republic of representative and direct democratic forums, all of which ought to be deliberative. Such forums would serve the function that John Stuart Mill envisioned for the Parliamentary office of the Committee of Grievances or Congress of Opinions: where positions and opinions would be spoken

in the face of opponents, to be tested by adverse controversy; where those in whose opinion is overruled, feel satisfied that it is heard, and set aside not by a mere act of will, but for what are thought superior reasons . . . where every interest and shade of opinion in the country can have its cause even passionately pleaded . . . can compel [others] to listen, and either comply, or state clearly why they do not. (1972, 259)

Thus, through my research, I have arrived at four central conclusions, which I argue for in the text: (1) the state has no right to demand that students exercise autonomy in public schools, yet the state can and should teach the skills of critical thinking through an education in deliberation; (2) citizens educated in deliberation who want to exercise full autonomy might well find that self-ruling is limited, and thus insufficient, because it does not include self-governing—that is, does not include at least some direct democratic decision making; (3) our representative system ought to include more opportunities for direct democracy, though the system cannot be entirely composed of direct democratic processes; and (4) any democratic process, direct or representative, needs to be deliberative to make certain that citizens exercise the critical thinking skills at the core of autonomy. The chapters that include the arguments used to arrive at these conclusions are laid out in the following way.

Should we involve citizens in direct democratic decision making, regardless of how deliberative the process? From the outset the Framers of our Constitution sought to exclude the people from exercising direct democratic decision-making. They did so for two primary reasons: they thought that the people were unvirtuous—and thus not fit to govern—and that the new nation was too vast. Chapter 1 contrasts two competing democratic visions extant around the Founding. One is Madison's idea of a republican framework for governing the nation, a system in which representation came to be seen not as a "democratical" element in a mixed constitution, but as the basis of an entire democratic political system;[3] the other, Jefferson's vision of the "two hooks of the republic"—ward democracy and democratic education. We know which vision won out, and it led to the rise of a particular kind of liberal democracy, which is the foundation for our contemporary democratic system. The result, at the Founding and now, is a system in which the political arena seems of secondary importance to citizens, most of whom were and are all too willing to turn over res publica to elected representatives.

To liberals, then, the private side of life became paramount, and autonomy—the control of one's life—was a value central only to private life. In chapter 2 I take up the meaning of autonomy, especially for liberalism. By examining the social nature of autonomy, the requirement that autonomous persons engage in dialogue, or deliberation with others, about their self-reflective decisions, positions, and actions, we can come to see that autonomy is a value that can lead us back into the public or political realm in the name of self-ruling or self-government.

Another important issue taken up in this chapter is whether the liberal state is really neutral or is instead promoting a kind of culture that in turn promotes liberal democratic values. The answer to that question turns on whether we see those values as constituting a specific culture or whether we see them as serving as the very ground necessary for establishing some kind of culture meaningful to those involved.

Deliberative democratic participation is essential, I argue, to persons who wish to be self-governing; who wish, that is, to be fully autonomous. Chapter 3 discusses what deliberation entails within the context of a more participatory democratic system. I look in depth at the ideas on deliberation of James Fishkin and George Will, and I propose a "politics of initiative" as a counter to their views and as one prospective deliberative democratic "forum." Such a politics combines representative democracy with a form of direct and deliberative citizen participation in political decision making. It enables citizens to be fully autonomous, by extending its exercise into the public realm.

In chapter 4 I place an education in deliberation in the context of recent discussions of civic education among political theorists. In particular, I focus on Amy Gutmann's views of democratic education and compare and contrast those views with my own and with the views of William Galston. Within this discussion I include a section on my distinction between teaching deliberation or the skills of critical thinking, which I endorse, and teaching autonomy or the requirement for students to be critically self-reflective. This is a distinction that has animated, if not divided, theorists Stephen Macedo, Eamonn Callan, and Harry Brighouse in their most recent works, and I discuss those differences and my response to them in some detail.

In chapter 5 I turn directly to the central component of an education in deliberation: critical thinking. I begin by examining the current debates among three of the most prominent philosophers engaged in arguments about critical thinking: John McPeck, Harvey Siegel, and Richard Paul. The perspective I develop is that writing is the best way to teach students to think critically. In this context, writing could be seen as "the core across the curriculum"; that is, it is both a methodology suitable for exploring any content area, and thereby developing critical skills, and the core around which a coherent curriculum can be formed. Thus two prominent movements are married into one: core curricula and writing across the curriculum. Thus I argue that the best way to teach these skills is through teaching writing across an integrated curriculum, K-12.

In chapter 6 I explore how schools might implement the integrated curriculum into a setting that I call "democratic schools." The first half of the chapter deals with how to implement the core across the curriculum through a language arts program; the second half explores ways to bring democratic practices into our schools through various levels of, and experiences in, democratic discussions, democratic classrooms, and democratic assemblies. All involve practice in deliberative decision making that uses the skills of critical thinking and does so in a setting where actual decisions are made and where students' voices make a difference.

Chapter 6 involves more practicality than theory and abstraction. It looks at how schools might reform, or improve on, policies and practices. Teachers and administrators, I think, can learn much from political theorists about the need and the conditions for creating not only a democratic ethos, but also real participatory practices in our public schools. At the same time, political theorists have much to learn from teachers and educational theorists about how to structure dialogue and deliberation in small, and not-so-small, group settings. Therefore, political theory and practice are interactive, or ought to be, with educational theory and practice. Within the particular context of this book, that interaction takes place around the subject of deliberative democracy and democratic schools. Schools from elementary school through college need to reflect and practice the value of active, real democracy; democratic politics needs to look like or even mimic good classroom discussions.

However sublime and compelling the proposed reforms, they stand little chance of succeeding as long as we as a nation are reluctant to fund our schools equitably. This is the topic of the epilogue, which is more rhetorical than the chapters. The mission of public education is daunting: we are to provide to a student population diverse in background, beliefs, socioeconomic circumstance, ethnicity, race, motivation, and ambitions a quality education to the heights, or depths, of each student's variegated ability and desire. A requisite for activating, let alone achieving, this mission is equality, at least equality of democratic standards to which all can reasonably aspire and to which schools are held accountable.

Yet equality of standards is not enough. Also required is equality of conditions for which America, certainly at one time, was notable. (See Tocqueville's *Democracy in America.*) The specific conditions in this case are those to be found in our schools: adequate if not abundant resources, well trained and motivated teachers and principals, and students who feel safe in buildings that are safe. The last is the most difficult of all to meet, for the conditions inside our schools, however equitable the funding to all our schools, do not speak to the conditions surrounding them—the nature and shape of the families of students; the level of crime, violence, and abuse in the family and on the streets; the socioeconomic resources of the family and the neighborhood; the extremes of degradation and prejudice confronted daily by the students.

These are conditions ineluctably tied to the healthy, successful functioning of students, teachers, families, and schools. Addressing them is beyond the scope of this book, and so I settle for arguing that we need to make our public schools, and our inner-city schools in particular, safe havens in a hostile world. But the topic cannot be beyond the scope of our mental and physical resources as a nation and beyond our compassion as a people.

This work is a study in liberal idealism or ideal liberalism with autonomy as its foundation. It is therefore clear that this liberalism is not for everyone. There are reasonable comprehensive doctrines, in Rawls's parlance, that are nonautonomous. They can survive and even thrive in an autonomy-based liberal democracy. But, equally clearly, some values will be preferred to, and even favored over, others. Autonomy is one; liberty, equality, and tolerance are some others. The liberal state that I have in mind assumes that citizens, all citizens regardless of their particular persuasions, are autonomous. They are not required to be, not even when they take an active part in public deliberations. In those deliberations, however, those who do not value autonomy may be required to exercise autonomy in defense of their positions and interests. They may be asked to explain their position as it relates to their identity or to the way of life, or ways of life, of the community. Participation is, hence, risky. Yet there can be no foregone conclusion that one's participation will be challenged in this way or on every issue. Democracy is the exercise of autonomy in that those autonomous choices made or worked out privately are subjected to public scrutiny, and possible ratification through democratic procedures. That is one point of political deliberation. Another point, as already stated, is that the "self" examined in public deliberations is the collectivity itself, however it is defined.

Two additional points follow from these observations. First, the liberal state is not neutral but is only "softly" neutral. (See chapter 2.) Second, because it is not fully neutral, some ways of life or conceptions of the good are ruled out as inadmissible. This is what Stephen Macedo calls "liberalism with spine" (2000, 5, 85). Although nonautonomous good lives are not categorically among the inadmissible, some lives that might be autonomously chosen are. Cannibalism, for example, would be, as would be those ways of life that precluded teaching the skills of deliberation. But the list will be and ought to be short, for it is not autonomy that rules out some ways of life, but the fact that some ways of life violate the individual rights guaranteed in our liberal democracy. That is the point of the marriage of the two political terms, *liberal* and *democracy*. This ought to have no effect on those who wish to live traditional, or even nonautonomous, lives. Liberals will continue to honor pluralism, will continue to try to persuade the nonautonomous of the merits of autonomy, and will continue also to recognize the presence of, the need for, and even the value in resistance, as traditional ways of life strive to protect the integrity and continuation of those good lives.

In the pluralist world, therefore, liberalism requires autonomy in the same way that liberalism requires individual rights: "as a wall against oppressors" (Berlin, 1969, xlv). Liberalism needs that wall, though perhaps a low wall, as a boundary against the predations of overzealous democratic majorities, especially when majorities, or any group, seek to impose a specific conception of the good. Parents, too, can be oppressors when they seek to keep their children in what Eamonn Callan calls "ethical servility" (1997, s152ff). An education in deliberation will militate against that.

Liberals in my view will argue, or should, that the values they strive to perpetuate and protect do not so much constitute a good life but serve as the ground for establishing and living out a conception of the good life in the face of plural-ism. Rather than seeing only that choices among conflicting values cannot be avoided (Berlin, 1969, li), the liberal is one who sees the value in actively pursu-ing difference and making such choices self-reflectively in the full light of clash-ing values.

Students, as future citizens, need to learn to make such choices. Still, an edu-cation *for* autonomy but *in* deliberation does not force students to examine their own lives. Such an education seeks to create the conditions by which students might or might choose to do so.

Is this in itself too much of an ideal to strive for; in essence, to make every citizen through this civic education a deliberative citizen? Do we want our citi-zens to be like that? Could they all be like that? If all cannot, then do we do nothing through this education but prepare an elite and frustrate the majority?

Which citizens among us cannot attain this ideal? Can we identify them? Which would not benefit from striving for this ideal? As a society, we have not reached the point where we ask, "How many deliberate, and deliberative, think-ers do we need?" When we do reach that point, it will be the end. Or will it be the beginning?

An education in deliberation is important not only to persons seeking to au-thor their own private lives, but also to all democratic citizens who need to par-ticipate in those collective, or political, decisions that help make those lives good lives. It must be an education for all of our future citizens. But elitism dies hard; a steady elite always learns to operate, as well as to operate successfully within, the system. Some will always learn to learn on their own. Representative democracy gets by. So where is the urgency to transform education and our po-litical system?

There isn't any. This has all the earmarks of a conspiracy, as elites manipu-late the system to perpetuate and to protect their wealth and power. But there are no sinister forces behind the scenes manipulating the system. The heart of the problem is that too many of us have not been educated to think critically. There-fore we look for conspiracies and other easy scapegoats, when what is required is the hard work of slow reform of both education and democracy. What we need is an education in deliberation, the best way to educate all democrats.

Notes

1. Much was made in the presidential election of 2000 about having all the votes counted. This does not detract from the notion that while all votes should count, and be counted, no vote will make a difference. While the final official tally in Florida had Gov-ernor Bush winning the state by some 320 votes, we know that all of the votes were not counted. In a state in which over six million people voted, no single vote probabilistically will make a difference.

2. Lynn Sanders, if I may understate the case, also concludes differently. In "Against Deliberation" she lays out several potential problems should a polity move toward or into a deliberative democracy. She warns, for example, that deliberation can exacerbate problems of alienation and disaffection by disregarding in democratic deliberations those whom we know already have been systematically disadvantaged, no matter how reasonable their arguments. The disadvantaged might include women, minorities, the shy, and the inarticulate. The hope of my perspective is that an education in deliberation helps not only those who wish to raise issues, but also those who need to overcome prejudices in order to listen. See Sanders, 1997, especially 353.

3. Nathaniel Gorham of Massachusetts described this framework as "a perfectly democratical form of government" (Wood, 1980, 15).

1) does democratic deliberation really demand autonomy? If so, mustn't this either strain the meaning of autonomy? or make the practice of democracy far too demanding?

2) wouldn't autonomy often enough lead to the rejection of democratic politics, even if the best sort? would the autonomous individual recognize the need to subject herself to democratic scrutiny?

Chapter One

The Rise of Liberal Democracy

As is evident even to a superficial observer of our democratic system, there are too few deliberative opportunities available to citizens. Deliberating only within oneself in a democratic system is a poor substitute for collective deliberation on substantive public issues among democratic participants. When citizens weigh evidence for and against their positions, when they form and advance reasoned arguments on behalf of their interests or against the interests of others, when they consider divergent perspectives and compare or contrast them to their own, then will their decisions and judgments be grounded and even acute. Such deliberation enables citizens to arrive at binding decisions, even when the decision goes against their views, because participants have had a chance to articulate their interests and argue against those interests that they oppose. Thus can deliberation strengthen the legitimacy of democratic decisions and thereby improve democracy.

If all of this were so, if deliberation did improve public, and even private, decision making, and I shall present arguments throughout the text to show that it does, then it would seem that my task should be simply to lay out an education in deliberation to encourage, if not engender, this improvement. But neither democracy nor autonomy is without some controversy, as I suggested in the introduction.[1] Therefore, I need to give an account of both ideas. I discuss my view of our democratic system in this chapter and discuss the nature of autonomy in the next.

The willingness, and capacity, of citizens to deliberate politically has been at least since the ancient Greeks a central concern of political theorists and politicians, and no more so than during the founding of our own democratic republic. The founding announced the rise of two significant versions of democracy: representative democracy, which essentially focused citizen deliberation on candidates for office, and liberal democracy, which signifies the marriage of two previously unattached political, if not ideological, notions: private rights and popular rule.

The rise of liberal democracy provided the Founders with strong reinforcement of their idea that any effective democratic system would have to be a representative one. The Founding Fathers' argument on behalf of representation
made it difficult to institutionalize, as is also true today, direct and deliberative
democratic procedures. The basis of the argument was that citizens, by and
large, being unable to transcend their selfish interests, would be able to pursue
those interests outside of politics, while elected representatives attended to the
public good. Thus were both deliberation and autonomy relegated to the private
sphere, from which I hope through my argument to retrieve them. To understand
how they were so relegated, and how they can be retrieved, I begin my account
with the rise of representative democracy.

Representative Democracy: Personal Interests versus the Common Good

In *Federalist* 10 Madison criticized directly the idea of "pure" or direct democracy and argued that a republic, or what he called "the scheme of representation," was to be preferred. To the Federalists there were essentially two telling
reasons for the preference. First, the people were not fit to rule, or, in the most
positive light, were not as fit to rule as representatives; second, the great size of
the territory, and concomitantly the number of citizens living there, militated
against gathering all the people together to rule the nation directly (126).

In Madison's view the national government, having far fewer seats than the
state legislature and many more citizens electing the men who would occupy
those seats, would attract those of "fit character": "men who possessed the most
attractive merit and the most diffuse and established characters" (127). "If the
people of a state, New York, for example, had to select only ten men to the federal Congress in contrast to the sixty-six they elected to their state assembly,
they were more apt in the case of the few representatives in the national government to ignore obscure ordinary men with local reputations and elect those
who were well bred, well educated, and well known" (Wood, 1980, 13). With
only a few seats available, "only established social leaders would be elected by a
broad constituency. . . . The men who would sit in the federal legislature, because few in number and drawn from a broad electorate, would be 'the best men
in the country'" (*Federalist* 3, 95).

Madison, and the other Federalists, did not mean by the criticism that the
people were not smart or at least savvy, though there is evidence that the "aristocracy" of America, natural or otherwise, before the Revolution, looked down
on the common people.[2] The Federalists admitted that the people had insight. As
a collective unit citizens were capable, at times, of "cool and deliberate sense."
Yet they would also suffer lapses, falling temporarily into "errors and delusions"

(*Federalist* 63, 371). The election of these men of fit character would offset the uneven qualities, "the factious tempers . . . local prejudices, or . . . sinister designs" (*Federalist* 10, 126) of many in the electorate.

While the Federalists "remained confident that . . . the people would 'choose men of the first character for wisdom and integrity'" (Wood, 1980, 16-17), they remained doubtful that the people themselves could wield political power, for when the Federalists looked at the composition of the various state legislatures, they were frightened by what they saw. The "legislators were too often too much like the people they represented" (12). While they represented other white, property-owning males, these were citizens of the "nongentry" sort: rough-hewned, rural, less educated, and bearing parochial interests. They were "[s]pecious, interested designing men . . . men respectable neither for their property, their virtue, nor their abilities . . . men without reading, experience, or principle." (Quoted in Wood, 1972, 477.) These lawmakers seemed to favor heavily the pursuit of private and parochial interests. The national legislature, the Founders thought, could not have a similar composition.

What excluded the ordinary man from participating directly in governing the nation and should, in the Federalists' view, have kept them from governing the states was their lack of virtue; that is, their ability to think beyond, and to sacrifice, their own narrow self-interests for the good of the whole society. This view combined the Platonic criticism of democracy with the classical republican notion of virtue, a notion thought by the Founders to be essential to the preservation of American society. "The American people seemed incapable of the degree of virtue needed for republicanism. . . . [They] were too deeply involved in trade and moneymaking to think beyond [themselves] or their neighborhoods" (Wood, 1992a, 229). "It was their deep involvement . . . their very interestedness" in business or their occupation or trade that made them unsuitable. "They lacked the requisite . . . disinterested, cosmopolitan outlook." The message conveyed to the Federalists by the ordinary man was that "the object of government was the pursuit of private interests instead of the public good" (247).

Madison's men of fit character were members of the landed gentry or of the learned professions and were thought to be free of concerns for or about their pocketbooks. As a result, once in government, they would transcend parochial interests and thereby find the common good for the entire community. "The representatives of the people would not act as spokesmen for private and partial interests, but all would be 'disinterested men, who could have no interest of their own to seek.'"[3]

The realities of politics were not quite so straightforward. Unlike classical republicanism, which rested on the virtue of the citizenry, the American republic would be devised around the reality that the people were unvirtuous, that they were, in fact, motivated by self-interests. It was unrealistic, if not impossible, Madison argued in *Federalist* 10, to keep from government the voices clamoring for private or for factional interests. The genius of the American Constitution would be that faction would counteract faction so that no private or local interests would dominate the business of national government. There would be so many competing interests and parties in this "extended republic" that no single interest could dominate the majority. The threat of tyranny would be dissolved. And because the elected representatives would be men of virtue and fit character, the problem of the people ruling, and ruling on behalf of selfish interests, would also be solved. With special interests neutralizing themselves, "rational men [could] promote the public good" (Wood, 1980, 11). Thus the machinery of government would rest on the fact of competing interests, not on virtue or honor. Separating governmental powers, and not reliance on a commitment by representatives to the public interest, would handle the problems of corruption—that is, the focus of government on luxury and commercial interests.

Gordon Wood's interpretation emphasizes that Madison was not arguing that the public good would be made from the outcome of clashing factions, as pluralists such as Robert Dahl have argued in a contemporary context. Instead, Madison thought that factions, having neutralized one another, would create a political space in which representatives might both perceive and pursue the public good. When factions cancel out one another, there is little recourse but to seek, and no reason not to seek, the public good through virtuous action. Martin Diamond captured the sense of how interest cancellation worked: "As the extremes of selfishness are moderated the representative can become free to consider questions affecting the national interest on their merits. The jostling of innumerable interests gives him a margin of freedom from any single interest group. He is thereby enabled, to some extent, to pursue the national interest as he comes to see it in the instructive national arena" (1966, 75).

But if elected representatives were virtuous, why the need for factions to negate or offset factions? Why couldn't representatives simply transcend their partisan interests through their virtuous concern for the public good? Because, as Madison said in *Federalist* 51, men are not angels. In other words, Madison recognized that the virtuous representatives would themselves not be free from faction. They had, however, the virtue, the wisdom, and the character to recognize when factional pursuits were feckless.

Yet if faction offsets faction, why the need for men of virtue? The response is the same: men of fit character would recognize the futility of pursuing partisan interests once "opposite and rival interests" (*Federalist* 51) arose to oppose and negate those interests. At that point, the virtuous would seek some mutual course of action (Wood, 1972, 606). Men of fit character would rise above self-interest and deliberate on the common good; the unfit would simply continue to squabble.

The American version of republicanism shifted the meaning of democracy. Democracy was not only a new form of government, but was also "a new social order with new kinds of linkages holding people together" (Wood, 1992a, 232). Replacing the monarchical social hierarchy were democratic social bonds and attachments based on the idea of equality. "Once invoked, the idea of equality could not be stopped, and it tore through American society and culture with awesome power" (232), a phenomenon studied in mid-nineteenth-century America by Tocqueville.

In political terms this meant that the people were capable, and equally capable, of selecting for office men of integrity and merit. But they had capacity politically for very little else. The people were thought capable of exercising judgment singly on the assessment of a candidate's character. Thus the founders had to create a system of electoral politics that would tape the people's capacities but not stretch them beyond their limits. By the time of the Constitution there was little danger of that. In the Federalists' scheme, the limited number of national seats meant that only men of high reputation would be elected, since they were the ones who would stand out in their state legislatures.

The scheme was highly egalitarian: let every citizen's vote—aristocrat or democrat—count for one and no more than one. To offset any potential manic passions of the under- and uneducated, let only the "aristocrats," the "better sort," the "fit characters," run for office, while guaranteeing that all citizens— those white males with requisite property qualifications—would have equal votes.

The system of electing dignitaries worked. Representatives at the end of the eighteenth century continued to be "clusters of local notables" (Wiebe, 1995, 18). As Wiebe points out, "[t]he American Revolution actually enhanced the authority of the patriot elite who had directed it and who as a consequence could draw on large reservoirs of gratitude in public life" (20).

Once America defined its aristocracy in terms of property, however, and not in terms of heredity or rank, then money spoke in politics. The rich supplanted the well born as the foundation of our aristocracy, and in such a democratic society money was, and is, the great signifier of acceptable, even invidious, inequality.[4] "For many Americans the ability to make money . . . now became the only proper democratic means for distinguishing one man from another" (Wood, 1992a, 342). In America, which lacked Europe's inherited nobility, property had quickly become the criterion of merit and character. Citizens quickly latched onto the idea, in this egalitarian climate, that since any enterprising man could make money, any and every such man could become one of the better sort.[5]

There was, therefore, growing suspicion among many citizens of their representatives, both state and national. Those elected did not seem to be representing anyone but themselves or any interests but their own. In 1786 Benjamin Austin said that it was time that "the majority of persons should be cautioned against *acquiescing* in the sentiment of placing *implicit confidence* in their Representatives" (quoted in Wood, 1972, 257, 367; emphases in original).

"The Constitution," as Wood concludes, "was intrinsically an aristocratic document designed to check the democratic tendencies of the period" (1972, 513), and the democratic rhetoric used to bolster and justify the document emanated from the broad social egalitarianism following from the Revolution. Yet, in truth, through the Constitution the Federalists "offered the country an elitist theory of democracy" (517). There was, wrote Sidney Aronson, an "absence of real choice among candidates and programs." As Josiah Quincy asked of the South Carolina legislature around the time of the Founding: "Who do [our representatives] represent? . . . The laborer, the mechanic, the tradesman, the farmer, the husbandman or yeoman? No, the representatives are almost if not wholly rich planters."[6] If representatives had failed at the state level to promote any interests but their own, what would happen at the national level where the stakes and the possible take were even greater?

A great deal—indeed, everything—hinged on Madison's emphasis on the wisest, most prudent, most talented citizens being elected to Congress and then acting virtuously in a political climate that was at first blush, and perhaps through and through, unvirtuous. The Anti-Federalists pointed out that there was no "disinterested gentlemanly elite" able to do this; the gentry simply "had its own particular interests to promote" (Wood, 1992a, 255). If this were so, if there were no group of citizens better able than ordinary citizens to promote the public good, if all groups were only and always in pursuit of their own interests, then why shouldn't everyone, mechanic and gentleman alike, share in making the laws for society? Perhaps because the ways of making laws, the requirements of deliberation and compromise, were beyond the ken of the ordinary or average man. The best educated and the most experienced should rule, not because they were the most virtuous, but because they were apt to be the most thoughtful— that is, the most able to form and advance arguments for and against different positions and interests.

Indeed, it was the Senate, said Hamilton, that should do just that: use sedate and cool deliberation to offset the passions of the people. But, he conceded in *Federalist* 71, the people were also capable of right reason. It was simply that on occasion they would be carried away "by the wiles of parasites and sycophants, by the snares of the ambitious, the avaricious, [and by] the desperate" enactments that in more reflective moments the people would recognize as divisive or deleterious. Yet if the people at large were capable of such reflection, then why not establish democratic procedures or conditions that required such reflection, that would emphasize reason and discourage zealotry and emotional appeals?

As it turned out, the elections for the First Congress in 1788 proved the Anti-Federalists' point. The elections "revealed the practical realities of American democratic life that contradicted the Federalists' classical republican dreams of establishing a government led by disinterested educated gentlemen" (Wood, 1992a, 259). Men elected to that Congress pursued unbridled self-interests. So Federalists like Hamilton proposed "'corrupting' American society [by creating] new hierarchies of [commercial] interest and dependency that would substitute for the absence of virtue and the apparently weak republican adhesives existing in America" (263). In other words, in the absence of both a virtuous citizenry and virtuous representatives, the pursuit of self-interests, especially commercial interests, could proceed full bore. This form of perversity, this turning away from classical republican virtue toward commercial self-interest, the very enemy of virtue, as the means of binding people to their government, meant that the men of property came to see that they had a vested interest, a personal interest, in the prosperity of the government.[7]

The result of resting government on self-interest was, as Wood points out, that "the Federalists laid virtually no civic foundations for their scheme and weakened their ability to justify their peculiar disinterested leadership."[8] Peculiar indeed, for it turned out that "many of the Federalist leaders themselves . . . were deeply involved in speculative schemes and were busy making money out of their public connections and offices."[9]

In light of such developments, what could be the basis of an argument for representation? It was conceded that there were too many interests to have them all represented. It would have to be conceded also that virtual representation was out as well, for the virtuous gentry, now seen to be in pursuit of their own narrow self-interests, could hardly pretend to search for "the single common good," as Samuel Adams phrased it (Wood, 1972, 58), for the whole society.

The Madisonian model, however, might still hold. Those elected, seeing that their own interests were thwarted or offset by competing interests and thus could not be pursued, might therefore find that their only recourse was to think about what would be good for all. (The concept of governmental gridlock was obviously not yet in vogue.) Madison, and others, would not have to concede that there was no natural aristocracy capable of, if not continually reflecting, republican virtue. "[O]ut of the clashing and checking of this diversity . . . the public good, the true perfection of the whole, would somehow arise. The impulses and passions would so counteract each other . . . that reason adhering in the natural aristocracy would be able to assert itself and dominate" (Wood, 1972, 604-5).

Who constituted this natural aristocracy? How was the merit at its core to be determined and judged? By whom? Property was no longer the defining condition. Indeed, if property were just another interest, and if everyone were in pursuit of his own interests, why have representation at all? Clearly fitness as discussed by the Framers could no longer be the issue. If the system enabled reason to rise above countered impulses, passions, and narrow interests, then why could it not do so in a direct democracy rather than a representative one?

The question harkens back to 1776 when the radical democrats of Pennsylvania asked why there should be representation in any form. Interests, they argued, cannot be represented. Who knows one's interests better than the person himself? Such thinking led the New York mechanics to declare in June, 1776, that "every man out-of-doors 'is, or ought to be by inadmissible right, a co-legislator with all the other members of that community.' Only the people-at-large were 'the sole lawful legislature'" (Wood, 1972, 366). This seems especially true if government is nothing more than the pursuit of self-interest, and ordinary people know their own interests best. As revolutionary leader Nathan Chipman said, "[E]very man is, under the best regulated government, of right allowed to be the judge of his own interest, and an actor in his cause" (417). How can he be "an actor in his cause" when his sole responsibility is to vote for a representative? Why must he be, why should he be, *represented?*

Thomas Jefferson's Competing Democratic Vision

Thomas Jefferson proposed two strong remedies for, or two strong answers to, the Madisonian arguments that the nation was too vast and the citizens unfit for direct democracy. In fact, he thought so highly of these remedies that he referred to them as "the two hooks of the republic": education and ward democracy.[10]

Instead of seeing a republic as composed of elected representatives, Jefferson considered "a government [to be] republican in proportion as every member composing it has his equal voice in the direction of its concerns."[11] Jefferson seemed clearly out of step. The Framers saw that such a system of equal legislation would be suitable only for small communities. The size of the United States made it "impracticable *for all* to meet in One Assembly."[12]

But who said that all had to meet in one assembly? It was in the spirit of Pennsylvania's "little republics" that Jefferson proposed his "wards." A ward was the division of

> every county into hundreds [100 adult citizens or males], with a central school for all children, with a justice of the peace, a constable and a captain of militia. These officers, or some others within the hundred, should be a corporation to manage all its concerns, to take care of its roads, its poor, and its police by patrols. . . . Every hundred should elect one or two jurors to serve where requisite, and all other elections should be made in the hundreds separately, and the votes of all the hundreds be brought together. . . . These little republics would be the main strength of the great one.[13]

When Jefferson mentions "all other elections," he has in mind those political decisions that the 100 citizens would reach together.

> We of the United States, you know, are constitutionally and conscientiously democrats. We consider society as one of the natural wants with which man has Been created; that he has been endowed with faculties and qualities to effect its satisfaction by concurrence of others having the same want; that when, by the exercise of these faculties, he has procured a state of society, it is one of his acquisitions which he has a right to regulate and control, jointly indeed with all

those who have concurred in the procurement, whom he cannot exclude from its use or direction more than they him.[14]

Politics is part of the ordinary life, comments Jefferson, and thus does not require intelligence over a level of common sense. The citizens are competent to judge and decide. When a republic grows too large, divide it into wards. He wrote to Dupont de Nemours: "[B]oth of us act and think from the same motive, we both consider the people as our children, and love them with parental affection. But you love them as infants whom you are afraid to trust without nurses; and I as adults whom I freely leave to self-government" (1905, 489-90).

Since the common folks are competent judges of facts, claimed Jefferson, let the citizens rule. He imagined tiers of government, with the wards having an essential place:

> [T]he way to have good and safe government, is not to trust it all to one, but to divide it among the many, distributing to every one exactly the functions he is competent to. Let the national government be entrusted with the defence of the nation, and its foreign and federal relations; the State governments with the civil rights, laws, police, and administration of what concerns the State generally; the counties with the local concerns of the counties, and each ward direct the interests within itself. It is by dividing and subdividing these republics from the great national one down through all its subordinations, until it ends in the administration of every man's farm by himself; by placing under every one what his own eye may superintend, that all will be done for the best.[15]

The elementary republics of the wards, the county republics, the State republics, and the republic of the Union would form a gradation of authorities,

> Standing each on the basis of law, holding every one its delegated share of powers, and constituting truly a system of fundamental balances and checks for the government. Where every man is a sharer in the direction of his ward-republic, or of some of the higher ones, and feels that he is a participator in the government of affairs, not merely at an election one day in the year, but every day; when there shall not be a man in the State who will not be a member of some one of its councils, great or small, he will let the heart be torn out of his body sooner than his power be wrested from him by a Caesar or a Bonaparte. . . . As Cato, then, concluded every speech with the words, *"Carthago delenda est,"* so do I every opinion, with the injunction, "divide the counties into wards."[16]

Wards are for local administration and the resolution of local political problems. "Divide the counties into wards of such size as that every citizen can attend, when called on, and act in person. Ascribe to them the government of their wards in all things related to themselves exclusively." Such division thus makes "every citizen an acting member of the government."[17]

Americans were no strangers to Jefferson's wards. Indeed, the ward model was for many Americans right in their midst. "These wards, called townships in New England, are the vital principle of their governments, and have proved themselves the wisest invention ever devised by the wit of man of the perfect exercise of self-government, and for its preservation."[18]

Why, then, did Jefferson not propose that the wards participate in matters beyond their locale? Because, argued Jefferson, the people are not competent to judge matters beyond that scope. But why not?

"I am not among those who fear the people," Jefferson commented to Samuel Kercheval,[19] perhaps because Jefferson placed so much value in, and thus emphasis on, education. He thought that the people could be educated so as to be capable of even more democracy. The wards themselves were to be the sites not only of politics but also of education. Each ward would provide the base for public education: the captains would "muster" the ward and "put to their vote whether they will have a school established, and the most central and convenient place for it; get them to meet and build a log school-house; have a roll taken of the children who would attend it, and of those of them able to pay. . . . Should the company, by its vote, decide that it would have no school, let them remain without one."[20]

Jefferson did not imagine that citizens needed schooling to deal with the local issues that would arise in the wards. These issues were within the purview of any citizen, falling as they did within each citizen's daily life. But if we wish today to expand that exercise of citizen control to more self-government, to more tiers of government, then we must make sure that they are prepared to take on more control. To do so, we must, as Jefferson admonished, "inform the people's discretion."

This is one of Jefferson's most powerful and reverberant statements: the only "safe depository of the ultimate powers of the society" was "the people themselves; and if we think them not enlightened enough to exercise their control with a wholesome discretion, the remedy is not to take it from them, but to inform their discretion by education."[21]

Informing the citizens' discretion would enable them to practice more self-government by increasing their competence, which rested on making citizens themselves the depository of powers respecting themselves. What, exactly, is it to inform one's discretion? It is not just the transmission of knowledge, though that, too, is important.[22] It is close to the capacities associated with autonomy: "the power to decide or act according to one's own judgment." What would give rise to this power? Part of the answer is an education in thoughtfulness or critical thinking: learning how to form and advance arguments; to follow lines of reasoning; to differentiate opinions from facts, assumptions from evidence, and reasons from assertions; to engage in critical and creative thinking; and to find, and experiment with, various methods of articulating one's perspectives.[23] Another part of the answer lies in learning and practicing deliberation. This, as Jefferson knew and John Stuart Mill was to argue later, would be the experience of citizens in politics: their discussions of political issues could elevate their competence and confidence, perhaps in a way that nothing else would, so that they might take on broader political issues. "Forty years of experience in government," wrote Jefferson, "is worth a century of book-reading."[24]

Yet Jefferson overlooks discussion within ward politics. Even though the ward is the site for settling local political issues, it is not a setting for deliberation. It resembles, rather, Rousseau's democratic assemblies where the citizens, without deliberating among themselves, meet to inspect and vote their consciences.[25] "The mayor of every ward, on a question like the present, would call his ward together, take the simple yea or nay of its members, convey these to the county court . . . and the voice of the whole people would be thus fairly, fully, and peaceably expressed, discussed, and decided by the common reason of the society."[26]

The Rise of Liberal Democracy

Jefferson's concept of ward democracy was a way to overcome the problem of the vast republic; education to "inform discretion" was a way to elevate citizen competence. But it was the Madisonian vision that won out. Perhaps political deliberation would not have been any more developed under Jefferson's ward system than it is under our current liberal democracy, yet surely an opportunity to involve the people directly in political decision making was lost. With the Founders' representative system came not just a new understanding of democracy, but also "the beginnings of liberal democracy" (Wood, 1992a, 296), a kind of democratic politics based on the aggregation of interests: coalition building for the purposes of realizing one's own, or one's group's, interests.

Under this version of liberal democracy citizens had simply become too busy making money to focus on politics. Liberalism, now joined to democracy, meant that citizens could be represented by persons pursuing mutual interests, while the citizens themselves could turn away from politics and concentrate on their private, usually commercial but sometimes philanthropic, interests. Here the marriage of liberalism and democracy meant more than the protection of individual rights by limiting the scope of democratic majority decisions. It signaled a perversion of democracy, as liberalism enabled citizens *to turn away from,* if not abandon, politics altogether. Representatives could attend to public business and protect personal interests where need be, while others pursued their private interests in their own way.[27] Democracy, through this marriage with liberalism, had become a regime of producers and consumers, not of citizens.

So, while it was acknowledged that there were too many interests to have every interest represented in Congress, people also came to acknowledge that there was no possibility of finding, and therefore electing, disinterested men who would strive to attain the common good. Left to the citizens of this liberal democratic republic was the challenge of electing men who represented their interests over those men representing others' competing interests. If Congress cannot represent all interests, nor "no" interests, then let it represent *my* interests. The Federalists had to accept the idea of bringing one's own cause or interests into politics, for there was no explicit common good or public interest, and even if there had been, there was apparently no patrician disinterestedness to discern it.

Remaining constant amidst all of these changes in thinking, in rhetoric, and in American politics was what Madison called the "true distinction" of American government: "the total exclusion of the people in their collective capacity, from any share" in their government (*Federalist* 63, 373, emphasis in the original). "In other words," wrote Forrest McDonald, "'the people' were not in any part of the multi-leveled government allowed to act as the whole people" (1968, 193). They were individual citizens, individual voters, individual consumers; they were not a collectivity. Thus, the government "would be of (that is, from) the people; hopefully it would be for the people; but by no means would it be by the people" (194).

The Federalists now had a different response for those like Jefferson who argued for "simple democracy" in which the people made the laws that governed society and their lives. That response was not that the people were unfit, that they lacked adequate virtue or insight. Instead, it was that the new nation could not be governed by the people directly because the people's interests were not in politics but were largely in the marketplace. Therefore, let our representatives fight for our interests, let them keep the government free of the market, so that we can pursue our commercial interests unimpeded. Politics, in this liberal view, might be unavoidable, but it is handily minimized. Representative democracy demanded little from its citizens and left them ample time to aggrandize their property, which the government would now protect.

Thus our democracy remains, as it was originally devised toward the end of the eighteenth century, a system, to repeat Forrest McDonald's observation, "of (that is, from) the people; hopefully it [is] for the people; but by no means [is] it by the people." Representative democracy, in practice, is the rule of political parties and government bureaucrats *over* the people. Ours is a democracy that Sheldon Wolin, casting back to Plato, calls "guardian democracy" in which constitutional structures are favored over democratic politics and some political institutions are used "to check the demos" (1996, 100). In this democracy, as Gottfried Dietze points out, the syllable "re" in *representation* does not mean "again," but means "instead." To *represent* in this case does not mean that the people assemble again, but that elected officials meet instead of the people. "The actual presence of the people becomes a fiction. . . . One arrives at the conclusion that representation amounts to falsification, that representative democracy is a falsified democracy not a real one" (1993, 176). This has been so since the Founding.

Dietze, however, exaggerates. The presence of the people making legislative decisions is a fiction, but that presence exists still in elections, in the equality of our rights and liberties, in our freedom to pursue private interests, and in the choice we have whether to vote. People throughout the globe struggle to achieve this right to vote for representatives, a right, it seems, that many in the West take for granted to such an extent that in the United States fewer than half of those eligible vote in most elections. Still, we can agree with Dietze when he comments that "[d]emocracies as concrete forms of government known to us so far [are] mere steps toward democracy proper . . . that is, a democracy in which all people, without exception, rule" (166). What we observe around the globe and at home are not "full-fledged democracies" but stepped-down democracies. Therefore, concludes Dietze, all of us, East and West alike, are living not in an age of democracy, but only in an age of democratization (166).

The picture is not so stark or so dreary. We would move further along the path of democratization toward "democracy proper" by involving the demos in more deliberative, political decision making. But an obvious first step before that involvement, for any nation, is to follow the Founding Fathers and marry democracy and equal liberal rights.

The representative democracy, the democratic republic, established by the Framers recognizes the political equality of all citizens—though many in the Framers' era were not citizens. Upon what does that equality rest? It rests on the assumption that all possess rights equally, which the Framers described as natural rights. How else might men be equal? In strength? In virtue? In wisdom? In none of these will all be equal. Because of the great disparities among men in the caliber and expression of these characteristics, a political system would have to be established in which these disparities did not negate the equality of the citizens. If, for example, the system relied upon the virtue of the citizens, then the most virtuous would gain at the expense of the less virtuous. Therefore, a system had to be devised in which it did not matter substantively what qualities citizens brought to their participation in it. If men were restricted in their political decisions to choosing between only the best candidates, then it would not matter how they voted. The nation would be assured, regardless of the voting, of having outstanding representatives. Only in this way could the Framers be certain that the vote of an ignorant backwoods farmer would be equal to that of the wealthy, sophisticated merchant from Boston and would do no harm.

Yet the constitutional framework, resting on the acknowledgment by the Framers of the unvirtuous nature of the people, did little to follow Jefferson and improve the reasoning of the citizens. Instead, the Framers sought protection from the lack of virtue by designing a system that demanded little of the citizens. By limiting participation to the periodic casting of votes, the Framers left the bulk of society's members as the Framers found them. Neither the government's operations nor the elections were necessarily educative. Through politics the citizens were not necessarily improved.

Nothing was required for eighteenth-century citizenship but to be white, male, and property owning. As suffrage became more inclusive, the requirements broadened but the demands on citizens remained the same. So today even Ronald Beiner's alternative to the model citizen can vote: "Someone hooked on cocaine, committed above all to the satisfying of his or her physical urges, apathetic as regards public affairs in one's own society and beyond, and indifferent to the plight of other human beings" (1992, 132). Provided this citizen is at least eighteen, has a residence, and has registered, he or she can stumble into the voting place, if only to get warm; and knowing nothing of any of the candidates, can vote on the basis of name euphony. When that ballot slips in next to the Nobel Prize winner's, a woman with a passion for politics, the two ballots are completely equal.

What every citizen is certain of is that she is guaranteed the right to cast a ballot, regardless of who she is, what she knows, where she is from, or what she cares about or is indifferent toward. Voting is one of our fundamental rights as citizens, but it is no more significant than any of our other fundamental rights. Indeed, if the government exists to protect my rights, and I perceive that it is doing so, then voting is one right that I need not bother to exercise. Moreover, as the Framers noticed, the pursuit of my interests may not bring me into politics at all, especially if my representatives are protecting—and from the cynical point of view, even enhancing—that pursuit. This leaves citizens of our modern liberal democracies as nothing more than "self-regarding individuals who are prone to count their entitlements as benefits and their duties as costs" (Hollis, 1991, 29).

When politics is reduced to little more than casting votes, then "the locus of people's activities will be the 'private' realm of civil society" (Held, 1987, 289). The private realm, the Framers realized, had become the focus, and the locus, of the citizens' activities as they pursued their economic and commercial self-interests. This focus continues today, and this perversion of democracy, this turn away from politics to the private sphere, is well summarized by Charles Krauthammer: "Remember that indifference to politics leaves all the more room for the things that really count: science, art, religion, family, play" (1990, 82).[28]

The point, obviously, is not that these things don't or shouldn't count. On the contrary, they can be fundamentally important to one's good life. The point is that politics ought to count for more, for political issues and their repercussions are fundamentally important as well. But in our political system we don't do enough of the deliberating and deciding. Instead, our politics leaves us at best with "choosing a candidate on the basis of his views on monetary policy" (82). Because we do not do the decision making, "it is easy for a citizen . . . to wash her hands of any responsibility for any decision taken by any public officials. . . . It was not our decision, we think, and so whatever the harm done by it, that was not of our doing" (Baier, 1993, 234).

What is our responsibility is the choosing of candidates for political office. As in the time of the Framers, that choice more often than not revolves around issues of character. Look, for example, at the kinds of questions one writer lists as those that give voters pause on election day as they consider the candidates: "How can they know the heart of this man who offers himself for office? What are his motives? What are the hidden purposes of his life? How will he behave under temptation? How will he resist the corruption of power? Will it be better or worse for voters and their families if this or that official is elected?" (Tallian, 1977, 2).

Notice that only the last question even hints at the candidates' positions on the issues. In the context of this list of questions, one might well ask just how much the people, even influential people, need to be informed on the issues to exercise well our democratic right to vote. It strikes me as nothing short of wishful thinking to suggest, as Thomas Cronin does, that our democratic system permits "large numbers" of citizens "to participate in the great debates about crucial public policy decisions" (1989, 21). Aside from the one-sided debates among candidates for office, where citizens are at best spectators, there is only the recourse of writing one's representatives, or of writing letters to the editor, expressing the views that one's representatives ought to hear. Neither of these can be construed, however generously, as participation in political debates, to say nothing of public debate, on policy issues.

The candidates themselves often focus on character and not substantive issues. They project themselves as persons above reproach, as they vilify and derogate their opponents. They launch emotional appeals rather than reasoned arguments. Candidates, feeling the need to shape public opinion, rely on images and symbols. Since all candidates use this approach, the democratic process becomes a spectacle or display. Sheldon Wolin, editorializing in the first issue of *democracy,* referred to elections as "rituals of despair. . . . At the same time that vast sums of private money are being spent to buy candidates, public millions are, in effect, handed over to the public-relations and public-opinion industries so that their flacks can purchase the right to debase public discourse during prime time and encourage a level of political deliberation somewhere between idiocy and prolonged adolescence" (1981, 3).

This is part of the genius of the American democratic system. If people's attention is directed to the private sphere, and, simultaneously, we want an egalitarian system in which all citizens are competent to take part, then what could be better than limiting participation, for the most part, to voting for representatives? "The work of selecting a score or two of public officials from [even] an army of candidates is not a problem of intelligence at all. It is a mere guess, a flipping of coins, and in the nature of the case can be little or nothing more" (Wilcox, 1912, 253).[29]

The system, as it was designed in the eighteenth century and as it works today, brilliantly addressed the concerns of the Framers about the character and fitness of the people. They devised an egalitarian, representative democracy for people who were noticeably unvirtuous, not the least reason for which was their liberal interest in activities other than politics. And the design, now as then, was equally impressive as a solution to the dilemma of the nation's size. Representative democratic politics in the modern era, based on the size of our nation alone, became the domain of political parties.

Parties were a method of recruiting and training future representatives, of articulating and circulating political ideas and interests, and of managing the process for blocks of voters, many of whom needed, or looked to, the parties as a mediator between citizens and government. But historically the electorate has been nervous about the power of political parties. The fear was, as David Wooton writes, that "[I]n representative democracies, it is not the people who govern, but political parties. . . . [T]hey also reflect the priorities of interest groups while simultaneously seeking to articulate the concerns of the wider public" (1992, 79). In brief, the fear was that in representative democracy rule by the people becomes rule by the few, the party elites. But did the parties control who would run? In many ways they did. Up to our contemporary era, party leaders determined who the best candidates would be for which offices or, worse, simply rewarded a party worker's dedicated, protracted service with party backing for an office.

John Burnheim argues that things have changed little today. "Whatever the various methods used by parties in selecting candidates, in practice the decisions are made by a small number of people, whether they be a central committee or the local branch activists or the party backers who support candidates in primary elections. These groups almost always represent a quite narrow range of interests and make their choices on strategic or tactical grounds rather than on the merits of the candidates " (1985, 100).

It would be useful in arguing against representative democracy to take Burnheim's view. But in support of his view Burnheim offers no evidence or citations. If he is not flatly wrong in what he says,[30] then at least the issue is more complicated than he makes out. For steps were taken in our system to minimize party control of candidates by introducing direct primaries. Yet the results of these steps may have had an outcome more deleterious than the system the changes were meant to improve.

One cannot simply assert, as Burnheim does, that "party politics breeds mediocrity and corruption," however inclined we might be to agree. One could, on the other hand, follow Thomas Ferguson and Joel Rogers (1986) who argue that financial contributors drive the national primary process. Financial contributors provide funds to front-runners who can then saturate primary states with television campaign advertisements, thereby forcing other candidates into a frantic financial and advertising race to catch up.[31]

What drives and controls campaigns and candidates is, therefore, money. As party control of candidate recruitment waned with the introduction of primaries, emphasis within parties shifted to fundraising and control of money.[32] The result is that "one important strategic consideration weighed by rational candidates entertaining thoughts of running for Congress is the availability of money" (Jacobson and Kernell, 1981, 35). One observer and critic of our political system has gone so far as to say that parties no longer perform the basic party functions of the past. They are now little more than "a mail drop for political money" (Greider, 1992, 247).

Today in politics money makes a difference not only in whether a candidate wins, but also in whether a candidate will run. "[I]n fact, a good deal of party money is controlled by incumbent members of Congress who . . . are unwilling to forego [sic] their share in order to pursue the collective interests of the party" (Jacobson and Kernell, 1981, 37). Incumbency as expressive of entrenched political interests was a scourge of representative democracy that was identified as early as the Founding. What commentators in Pennsylvania said in 1776 about the other states' legislators is true of many of our incumbents today: "[M]en have become too careless in the delegation of their governmental power . . . [and] suffered it to continue so long in the same hands, that the *deputies* have, like the King and Lords of Great Britain, at length become *possessors in their own right;* and instead of *public servants,* are in fact the *makers* of the public" (quoted in Wood, 1972, 299; emphases in original).[33]

Incumbents, wishing to retain their political power, strive to stay in office. Since fundraising is integral not only to running for office, but also to staying in it, incumbents spend significant amounts of time raising money for the next campaign. Holding office, and the power and recognition that derive from it, provides a fundraising and campaign advantage that challengers do not have. In addition, the party, which is in the business of maximizing good outcomes—that is, electing their candidates to office—uses its organization on behalf of the incumbent. Thus challengers, inside and outside the party, can be discouraged by an incumbent who is awash in cash. Money and political experience are difficult to beat. Candidates with those two "attributes" will be the parties' nominees, since parties are interested in nominating the most electable candidates. These are not necessarily the most distinguished or meritorious ones. They are not necessarily the candidates of "fit character."

Incumbent success in reelections has been the story throughout our history. In the entire history of the House of Representatives there have been only two elections when voters returned less than 80 percent of the incumbents. In those two elections—1938 and 1948—the percentages were 79.1 and 79.3 percent, respectively. The Framers might not be able to rest comfortably in the knowledge that the wisest and most virtuous were serving the public in the federal government, but their scheme had surely succeeded in narrowing the pool of possible winners: between 1790 and 1810 reelection rates for incumbents exceeded 90 percent.[34]

The Framers blamed obsessive moneymaking and excessive concern with commerce for diverting attention away from politics. This made pursuit of the collective good a virtual impossibility. Liberal democracy might protect our individual rights, but it also made politics secondary to pursuits in the private sphere. Yet money became a sign of distinction, the only way to differentiate oneself from others.[35] But money also intruded into politics, as it became the way for incumbents, and candidates of all sorts, to differentiate themselves from others—not by having money but by using it in campaigns.

The Framers, finding the people focused on self-interest, and thus unvirtuous, devised a political system that citizens could participate in amidst their liberal—by which the Framers meant private—concerns for markets and commerce. The result is that citizens since the Founding have been asked to do very little politically. This may have been a self-fulfilling prophecy: the people, interested in private pursuits and not politics, withdrew even further from politics as it demanded little of them. As Walt Whitman concluded: "To be a voter with the rest is not much" (*Democratic Vistas*).

Perhaps the results would have been quite different if the Framers had followed Jefferson and had not been satisfied to leave the people as they found them. But to their minds, with self-interests dominating the people and with a nation extending over a vast territory, Jefferson offered no alternative if there were to be a semblance of an efficacious republican government. The people could not rule themselves; they would have to elect representatives. Yet we should heed the advice of the ideologists of Italian city-republicanism: "[I]f we remain content to leave the business of government to ruling individuals of groups [and not ourselves], we must expect them to rule in their own interests rather than in the interest of the community as a whole. . . . The moral . . . is that we must never put our trust in princes" (Skinner, 1992, 69), not even in princes we elect.

Notes

1. See the references there to Gutmann (1993b) and Sanders (1997).

2. For example, "George Washington called ordinary farmers 'the grazing multitude.' Colonel Landon Carter, a leader of one of Virginia's most distinguished families, saw little to respect among ordinary people and thought that some of them were 'but Idiots'. To Nathanael Greene 'the great body of the People' were always 'contracted, selfish, and il-

liberal'. Even John Adams early in his career referred to them as the 'common Herd of Mankind'" (Wood, 1992a, 27).

3. Boston *Independent Chronicle,* 10 July 1777; quoted in Wood, 1972, 59. See also 58.

4. In 1791 geographer Jedidiah Morse described what he had seen in New England as the likely future of all of America: a man was "weighed by his purse, not by his mind, and according to the preponderance of that, he rises or sinks in the scale of individual opinion." *Geography Made Easy: Being an Abridgement of the American Geography* (Boston, 1791), 65; quoted in Wood, 1992a, 243.

5. For a general discussion of egalitarian democracy in the United States, see Robert Wiebe's *Self-Rule,* in which one of his themes is "the tension between the inherent radical nature of democracy, which entails an equality among all participants, regardless of their standing in other settings, and ongoing attempts to use the institutions of democracy to limit or nullify its effects" (10).

6. Both quotations are from Sidney Aronson, *Status and Kinship in the Higher Civil Service* (Cambridge, Mass.: Harvard University Press, 1964), 49.

7. Joyce Appleby argues that in the eighteenth century the meaning of virtue underwent a dramatic shift away from the idea of serving the common good. Virtue became "a private quality, a man's capacity to look out for himself and his dependents." This is, of course, "almost the opposite of classical virtue." Indeed, this quality is what Tocqueville called in the 1840s "individualism." See chapter 4 of this volume. Appleby, 1984, 14-15.

8. Wood, 1992a, 264. "By limiting popular participation to the selection of leaders," comments Russell Hanson, "the Federalists consigned the population to a state of civic lethargy, in which citizens failed to develop a sense of moral and political responsibility that, according to classical republican theories, accompanied civic involvement" (1989, 77, n. 18).

9. Hanson, 1989, 77. n. 18. There is an irony in this result. The success of the Federalists' arguments reposed not on their superiority to Anti-Federalist arguments, but on the grounds that the Anti-Federalists were, as Wood says, "overawed" [1972, 487]. They lacked within their own ranks men of "social distinction and dignity" the kind of men who spoke for the Federalists.

10. 1905, Volume 12, Letter to Governor John Taylor (26 May 1810), 525-26.

11. 1905, Volume 15, Letter to Samuel Kercheval (12 July 1816), 37.

12. Quoted in Wood, 1972, 164; emphasis in the original.

13. 1905, Volume 12, Letter to Governor John Tyler (26 May 1810), 391.

14. 1905, Volume 14, Letter to Monsieur Dupont de Nemours (24 April 1816), 487-88.

15. 1905, Volume 14, Letter to Joseph C. Cabell (2 February 1816), 421. See also Letter to Samuel Kercheval (12 July 1816), Volume 15, 37.

16. 1905, Volume 14, Letter to Joseph C. Cabell (2 February 1816), 422-23.

17. 1905, Volume 15, Letter to Samuel Kercheval (12 July 1816), 37-38.

18. 1905, Volume 15, Letter to Samuel Kercheval (12 July 1816), 38.

19. 1905, Volume 15, Letter to Samuel Kercheval (12 July 1816), 39.

20. 1905, Volume 14, Letter to Joseph C. Cabell (2 February 1816), 419-20.

21. 1905, Volume 15, Letter to William Charles Jarvis (28 September 1820), 278.

22. The human condition, concluded Jefferson, is "susceptible of much improvement." The "diffusion of knowledge among the people is to be the instrument by which it is to be effected." Letter to Monsier Dupont de Nemours, 14 April 1816, Volume 14, 491-92.

23. Discretion is derived from *dis* "apart" and *cerner* or "separate." See *The Oxford Dictionary of English Etymology,* 1979, 271-73.

24. 1905, Volume 15, Letter to Samuel Kercheval (12 July 1816), 40.

25. "From the deliberations of a people properly informed, and provided its members do not have any communication among themselves, the great number of small differences will always produce a general will. . . . [I]f the general will is to be clearly expressed, it is imperative that . . . every citizen should make up his own mind for himself." (*Social Contract,* book 2, chapter 3). Here Rousseau implies that deliberations are to be individual, not group, acts. See the discussion below on the etymology of the term "deliberation."

26. Rousseau, *Social Contract,* book 2, 43.

27. The Whigs, according to Gordon Wood, themselves considered "each man doing what was right in his own eyes" as "a perversion of liberty" (1972, 23).

28. My colleague Rich Dagger reminds me to recall John Adams's statement that he engaged in politics so that his children might engage in scholarship and the arts.

Is it too cynical to suggest that the Federalists, some at least, saw in the national government an opportunity to create around the state a "clerisy" tantamount to the Church hierarchy of the Middle Ages, one that would retain power and control of the nation while maintaining for the people the structure of law and order to enable them to pursue private affairs with only a modicum of attention to public concerns?

29. "Votes . . . are stylized answers to standard questions. Voting is therefore a somewhat passive activity. Other people propose, and the voters can do no more than dispose" (Lucas, 1976, 166).

30. See, for example, John G. Geer, *Nominating Presidents,* Greenwood Press. Geer shows that in the United States changes in how presidential candidates are nominated undercut Burnheim's view.

31. Steve Forbes, the multimillionaire publisher who ran for the Republican Party presidential nomination in 1996, and ran again in 2000, spent approximately $100,000 in 1996 for each of the 39 delegates he won in Arizona. "The Power of Rich Candidates," *New York Times,* 2 February 1996, A4. For a thorough treatment of the effects of money spent on campaign advertisements in Senate races, see Kahn and Kenney, 1999.

32. See Gary C. Jacobson and Samuel Kernell, *Strategy and Choice in Congressional Elections* (New Haven, Conn.: Yale University Press, 1981). Direct primaries seemed to be the solution to having nominees ordained by parties. See Paul Allen Beck and Frank J. Sorauf, *Party Politics in America,* New York: HarperCollins, 1992, ch. 9. But parties retained methods and introduced new ones for attempting to control nominations. Methods consist of endorsement conventions; attempts by party leaders to arbitrate among prospective nominees by offering patronage positions or support if a candidate runs at another time; or blocking access to campaign funds or to other party resources such as campaign workers, election expertise, and advertising. However, "it is impossible to write

authoritatively of the frequency of party attempts to manage or influence American primaries. Practices vary, not only from state to state but within states, and descriptions of local party practice are hard to come by" (246). The point is, as Beck and Sorauf imply, that parties do attempt, though in various ways, to influence if not control nominations. "[T]he result tends to be a nomination politics of a limited scope more easily controlled by aggressive party organization" (246).

33. Gouverneur Morris advocated holding Senate seats for a lifetime so as to secure "the rights of property against the spirit of democracy." Max Farrand (ed.), *The Records of the Federal Convention of 1787* (rev. ed.), Volume 3 (New Haven, Conn.: Yale University Press, 1966), 499.

34. See David C. Huckabee, *CRS Report to Congress: Reelection Rates of House Incumbents, 1790-1988* (Washington, D.C.: Congressional Research Services, 1989). Rates for incumbents in senatorial races are lower than those in House races, fluctuating between 55 percent to 93 percent between 1946 and 1988, but usually over 70 percent. See Gary C. Jacobson, *Politics of Congressional Elections* (Boston: Little, Brown, 1992).

35. See Tocqueville, 1966.

1) are we missing the point when we equate 'liberal' with 'private'? ~~Some~~ Most 'liberal' rights do not concern themselves w/t property or its pursuit.

2) like most books of its kind, midwife is unclear about where, exactly, deliberation will be practiced, other than in local 'settings' associated w/t initiative + referendum procedures.

Chapter Two

Liberalism and Autonomy

Many of the revolutionary leaders around the time of the Founding, facing the realities of self-interest in postrevolutionary life, conceded that the people were more concerned with liberal pursuits, with moneymaking and commerce, than with politics. With citizen attention prescinded, direct democracy would then seem the least popular form of government, while representative democracy, with elected officials protecting citizen interests and rights, the most popular. The citizens' focus had definitely shifted, as Benjamin Constant commented, from "active participation in collective power" to "the peaceful enjoyment of individual independence."[1]

Whether representative democracy caused a retreat by many citizens into the private and commercial spheres, or simply reinforced it, these became the foci of activity and even of deliberation. Today liberal democracy signifies, as it did earlier, a placing of limits on the kinds, and scope, of decisions that democratic majorities can legislate. In addition, liberalism provides democrats with the theoretical or ideological underpinnings for an egalitarianism that assures all citizens of legal and political rights, irrespective of their birth, wealth, race, sex, ethnicity, or education. Finally, it assures the people that government, being limited, will not interfere in the private lives of the citizens.

We carry forward from the Founding these guarantees and this idea of limited government. Citizens rest content, so it seems, in their individual independence. Yet a liberal focus on autonomy, here relegated to the private realm, can change all of that.

While the structure of our democracy, the Constitution, is the same today as it was at the Founding, the sociopolitical environment in which that structure is set looks quite different. Liberal democracy today is also a reflection on a different reality, the reality of pluralism or diversity in ways of life. Slavery notwithstanding, there was at the Founding a homogeneity to citizens and their concerns. But citizenship now includes groups previously and intentionally shunned: women, Native Americans, Blacks, the propertyless, the young. The

[handwritten marginal note: Consistently equated commerce + moneymaking with (Liberalism)]

result is a greater need to try to understand the circumstances, values, goals, and beliefs of the people, because the people are now a variegated lot.

Thus liberal democracy needs to accommodate diversity. Does it do so? By directing the attention of citizens not to the political arena but to private life liberalism seems to eschew the politics of diversity. Politics is at best instrumental; that is, it is only useful for aggregating preferences into winning coalitions so that my/our interests, and not yours, are enacted or protected. On this account, liberal politics has little to do with participation and even less to do with accommodating diversity. Liberals might tolerate differences, but that is the extent of their accommodation.

But if autonomy is placed at the center of liberal values, then liberal democracy can come to mean both accommodating diversity and active participation within democratic politics. For central to autonomy, as I shall argue, is the need to give an account to others of our reasons for making what we construe to be autonomous decisions. Giving such an account then opens up possibilities of public dialogue and therefore deliberative democracy.

The Meaning of Autonomy

The values that constitute the set central to liberalism are those that liberals rely upon to live a good life, which is a concern of every person. These values read like a list of traditional liberal values and rights: reasonableness, tolerance, openness, mutual respect, liberty, and, above all, autonomy. It is important to note here that these liberal values—and I would include as well the welfare state, domestic tranquility, separation of public and private, as well as individual rights—are not of themselves liberal ends. Rather, they are necessary conditions for enabling citizens to make and control their own lives, which is essential to liberals in living a good life.[2]

Using these values, liberals evaluate and choose among plural or diverse ways of life. These values are essential, therefore, to choosing a good life, a life a liberal thinks is good. Some values, or virtues, are thus clearly better than others. Tolerance and reasonableness, for example, are better than some other values liberals do not cherish, because these are crucial for choosing a good life; that is, for deciding, among myriad kinds or ways of life, which kind or way is good and best. Liberals thus favor those conditions and values that enable persons to identify, define, and choose a good life, but that do not define the substantive features of that good life. Liberals agree with Charles Taylor that they have a duty to protect the society or social conditions conducive to evaluation and choice of a good life (1985, 204-7). Persons who want to live a good life, and that is everyone, should support the society or social conditions that enable them to do so, irrespective of their own conception of the good life.

All of these liberal values and rights could be subsumed under the right to autonomy, for autonomy captures or makes use of the essences of all of them. It involves reasonableness, tolerance, openness, liberty, and mutual respect.[3] It is autonomy that enables persons to choose from within pluralism the life one thinks is good. Liberals value autonomy—indeed, even base liberalism on autonomy—because they value that people control their own lives. They also recognize that not everyone values autonomy. Those, for example, who live according to unquestioned doctrinal authority or religious practices, perhaps in a tightly knit ethnic community, will not welcome the critical evaluation of their way of life that autonomy requires.

Autonomy is obviously not part of every conception of the good life. Yet it is indispensable to liberals if they are to live a life that they think is good. This is so because it is autonomy that enables one to step back reflectively and requires one to step back reflectively; that is, to gain some critical distance from the norms and practices, the goals and beliefs, of one's society or social milieu. The ability that permits this stepping back or critical distance comes with the unfolding of what developmental psychologist Jean Piaget called "formal operational thought," the mental level of abstract logic and rationality. With this unfolding come the capacities to express relations in terms of linguistic propositions; to consider systematically the relations of propositions to one another; and to generate counterfactuals, to make hypotheses, and to draw inferences. Able to operate on the world propositionally, hypothetically, and abstractly, the person can step back not only from her social milieu, but also from her own thinking. She comes thereby to realize that her own group or social order is only one possibility among many. In addition, she can now imagine ideal states and worlds that do not exist in reality.[4]

This kind of full-blown perspectivism means that she can separate from and thus act on the group and its norms and practices. With formal operations comes, for the first time, *self*-reflectivity when she can think about—that is, take as an object of her attention—her own thinking. This is both a blessing and a curse. Not only is her world now one of open possibilities, not only can she consider different ways of life, but now her self-definition is also open. Because her self-definition is no longer something given or something found but is something created—created by choices, deliberations, analysis, and self-reflection—the person becomes the author as well as the owner of her actions and values. All of this is made possible by the unfolding of formal operations, but unless sssthese mental operations, these abilities, are put into action, it does not follow that this potential is realized. Autonomy is that action; it is self-reflective choice, especially involving the nature of one's way of life and self-definition.[5]

Autonomy is not new to liberalism. Its flavor is captured in John Stuart Mill's notion of freedom: "The only freedom which deserves the name, is that of pursuing our own good in our own way"[6] (*On Liberty*). We can do so, because with formal operational thinking, we have the capacity "to reason self-consciously, to be self-reflective and to be self-determining. [Autonomy] involves the ability to deliberate, to judge, choose and act upon different possible courses of action in private as well as public life" (Held, 1987, 270).

Few would disagree with such definitions,[7] or with the notion that autonomy captures those aspects of living that liberals think essential to the good life in liberal democratic polities: our lives are self-directed; we choose the ways of life we direct; and we take responsibility for how they go. Here is the literal meaning of autonomy: self-ruled. Less celebrated, however, is the understanding of how people rule themselves, how they make autonomous choices and decisions.

More than a kind of choice, autonomy is an activity, a process of choosing. That process must involve both rationality—which here means the ability to give reasons for one's choices—and self-reflectivity, which contains the idea of having some critical distance from the range of choices offered. Indeed, as Stanley Benn comments, the content of the choice is at best secondary: the emphasis in autonomy is "on processes and modes of consciousness [or self]" and leaves "out of account the content of the autonomous man's principles and ideals." Benn continues: "There is no reason why an autonomous man should not be deeply concerned about social justice and community—but I have said nothing to suggest he will be."[8] Instead of content, argues Benn, autonomy rests on rationality and self-reflectivity, otherwise "the *nomoi* that govern him can be those absorbed uncritically and unreflectively from parents, teachers, and workmates. . . . Such a person . . . governs himself, but by a *nomos* or set of standards taken over from others" (123-24).

An unreflective and uncritical rational chooser Benn calls heteronomous (123-24). This chooser lacks rational reflection and self-reflection. Every theorist who discusses autonomy grants that rationality in part constitutes autonomy; otherwise, one who claims to make decisions on whim or preference or flipping coins could claim to be autonomous.[9] But why *self*-reflectivity or *self*-reflection?

Benn is certainly talking about critical reflection, but why does he insist that autonomy emphasizes "processes or modes of consciousness [or self]"? The critical reflection central to autonomy must be self-reflection because it consists of thinking about one's own thinking. Thus, when the individual can take *herself* as an object of attention—that is, can think about her own thinking—then she simultaneously objectifies and relativizes her sodality, its norms, roles, and *nomoi*. The "autonomous agent must also have distanced himself in some measure from the conventions of his social environment and from the influences of the persons surrounding him. His actions express principles and policies which he has himself ratified by a process of critical reflection" (124). It is self-reflectivity that provides the critical distance.[10]

This distancing or separation or stepping back reflectively is not simply from one's own thoughts but also from oneself. To scrutinize one's own thought requires taking a perspective that is not, or is not yet, one's own. To scrutinize one's own thought—one's own principles, actions, decisions, rules, roles, standards, ideals—from a position outside that thought is also to scrutinize one's self constituted by such thought. Stanley Benn conveys the point through the image of a potter: "[I]n judging his own pots, knowing them to be his own . . . his judgment goes beyond assessing the pots, not merely to an assessment of himself as a potter but to an assessment of his life as a person, for being a potter is a central element in his being the person he is" (Benn, 1988, 178).

So the autonomous person, in critically thinking about his thinking, asks himself what it means to be a person who acts this way, holds these views, does these things. Moreover, he asks what he would be, what his life would be like, if he held different views and lived in a different way. Unless on scrutinizes one's thought—steps back reflectively from it—and thus steps back reflectively from one's self, one cannot be autonomous.

The way in which one steps back from one's own thinking, and one's own self, is not by assuming some universal and objective, some Archimedean, point. Instead, it is to take up the perspectives of others, to assume temporarily and reflectively the roles of others. Taking up such perspectives, especially those opposite one's own, and treating them seriously—to wit, as if they were one's own—is a significant skill or habit in autonomy. The presence of pluralism makes this skill or habit easier to use, since pluralism provides a backdrop of various perspectives. Otherwise, one must rely principally on one's imagination.

Through autonomy, if the norms and *nomoi* of the sodality are accepted, then they have been self-imposed, adopted as a set of standards arrived at through critical reflection. There is nothing in self-reflectivity that insists that the set of standards of the group must be rejected in whole or in part. The set must simply be scrutinized. Nor does autonomy require that one's rules or laws be created ex nihilo or de novo. Most likely they come as selective or modified versions of those of the sodality. They are combined, as is one's identity, into a form that is one's own. The group no longer constitutes the person; now he is constituted by those insights and principles by which he governs his life and makes his choices. So saying that a certain belief of mine is not autonomously held because it is the same belief as my father's is to miss the point of autonomy as a process. When I have scrutinized the belief and can give reasons for accepting it, then it is my belief and I am its author (for me), though I did not *create* the belief. Autonomy makes no such demand.

The autonomous person is therefore not only rational, but she is also independent. That is, she is separate from or independent of her sodality or social matrix and is now able to reflect on it. Autonomy is therefore not independence per se, but is independence from the need to follow the norms and rules and roles of one's social milieu. At this stage the person can see that "traditionally settled forms of life can prove to be mere conventions, to be irrational. . . . Role identity is replaced by ego [autonomous] identity; actors must act as individuals across, so to speak, the objective contexts of their lives."[11] The demand of identity at the autonomous level is to be able to go "behind the line of all particular roles and norms and stabilize [identity] through the abstract ability to present oneself credibly in any situation as someone who can satisfy the requirements of consistency even in the face of incompatible role expectations" (86). The acting subject is now what Habermas calls "context-free."

What can he mean by context-free? As an autonomous person one can no longer be thought of as an ensemble of specific roles, of role identity. Rather, he has the ability through employing rationality and self-reflectivity "to construct new identities in conflict situations and bring these into harmony" (90). The person is now free of any particular context, of any kind of traditional—what Habermas calls "imposed"—norms and can now distinguish and operate according to principles that generate norms. Not only can the person distinguish the general from the particular, the symbolic from the concrete, but now he can make such generalizations himself.

Now we have some substance to add to the literal definition: to be self-ruled one must be rationally self-reflective about one's identity and about the community's *nomoi;* that is, one must be able to step back reflectively from her social context to evaluate critically the norms and standards and ends of that context. Notice in this more substantive definition that there is no demand either to reject the social context or to flee from the voices of others.

It is not the case that all of one's life will be self-reflectively scrutinized, nor if we thought to do so could we do so all at once. Autonomy seems more an attitude, a need perhaps, to engage in the process of self-reflective choosing. When one looks within, one finds not just the conventions of one's life and group and culture; one finds opening out an array of alternative lives, groups, and cultures—some real and some imagined but originating outside of the self— as well as an infinity of possibilities emerging from hypothetical or modified versions of lives, groups, and cultures that the self by itself can create. When introspecting, one finds "an inner ocean," to borrow George Kateb's phrase (1992).

The Social Nature of Autonomy

Once the person's abilities for autonomy have unfolded, what responsibilities to the social matrix that spawned autonomy does the person have? Once she has, through psychological maturation and self-reflectivity, been able to internalize the voices of the many, on which she depends for her perspectivism and judgments, why does she any longer need the society? With the voices within, with her ability to imagine and invent dialogue and to reason abstractly, she can be self-sufficient.

To make our actions and judgments intelligible to ourselves, we not only translate them into language, but also form them through language. The only language we have available by and through which to think rationally and self-reflectively is one based on a cultural tradition.[12] There is implicit in every language, as part of that cultural tradition, a system of norms and standards that determines proper use. Thus to understand whether we are using the language properly—whether, that is, we are properly following the rules for structuring thought in that language—requires interaction with others using the same language, for only in this communication can we determine whether our reflection and reasoning are properly rational.

If we wish, therefore, to be taken as or understood to be autonomous persons, and if we wish our decisions to be taken as autonomous, then we must be seen and must know ourselves to be using the language properly and responsibly. That means that we must be in dialogue with others and must be taken by those others to be rational (and reasonable) persons. If this were not so, then we could not claim to know ourselves to be autonomous, or our decisions to be autonomous, for we would not know we were being rational—that is, using the language in the proper, responsible way.

Two points here need emphasis. First, to be autonomous we must conform to the implicit norms and standards of the language we use. To know that we are doing so requires dialogue with other language users—that is, requires us to interact socially and not just with our own internalized voices. Second, concepts invented or introduced that are foreign to the language may well not be intelligible to the persons with whom we are in dialogue and so cannot be validated as rational.

To be autonomous, argues Charles Taylor, is "to be self-responsible, to rely on one's own judgment, to find one's purpose in oneself."[13] To be responsible means "able to respond"; in this case it means able to respond to others. Giving an explanation is central to responsibility and to autonomy, and this should not be surprising since explanation is also central to rationality. To grasp something rationally, as Taylor says, "is to be able to 'give reasons' or 'give an account'" (471). Thus giving an account is not simply to give any kind of response; rather, following our earlier argument, it is to give an account in accordance with shared criteria.

The account, in other words, must be intelligible to others in our social milieu; otherwise, how can I know that I have been rational in my actions and/or decisions? Also, without giving such an account, how am I to know whether the action that I've just performed is the manifestation of a rule that I chose to follow or merely a necessary reaction to a group rule?

"How are we to judge," asks Steven Lukes, "whether the person who conforms to the will of others or to the norms of his culture or the requirements of his role is doing so autonomously" (1973, 128)? The only way is to ask him. His explanation enables me to determine whether the actions are the result of reflection, of whim, or of unexamined adherence to the rules of the group. The explanation also lets *him* know whether he has been autonomous.

Autonomy is not something that we can know and acknowledge by ourselves. The rationality and self-reflectivity essential to autonomy militate against that. Central to rationality is accountability, to be able to give reasons to others for actions or decisions. To know that an act is rational, one must give an account of it. As Taylor argues, really knowing something is different from really believing something. To know something requires giving an account, which can only be done by confronting my thought and language with the thought and language of others (1989, 168): do I know what I am saying? Do I know what I have done and why I've done it? Do I really grasp what I'm talking about? "[T]hat we know what we mean . . . depends on this relating" (37-38). Through dialogue, through this relating, one discovers and has validated the grounds of his actions and decisions. It is intersubjective validation and not subjective certainty that establishes one's autonomy.

Intersubjective validation is necessary only for those who claim to be autonomous, or for those who will claim of another that he or she is autonomous. For those who do not care whether they are acting autonomously, arguments for intersubjective validation will have little purchase. To be *your* action, it must be one that you intended. To have that intention conveyed to me, it must be an explanation that you can make intelligible to me. An autonomous person must follow some rules, and those will include self-chosen rules as well as the rules of reason and communication (rationality and language).[14]

Liberals too often do not see that the point of autonomy is not simply to be self-ruled or the author of our own actions, though that is surely part of autonomy. It is to do so or to be so for a reason—itself autonomously arrived at—and that is to pursue the life that is good. Liberals also do not often see that autonomy requires giving an account to others of one's actions and decisions. That, for the liberal, is part of any life that is good, because it is an acknowledgment that one's chosen life is chosen autonomously, is one that can withstand scrutiny, and is one that is persuasively worth living. Therefore, liberals ought not to shy away from demanding such accounts from others or from giving such accounts to others on political, or public, matters. This, it seems to me, is not simply part of autonomy, but is also the hallmark of liberal democracy when autonomy is a central value. Where autonomy is central to liberalism, so too is dialogue; where autonomy is central to liberal democracy, so too must be political dialogue or deliberative democratic participation.

"Soft" Liberal Neutrality

Does liberalism actually favor certain conceptions of the good life, or does it remain neutral, and thus should liberals argue unselfconsciously for neutrality among competing conceptions of the good? I think that liberalism offers, or needs to offer, a position of "soft," even of an "antineutralist," neutrality. By this

I mean that liberalism does favor some conceptions that liberals think are central to the process of evaluating and living a good life. In other words, liberals think that a good life, even one that is inherited, can be critically evaluated, which does not necessarily mean abandoned or overturned. The process or power by which this is done involves the capacities for, or of, autonomy. Therefore, as a process but not necessarily a content—that is, as a means of structuring a good life and as a constitutive element in that good life, but not necessarily specifying the contents of that life—liberals favor any life plan and social arrangement that enables a person to be autonomous and to exercise autonomy.[15]

Autonomy, as I have argued before, is more process than content. Just so, liberals, in favoring autonomy, are suggesting that to live a good life persons must be able to evaluate and to choose that way of life. The abilities involved in evaluation and selection—the abilities of autonomy—are those that liberalism favors. But on what is evaluated and chosen, short of undercutting autonomy as a process, liberalism remains neutral. To translate one's chosen way of life into the chosen way of life for all citizens of a polity would require, in the liberal view, persuading all of those citizens through deliberative discourse to choose that way of life. Persuasion must be of all the citizens; otherwise, the arguing group attempts to impose a way of life on others that would violate the liberal rights guaranteed to all citizens and that safeguard one's chosen way of life.

Susan Mendus, in *Toleration and the Limits of Liberalism,* suggests that liberals who base their political theories on autonomy ought to have something to say about groups like the Amish or like the Muslim community in Britain, for "[w]hat needs to be established is what the liberal attitude will be to those forms of life which do not place a high value on autonomy" (103). One would think that liberalism, valuing not only autonomy, but also toleration and diversity, would have little problem establishing the liberal attitude toward diverse ways of life. Yet, argues Mendus, it turns out that liberalism favors only those ways of life that honor autonomy. It promotes, therefore, a version of cultural imperialism (105), as it imposes an autonomous way of life on its citizens and thus fails to promote toleration. Not only does autonomy-based liberalism fail to promote toleration, but on closer inspection one can see that it "ultimately contains no commitment to the value of diversity in and of itself. It justifies only those diverse forms of life which themselves value autonomy" (108).

It is difficult to see how a liberal state imposes an autonomous way of life on all of its citizens. Certainly no one is forced, or ought to be forced, either to live an autonomous life or to undertake a self-reflective examination of the kind of life one is living or wants to live. Thus autonomy is a value relative to the liberal's own way of thinking and to the reasons and evidence available when scrutinizing that way of life and way of thinking. Autonomy is not an absolute value that the state imposes; it is a relative value that the state protects, as it protects those values central to many nonautonomous ways of life.

To return to Mendus's example of the Amish: she describes the Old Order Amish as sharing "not merely a religious doctrine, but an entire way of life which is premised on the religious injunction to 'be not conformed to this world.' They seek to withdraw their children from the state education system in order to avoid their 'contamination' by outside influences, and thus they effectively deny their children the opportunity to participate in the wider society of American life" (103).

This example, it seems to me, presents no problem for liberals, unless the Amish claim to be liberals. The liberal state cannot force the Amish to participate in American life. The state might require the Amish to pay taxes, but it cannot force them to go to public schools and to become autonomous or act autonomously. Because the Amish enjoy the same rights as all citizens, they are entitled to organize their lives as they think best, provided that that way of life does not impinge upon the rights of other citizens. Should it happen that the Amish, or any group, had a conception of the good life that required them to impinge upon the rights of other citizens, then the liberal state would prohibit them from doing so, as it would with any autonomous-loving or autonomous-hating group.

Yet Mendus raises an excellent point: do the Amish deny their children *the opportunity* to participate in American life? If their form of organized education fails to prepare those children to carry out their obligations as citizens, then the state may have to intrude. The state would do so, because it also has an interest in the development of those children, for they will be future citizens. (I shall return to this topic in a later chapter.)

What if the Amish way of life, and their insistence that their children be exempt from public schools beyond the eighth grade, denied to Amish children the opportunity to become autonomous? Ian Shapiro points out that the Amish have designed their educational system to prepare their children to live in their communities, not in the outside, or secular, world by "actively discourag[ing] critical questioning of Amish values and beliefs" (1996, 141). So effective is this discouragement, comments Donald Kraybill, that the Amish think that they have made a choice to join the church when in fact by the time the choice is to be made, Amish adolescents have been "thoroughly immersed in a total ethnic world with its own language, symbols, and world view" (1989, 140). Since "abstract and rational modes of thought are simply not entertained in the Amish schools" (131), Amish adolescents have merely "the illusion of choice" (140). The liberal state, in promoting deliberative forums within democracy, as I am doing in this book, will have an obligation to intercede to make sure that the Amish children have the skills necessary to participate in democratic processes, even if the Amish choose not to exercise those skills. In short, as I shall argue in later chapters, the state has an obligation to see that all of its future citizens have met the democratic educational standards, whether those are met in public, private, or home schools.[16]

A liberal, however, would think the Amish way of life stultifying and less than the best life. It is a good life, of course, from the perspective of the set of values central to Amish society, and therefore it is worth living. But it is an autonomous life; that is, a way of life self-reflectively investigated and thereby committed to a way of life open to other possibilities or to the differences of others? If it is not, then forcing the Amish to look reflectively at their way of life might get some of them to change their minds. Yet the coercion itself is a violation of their rights and of autonomy, and thus it contradicts the very basis upon which that action was taken. A liberal thinks it best when persons pursue a life that they have come to think is a good life. Coming to this realization requires the exercise of autonomy. Simply because a way of life lacks that exercise does not provide justification for the liberal state to shut down or hinder that way of life. A liberal wants to persuade others of the best way to live; she does not want to force others to live any certain way.

Is the liberal state therefore neutral? Haven't I just and already argued that a liberal state favors autonomy over other values and principles? It does favor some principles over others, and this without question does make living other sorts of lives more difficult within a liberal state. Does that mean that the liberal state is not neutral? It is neutral but, again, in a soft sense: the liberal state wants to protect those values that make it possible to live a life a person thinks is good. That may be a way of life one has inherited from family and religion and community; it may be a way of life that one has committed to after lengthy, or brief, investigation of diverse ways of life. To arrive at one's way of life in the first way, through inheritance or tradition, requires that the liberal state protect diverse ways of life. The fact that all future citizens must meet democratic standards within an education for deliberation, the fact that schools must teach the skills of critical thinking, does not mean that persons must use those skills autonomously or self-reflectively. That is, the state does not require that persons turn those skills onto their own lives (an idea I shall discuss in depth later on). People are free, within conventional liberal limits, to live as they see fit. Other citizens must be tolerant of those ways of life, for they are protected by law.

But one cannot come to a conception of the good life in the second way, the autonomous way, unless the state also protects the exercise of autonomy. A liberal state does not simply protect the exercise of autonomy as it protects traditional ways of life. In the latter case it merely allows them to exist; in the former case, it favors those values that perpetuate autonomous choosing. In both cases, however, the state's actions have the same result. The liberal state does protect diverse ways of life without encouraging them. But it does not encourage a liberal way of life either, for there is no such set way of life. The liberal state permits autonomous choosing, and what is chosen autonomously are various ways of life, not a set liberal way of life. It would be nonsensical to suggest that there is *an* autonomous way of life. Values, ends, beliefs, and practices are autonomously chosen; they are not in themselves autonomous.

It is true that the liberal state protects the values that condition or constitute autonomy, but doesn't the liberal state do more than that? Doesn't it promote those values? There would seem to be two kinds of promotion: a thick kind and a thin kind. Thick promotion follows from a declaration that the values of autonomy themselves constitute a way of life. In this view, the liberal state would seek to establish for all of its citizens this way of life, because it is the best way of life. Such establishment would foreclose nonautonomous ways of life and thus cut across the values in autonomy-based liberalism: tolerance, openness, diversity, and the like. In the name of establishing autonomy as the basis for a way of life, the liberal state would have to violate its own principles or values. Some citizens could not live as they saw fit, but would instead have to conform to the requirements of autonomy. They would have to be autonomous and live autonomous lives.

Can there be an autonomous way of life, where those values that condition autonomy constitute the substance of that life? What precisely is the substance in this way of life?[17] Through a thin promotion of the values of autonomy the only ways of life that are excluded are those that violate persons' rights. Protection assures that no one's values, autonomous or not, are unnecessarily overridden; nonautonomous ways of life will be permitted and protected. But thin promotion favors the conditions and values of autonomy.

A liberal state sees the value in choosing a way of life, not simply in inheriting one. The state will therefore promote the values of autonomy in its institutions. This thin promotion is a form of "soft" neutrality. The liberal state is neutral in that it will not use political power to coerce persons to conform to a way of life, or even to coerce persons to choose a way of life; nor will it use its power to prevent persons from living as they see fit. But I agree with Stephen Macedo (2000): the liberal state is not neutral in the sense that it makes living in a traditional, closed community more difficult than living in an environment of autonomous choosing. Religious fundamentalists, for example, must withdraw their children from state education if they wish to instruct them as scripture demands. Presumably, if the state were truly neutral, there would be public schools teaching whatever specific groups wanted taught. There could be Muslim public schools, Christian public schools, or Jewish public schools, for the liberal state would not want to favor any way of life over others.

Technically, however, the liberal state doesn't favor any particular way of life; it favors a process for evaluating and choosing a way of life, regardless of the content of that life. The process is autonomy, and a liberal state promotes those values necessary for its development and exercise.

Thin promotion must be differentiated, therefore, from the thick variety. To say that the two are the same is like saying that the absence of an established religion in the United States favors or promotes atheism or secularism. Instead, the absence protects the ways of worship, and nonworship, of all. Thus a liberal state promotes the separation of church and state. That separation does not mean, however, that its mere existence denigrates those who worship, that the liberal state pushes people away from religion. Similarly, the liberal state that thinly promotes the values central to autonomy does not denigrate those who live, through choice or inheritance, a nonautonomous life. Indeed, thin promotion permits the establishment of Muslim schools and Catholic schools, for example, as private schools, which thick promotion might not.

But there will be public standards, which in the context of this book I am calling democratic standards, that all schools must meet. A liberal state has a definite interest in preparing future citizens for participation in society. A liberal society has both a public sphere and a private sphere. Private life is one's own business; that life certainly does not have to be a liberal life, whatever that may be. But one's public behavior is a matter of the state's concern. A liberal state wants its citizens to be able to participate in political activities—activities of the polity—and that will require liberal public institutions, and especially schools, to promote the conditions that underlie autonomy. Citizens should be prepared when deciding public business to act autonomously, but citizens themselves don't have to be autonomous.

What can that mean? How can one be prepared to be autonomous, but not necessarily have to be autonomous? Whatever the ingredients in autonomy, the liberal state promotes, and therefore offers, an education that develops the skills used in autonomy. But how those skills are applied, and whether they are applied, is left to the designs and plans of each person. There is no requirement to participate politically—indeed, one may autonomously choose not to do so—but a person who chooses to do so should be willing and able to exercise autonomy in the public sphere. If an Amish woman decides to exercise her rights of citizenship and vote in an upcoming election, then she must conform to the behaviors required of all citizens sharing in a public practice, regardless of her personal concerns.

The liberal's commitment to toleration and diversity is deeper than Susan Mendus thinks. While it is true that other ways of life help the liberal evaluate and choose a good life, that is not the only reason a liberal would support toleration and diversity. The support also rests on liberal uncertainty, often not a feature—to say nothing of a virtue—of fundamentalists, religious or political. Because the liberal lives a life she thinks is good, she is willing to persuade others of the value of that life. At the same time, because she lives a life she *thinks* is good, she realizes that other ways of life might be better. She is, therefore, open to persuasion herself. Diversity of ways of life, of beliefs, of goals, and of values, is more than a fact of life; it is a reminder of possibilities available to all, of the richness of human living, and of the need to reevaluate one's own choices, no matter how fundamental. Toleration is not simply the recognition of a right of others to live as they choose and to be left alone to do so. Rather, it is a recognition that others can make choices and commitments different from ours but just as deep as ours. It is a reminder that those who live, and choose, differently need to have that difference acknowledged, not just tolerated. That is the liberal virtue of openness, and toleration for liberals is the gateway to that virtue as well as to the virtue of mutual respect. Here difference is not just accepted as a fact of life; it is cherished also as a reminder of possibilities and as a reminder of the need to listen to and to take serious account of others who define themselves in different, even alien and execrable, ways.

Openness to other perspectives and a willingness, indeed, a requirement, to hold them reflectively and consider them seriously, which includes critique, is to pay a compliment to difference. It is a sign of respect, and even of dignity.[18] When I submit my ideas to you, when I am exercising autonomy, I offer you respect as someone who can understand where I stand and why I stand there. I treat you as a rational and intelligent person capable of hearing my arguments and responding to them in kind. By being accountable to others, I treat them with respect because I treat them, in Kantian terms, as ends and not as means.

Mendus's criticism brings up another facet of autonomy: the nature of commitment. Some citizens, as she points out, do not want to be autonomous and do not want their children to be so. Although liberals may think that evaluating and choosing a way of life are an essential part of any good life, and although they may think that adherents to any particular way of life should be willing to argue for that life on the basis of its merits, some citizens want to raise their children in a particular kind of religious or cultural climate that they do not want challenged, by their children or by others. Such challenges are not only disruptive, but can be alienating as well. To question the basic assumptions upon which that way of life is built is to undermine the fabric, the faith, of that way of life. Once that is done, then that life is never looked at, or lived, in quite the same way.[19]

Here, I think, the liberal distinguishes between devotion to a way of life and commitment to it. Devotion is adherence without deliberation, whereas commitment is a conscious bringing of oneself to something that at first is "other" than that self. Whereas devotion is the by-product of being embedded in a way of life such that one cannot separate oneself from that way of life, commitment is the result of self-reflective scrutiny.

The traditionalist's retort to this is that this liberal understanding of both commitment and devotion is a product of the very value system and way of thinking that the traditionalist might argue "isn't that as deep a commitment as anyone can make?" The liberal might then point out the difference between being raised in a way of life in which one's self *is* that tradition or culture and being raised so that one brings to a way of life a self that is separate, initially, from it. Commitment literally means bringing oneself to something or someone. This requires that there is a separate self or "I" that brings itself to the object—"to put [them] together." Two separate things are brought together. If I am required to swear an oath of allegiance to a leader, no one would say that the oath is a sign of my commitment to him.

Michael Sandel suggests that to make a commitment is to "establish a certain space between it and me . . . reflexivity is a distancing faculty" (1982, 58). Reflexivity is a distancing faculty because that is how one scrutinizes any object of attention, by gaining critical distance. Thus to make a commitment is to establish a certain space between it and me. It is the recognition of difference between the self and the "object" one is committing oneself to. One who is devoted, on the other hand, sees no space, and wants no space, between himself and the object of devotion. He cannot separate, therefore, from that object of devotion. This is why religious zealots often identify the leader not only as the "One" or the "Truth," but also *as himself*.[20]

Perhaps the liberal has more "faith" in traditional ways of life than do the adherents themselves, for liberals think that any way of life, if it is worthwhile, should be able to withstand scrutiny of its basic tenets. Is the traditionalist's fear of autonomous scrutiny, of self-reflective thought, that if adherents looked closely and carefully at how their people live and why they live that way, then they would question, and might even renounce, that way of life? Can many closed ways of life only survive if they permit indoctrination but not scrutiny? This would seem to be an admission on the part of the indoctrinators that, if faced with multiple choices, an adherent would live differently. Thus there is a need among some religious cults for mind-control techniques and the relinquishing of freedom.

Freedom is important to autonomy, but they are not synonymous. Freedom is the absence of restraints or restrictions that preclude one from pursuing or acting on her autonomous choices, especially those that pertain to one's life plans. In this view one cannot be said to be fully autonomous unless one has the opportunity to exercise autonomy and, once exercised, to act on those choices. Thus a prisoner could decide to become an investment banker and could take necessary steps in that direction—studying finance and banking practices, for example. But part of this being an autonomous choice is the understanding that his life sentence for murder and embezzlement prevents his taking the definitive step: gaining employment as a banker. He lacks the freedom to do so. Yet if he has considered that, if that realization has been part of his self-reflective thought, and if he finds that the study of investment banking is the crucial element in his life, regardless of his incarceration, then this could be an autonomous choice.[21]

He would have to admit, however, that the lack of freedom has altered his choice. He cannot *be* an investment banker, but he can study investment banking. He can act like an investment banker; he can know all that an investment banker knows; he can write fictional or even nonfictional accounts about investment bankers. Yet he lacks the freedom to be one himself. He does not lack the freedom to act on his desire, or need, to study banking, but he does lack the freedom to be employed as one. Nevertheless, the prisoner acts to the extent of his freedom, and the extent of his autonomy is bounded by that freedom.[22]

Liberals want to be fully autonomous. This means, given the preceding argument, that one must have the opportunity to act on the autonomous choices, as well as to make the autonomous choices, that guide and give meaning to her life and her identity. Anyone wishing to be autonomous must also give an account; must, that is, participate in dialogue with others. For many, even most, liberals this will involve democratic participation, where many important life decisions lie. Why this is so and one type of democratic participation that might suffice, at least for now, are the focus of the next chapter.

Notes

1. Benjamin Constant, *The Spirit of Conquest and Usurpation,* part 2, chapter 6, in *Political Writings,* trans. by Biancamaria Fontana (New York: Cambridge University Press, 1988) 102.

2. I have argued elsewhere, at length, about liberal values and the good life; I offer here a brief sketch of that argument. See Crittenden, 1992, 168ff.

3. In *Beyond Individualism* I differentiated between tolerance and openness. A short take on that differentiation is that tolerance requires that we acknowledge difference, hear the different opinions, and honor the right of different persons to speak. Openness encompasses tolerance but goes beyond it. Openness requires not only that we hear others and honor their right to speak, but also that we take their opinions seriously—that is, consider them as if they were our own. Rather than simply tolerating your differences, openness requires that I take on those differences and consider them seriously. I shall have more to say on this in the last chapter.

4. I have discussed at length the nature of autonomy as it pertains to political theory and to developmental psychology. What I offer here is an abbreviation of that discussion. For the full discussion see Crittenden, 1992, especially chapters 2 and 3.

5. I have written at length about the nature of levels of psychological development and their ramifications for political theory, especially as these pertain to autonomy. What I offer here, again, is the briefest outline of arguments made with evidence and in detail. See Crittenden, *Beyond Individualism,* as well as Crittenden, 1993.

6. Mill argued in *Utilitarianism* that there are "essential interests" which are to be protected as rights. Those interests are the moralities preventing persons from hurting one another, which include "either directly or by being hindered in [one's] freedom of pursuing [one's] own good" (59-60).

Mill is claiming that one has a right to noninterference in one's autonomy. John Gray points out that, with the exception of a letter to a correspondent, Mill did not use the term "autonomy." Yet Gray thinks that commentators are justified in using the term with reference to Mill, because Mill clearly argues for liberty as freedom of action, which, Gray says, is itself autonomy. However inadequate or underdeveloped this definition may be, I take Gray's point. See John Gray, *Mill on Liberty: A Defense* (London: Routledge & Kegan Paul, 1983), 54ff, and for a more thorough definition of autonomy, see 73-77, as well as Gray, "Political Power, Social Theory, and Essential Contestability," in *The Nature of Political Theory,* ed. D. Miller and L. Siedentop (Oxford: Oxford University Press, 1983), 40.

As Gray points out, Mill reserves the right to autonomy not to all persons, but to those who display the capacities of autonomous agents. At the center of those capacities are "the powers exercised in framing and implementing successive plans of life . . . the capacities and opportunities involved in self-critical and imaginative choice-making" (Gray, 1983a, 55). Says Mill: "He who does anything because it is the custom makes no choice" (John Stuart Mill, 1910, 126). Real choices must be, for Mill, autonomous choices. Likewise, "[a] person whose desires and impulses are his own . . . is said to have a character" (128). Mill implies here that only those who are autonomous have character, a point similar to Charles Taylor's distinction between agents and persons.

7. In the past few years there has been a veritable explosion of writing on autonomy and its relation to political theory. As a representative sampling see the following books on the subject: Richard Lindley, *Autonomy* (London: Macmillan, 1986); Robert Young, *Personal Autonomy* (London: Croom Helm, 1986); Lawrence Haworth, *Autonomy: An Essay in Philosophical Psychology and Ethics* (New Haven, Conn.: Yale University Press, 1986); Gerald Dworkin, *The Theory and Practice of Autonomy* (New York: Cambridge University Press, 1988); Joseph Raz's *The Morality of Freedom* (New York: Oxford University Press, 1986); John Christman, ed., *The Inner Citadel* (New York: Oxford University Press, 1989); Diana T. Meyers, *Self, Society, and Personal Choice* (New York: Columbia University Press, 1989); and Susan Wolf, *Freedom within Reason* (New York: Oxford University Press, 1990).

8. "Freedom, Autonomy and the Concept of a Person," *Proceedings of the Aristotelian Society* 76 (1975-1976: 129-30. My understanding of autonomy as process is similar to Gerald Dworkin's view of autonomy as "procedural independence." See Dworkin, *The Theory and Practice of Autonomy,* especially chapter 1.

9. See the theorists listed in note 6 above.

10. Diana Meyers argues that personal autonomy "requires living in harmony with one's . . . true—one's authentic—self," Meyers, *Self, Society, and Personal Choice,* 19. Self-reflectivity, on this view, is essential to understanding one's authentic self, for Meyers does not see the authentic self as static. Rather, it is the result of an introspective process whereby the person evaluates and adjusts commitments, wants, and beliefs according to the kind of self she takes herself to be.

Meyers, I think, makes too much of the idea of the authentic self, and too much of socially conditioned values or interests. For even if one's interests and values are the result of socialization, the ability to introspect, to examine these ideas in light of one's self-definition (i.e., self-reflectivity) means that the person can change these values and interests even if socialized and even if self-reflection itself is socialized. What if socialization predetermines the outcome of introspection? That possibility is why role-taking—

taking up the perspectives of others, especially those opposite yours, as if they were one's own—is crucial to self-reflectivity.

For another view of the importance of self-reflectivity to autonomy, see Robert Young, "Autonomy and the 'Inner Self,'" in Christman, *The Inner Citadel*, 81-83. For the importance of self-reflectivity to autonomy from the perspective of developmental psychology, see Crittenden, 1992.

11. Jurgen Habermas, "Moral Development and Ego Identity," *Telos* 24 (1975): 45.

12. Rationality is actually built into self-reflectivity, for it is by principles of reason, and logic, even if misapplied, that one reflects at all. For the sake of emphasis, however, I here separate them.

13. K. Baynes, ed., "Overcoming Epistemology," in *After Philosophy* (Cambridge, Mass.: MIT Press, 1987), 471.

14. What is the model of rationality involved here? As I said previously, logic plays a part in rationality but is not the only part. Rather, I am following Harold Brown's model of rationality in which judgment, and not simply the application of rules, is central to rationality (1988). This is, of course, associated with Jon Elster's view that "rational beliefs are those which are grounded in the available evidence; they are closely linked to the notion of judgment" in *Sour Grapes* (New York: Cambridge University Press, 1985), 2. "Judgment," argues Brown, "is the ability to evaluate a situation, assess evidence, and come to a reasonable decision without [deliberately] following rules" (Brown, 1988, 137). In addition, judgments are fallible and must be made on the basis of appropriate information.

Brown's "judgment" is related to Artistotelian "deliberation," an intellectual activity used when one cannot attain certainty, but needs to act, and can rely on relevant information (Brown, 1988, 143ff); see also *Nichomachean Ethics,* book 3, chapter 3, and book 6, chapter 5. Here is Aristotle's *phronesis,* "the capacity of deliberating well about what is good and advantageous . . . [about] what sort of thing contributes to the good life in general" (*Ethics,* 1140b, 25-30). Although Brown argues that *phronesis* is a narrower concept than his own concept of judgment, it appears that the only difference between these concepts lies in the range of the capacity, not in its nature.

The model of rationality as judgment amounts to this: rational claims are grounded in reasons; if we are to be rational, then we must believe on the basis of relevant evidence. "We expect a rational person to provide reasons for whatever conclusion she eventually arrives at even when no rules are available" (Brown, 1988, 184).

Therefore, a rational claim is one we can defend with reasons. These reasons must be good reasons or at least adequate reasons (Brown, 33). What constitutes good or adequate reasons? Not surprisingly, Brown argues that this is determined by "the community of those who share the relevant expertise for evaluation against their own judgments." Thus, rationality "requires other people—and not just any people—but other people who have the skills needed to exercise judgment in the case at hand" (Brown, 187). As with Thomas Kuhn's understanding of decision making during revolutionary periods in science, rationality as judgment is a socially mediated process rather than a formal, rule-guided process.

Rationality, then, is used as a counter to irrationality more than it is to indicate the necessity of logical proof, linguistic analysis, or anything resembling what professional philosophers do. But part of rationality, as was argued about autonomy, is also context-free, meaning outside of one's own social milieu. That is, one cannot be rational without following some universal laws of logic. Also, one can always step away reflectively from a given context, though not from all or every context.

15. Susan Mendus argues that autonomy is "a necessary presupposition of a life worth living, but not as a full specification of that life" in Mendus, *Toleration and the Limits of Liberalism*, 1989, 13. I think that that is precisely right.

My sense of neutrality has the flavor of that of Rawls in *Political Liberalism:* neutrality prevents the state from doing "anything intended to favor or promote any particular comprehensive doctrine rather than another" (193). By *comprehensive* Rawls means a way of life or set of thorough and encompassing life plans.

Stephen Macedo argues in *Diversity and Distrust* that "liberalism with a spine" will favor certain values over others and will thus make it more difficult for, say, sectarian ways of life to flourish within a liberal society. Therefore, he concludes, liberalism is not neutral and cannot be neutral. The theme of nonneutrality in liberalism is a subsidiary focus of his book. See especially pages 118-25, 180, and 185.

16. I discuss these standards in detail in chapter 4.

17. Stephen Macedo, echoing John Rawls in *Political Liberalism,* claims that autonomy is not a suitable liberal value because, like Mill's individuality, autonomy is a comprehensive ideal. But also like Rawls, Macedo fails to specify what about autonomy separates it from self-criticism, a liberal value that Macedo endorses but does not define, or what about autonomy differentiates it from "the ability to make *informed* and *independent* decisions about how [people] want to lead their lives in our modern world" (Macedo, 2000, 207, emphasis in the original).

18. This is similar to Habermas's notion of communicative ethics in a dialogue that is unconstrained and uncoerced, where participants can say whatever they want, but where what they say can be openly challenged. Habermas, *Moral Consciousness and Communicative Action,* 89.

The value of openness as I describe it may be an intermediate level between tolerance and the more demanding virtue of mutual respect. Where liberal tolerance, defined as "live and let live," may permit forms of discrimination, mutual respect, when defined as "reciprocal regard," demands too much of liberal democratic citizens. (See Gutmann, 1995.) It may well demand that ends that one finds noisome but tolerable must be promoted in order to accord the person who holds them appropriate mutual respect.

Gutmann argues that to avoid having different groups discriminate against each other, public schools in liberal regimes need to teach mutual respect rather than mere toleration (Gutmann, 1995, 561). Unfortunately, she makes no strong case that teaching mutual respect alone would have this effect. Besides, one could argue that toleration itself is based on a mutual regard for the dignity or worth of all persons; that is why we tolerate behavior abhorrent to us.

Gutmann seems to go further than this when she defines mutual respect as "a reciprocal positive regard among people who advocate morally reasonable but opposing positions in politics" (Gutmann, 578). There is ambiguity here. Does Gutmann mean that one must have a positive regard for people's *views,* regardless of what those views are? Additionally, if the notion that the views must be reasonable to be respected means that we need have no positive regard for, say, Nazi law, then it is also the case that religious fundamentalists need have no positive regard for laws protecting homosexuals when those fundamentalists hold that homosexuality is unreasonable.

Openness as an intermediate level requires persons to consider seriously the different, even opposing, perspectives of others—consider them, that is, as if they were one's own. This is not to say that one must then embrace those perspectives. One simply must hear them and be able to mirror them back in a way acceptable to those who hold them. The mirroring shows that the listener has heard accurately what the speaker said. (See chapter 6 for more on mirroring.)

19. One reason for favoring the position of the Amish in *Wisconsin v. Yoder* was to assure that Amish children would not be taken away from their community "physically and emotionally, during the crucial and formative adolescent period of life" (406 U.S. 205 [1971], 211). Requiring self-reflection or autonomous thought during adolescence might do that. This is why I argue against requiring *self*-reflective or autonomous thought of high school students. But that is not the same as requiring reflective thought. I have much more to say on this important distinction, and argument, in subsequent chapters.

20. This distinction between commitment and devotion, between a self separate from the object of attachment and a self inextricably embedded in and thus constituted by the attachment, does not mean that liberals are, as Sandel claims, "unencumbered selves" devoid of given identity. (See Crittenden, 1992, for a detailed argument on this point.) Iris Marion Young uses Heidegger's notion of "throwness" to describe group identity: "[O]ne finds oneself as a member of a group, which one experiences as always already having been." Yet implicit in Young's rendering is the idea of psychological distance. When one can take as an object of attention the group that constitutes identity, one is already at some remove, if only reflectively, from the group. The group has become the object of the subject's attention. Identity with the group must now rest on commitment, not embeddedness or givenness. Young recognizes this: "[I]t does not follow that one cannot leave groups and enter new ones. . . . Nor does it follow from the throwness of group affinity that one cannot define the meaning of group identity for oneself; those who identify with a group can redefine the meaning and norms of group identity. . . . The present point is only that one first finds a group identity as given, and then takes it up in a certain way," in Iris Marion Young, *Justice and the Politics of Difference* (Princeton, N.J.: Princeton University Press, 1990), 43-47.

21. Consider a Rawlsian grass counter who decides to devote his remaining years to counting grass in John Rawls, *A Theory of Justice* (Cambridge, Mass.: Harvard University Press, 1971), 432. He can present reasons for his decision and the actions based on the decision: "An inheritance provides materially for my family and me, so although I do not earn a living counting grass, I do not jeopardize anyone's welfare by doing so; I

might be listed in the *Guinness Book of Records* as the first 'full-time grass counter'; and I am not simply passionate about grass counting, but I also have expertise. I also have experience; I have counted the hairs on my head."

This decision strikes us as so odd that we might well think that this person is mentally disturbed. But on the evidence that we have, we must accord him the status of a person making an autonomous choice.

22. Mill also differentiated between freedom and autonomy. The freedom to associate with whomever one pleases is, says Mill, a classical liberal right but one which is only instrumental to the cultivation and practice of autonomy (Gray, 1983a, 55).

1) can individuals practice autonomy privately w/o practicing it publicly (i.e., through public justification)?

2) can individuals practice autonomy privately w/o practicing it publicly (i.e., through democratic deliberation in its free form)?

Chapter Three

Autonomy and Deliberative Democracy

Democracy is much like autonomy: it is a process for deliberating about and evaluating issues and for making rational judgments, decisions, and choices about those issues that can be translated into law. What is autonomy but "self-rule," and what is a law but a rule? Thus, most persons who are self-ruling—that is, who are autonomous—will also want to be self-governing—that is, to paraphrase Rousseau, will want to obey laws that they prescribe for themselves. As Hamilton said in *Federalist* 15, what is the one essential aspect of government but the making of laws?

Liberals, unfortunately, have historically limited the exercise of autonomy to the private sphere.[1] The result has been that politics, as we've seen, has often been for liberalism a world of issues to be eschewed. Those issues are better handled by representatives elected to address them. Liberalism thus grants to people the exercise of autonomy to enable them to be self-ruled in their private lives, but our liberal democratic system does not permit them to be self-governed, to be autonomous in our public or collective lives, where the "self" in self-reflectivity is the collectivity.

Yet politics involves issues important both to individual lives and to our collective life. Largely unavailable to liberal individuals interested in shaping and controlling their environments and lives—interested, that is, in autonomy—is the world of politics where the nature and scope of institutions, important social issues, and public/private boundaries are determined. Citizens can run for public office, can campaign for candidates, can write to their representatives or newspaper editors, and the like. The drawback to these outlets is that they either have little direct effect on putting one's positions into law, or, if they do have that effect—by serving in office—many of the requirements of the job, especially, the higher one goes, involve raising campaign funds and are ancillary to the issues that led one to run in the first place. Many persons will want to exercise their capacity for autonomy on public as well as private issues, if only for the reason that public issues often pertain directly to, if they are not identical with, private issues. In both arenas reside issues of fundamental importance to the kinds of persons we are and the sorts of lives we want to live, individually and collectively.

The two fundamental questions, according to Max Weber (1988), that citizens ask, or are idealized as asking, are what shall we do and how shall we arrange our lives. The translation of autonomy into political terms addresses these two questions. It means the use of self-reflectivity and rational choice in achieving understanding of and control over the circumstances of our social life and over the decisions that affect that life. Democracy, especially in this era of pluralism, of competing and conflicting interests and perspectives, requires dialogue or the public expression of responsibility—the need to give an account, to give reasons, for one's positions. As Amy Gutmann points out, liberalism and democracy converge in this kind of public dialogue, because the value of liberty, cherished historically by liberals, depends on the control that democracy enables persons to exercise collectively over their own lives (1993b, 151).

Such "dialogic" or deliberative democracy would involve airing positions, making judgments, and reaching agreed decisions, even where disagreement continues over the contents of those decisions. The emphasis would be on rational, self-reflective choice and on social interaction, both characteristics of autonomy. Stephen Macedo goes so far as to suggest that liberal citizens must "engage in public arguments if they wish to persuade others of the merits of their own interpretations of public norms" (1990, 272).

The emphasis on social interaction, on dialogue, solves another problem often associated with autonomy. Autonomy, some argue, encourages, if it does not demand, isolation. Once one is self-reflective and mentally independent, there is no reason to consult or interact with others. Instead, she can "retreat into [her] own deliberately insulated territory" (Berlin, *Four Essays,* 136), withdraw into her inner citadel where she can be alone, secure, and intellectually self-sufficient.[2] Indeed, in this view, the last place an autonomous person would want to be is in politics. There are too many voices arguing for personalized or group solutions to political problems. Politics is cacophonous, anarchic, combative, sleazy, and corrupt; far better, therefore, to keep to one's citadel, the private world that one can command.

Keep in mind, however, that autonomy requires persons to give an account, in dialogue, of their decisions, actions, and positions. Therefore, autonomous persons not only honor, but also seek out diverse ways of life. A liberal, believing that the life she is living is a good life, if not the best life, also harbors doubts about that life. Because she thinks this is a good life, she is open to possibilities and evidence of other, perhaps even better, ways of life. After all, she wants to lead a life that is good, not a life that is good for you or for me. If that were the case, if such relativism were acknowledged, then any life deemed good would indeed be good. But an autonomous person wants to determine what a good life is. How does she make determinations about the goodness, the quality, of her life? She must be willing and be able to reflect on the paths that she and others have taken; to scrutinize values and means and ends; to reconsider in the light of evidence, especially from other ways of life and perspectives on life and on life's issues, her own choices; and to give an account of that reflection and scrutiny.

She needs to hear the perspectives and objections of others and to consider those seriously.[3] She puts these, and her, views through what Galston calls "the most rigorous process of dialectical testing." This testing he calls "the dialectic of social inquiry" (1991, 37), which is similar to what Gadamer (1981) described as "social reasoning." It is what I call dialogic democracy; it is political decision making through collective reasoning.

But all of this seems beside the point, if not quaint or hollow. In a representative democracy laws and policies are made by officeholders who have won elections. Still, comments George Kateb, "the exercise of political authority is not only enabled but guided, in some way, by those who are to obey the laws and endure and experience the policies" (1992, 36). Kateb invokes two justifications for representative democracy offered by the Framers. First, representatives derive their authority from the consent, and sovereignty, of the people; second, if the people are displeased with the actions of their representatives, they can "guide" them out of office at the next election.[4] Political authority, in Kateb's and the Framers' view, is not guided by those who wield it, but, instead, by those who "choose those who wield it" (1992, 37). Thus, he concludes, "[T]he electoral system is a form of people's self-rule." In other words, the electoral system is a form of people's autonomy.

Yet if what I have said about autonomy is cogent, if not true, then this cannot be so, for the electoral system, by design, lacks the components that constitute autonomy: self-reflective, rational thought (implying critical distance and reasons) and social interaction or dialogue. Although our choices of representatives might be made autonomously, these can hardly serve as illustrations of what we mean by directing and authoring our own lives. Such choices do not constitute self-ruling or self-governing.[5] Kateb seems to accept the fiction that what representative democracy ought to do is educe the public exercise of autonomy. Autonomy can be exercised only by the person himself, and it can be exercised only in public by citizens themselves.

We are reminded, therefore, of Jefferson's concept of ward democracy as a way to overcome the problem of the vast republic and of education to "inform discretion" as a way to elevate citizen competence. Both, or variations of both, are necessary if citizens today are to exercise autonomy in public; that is, if they are to be democrats and we are to have more control over our lives through increased democratic participation. The key to gaining that control, however, revolves, as I see it, around deliberation, a value that Jefferson did not emphasize.

Deliberation

Talking together about political conflicts is essential both to liberal personhood and to democratic citizenship. The liberal needs to hear and consider different perspectives as a way of understanding the scope of the political issue and a way of finding a possible solution. Where deliberation is an essential element, the focus is not simply on finding an acceptable solution; it is also on coming to understand the various perspectives, the different perspectives, on the issue. The hope is that by considering all perspectives seriously, which includes criticism of perspectives, the participants can come to some "compound common good": a decision that all may not agree with but will agree to, since all have had an equal chance to participate and all who did participate think that they have been treated fairly.[6]

As Gutmann and Thompson (1996) point out, deliberation is not just talk, but a certain kind of talk, one in which participants must give reasons that others can understand and could accept. Such reasons enable participants to accept political outcomes, even when those outcomes go against the participants.[7] The authors go on to argue that laws adoped after deliberation of conflicting claims are more likely to be seen as legitimate than those enacted by other methods (41-43).

The immediate question, however, is why deliberation has anything to do with dialogue or discussion about different perspectives. Nothing in the term etymologically suggests that deliberation must be dialogic. Literally it means "to weigh thoroughly."[8] Yet today we add to the idea of weighing thoroughly, and carefully, the additional element of consulting or conferring, as in jury deliberations. What in autonomy requires consideration and consultation? As we have seen, autonomy requires that a choice or decision be rational, for with the requirement of rationality comes the commitment to discussion or deliberation, in both senses of the word. In short, we cannot be autonomous alone. Furthermore, the self about which we are deliberating is not just "I" alone but "we," the collectivity.

Some contemporary discussions of democratic deliberation resurrect concerns about the people's competence. Working within the confines of our current political system, George Will and James Fishkin propose an emphasis in democracy on deliberation, but only for a select few.

Will (*Restoration*, 1992) wants to reestablish the deliberative function, and purpose of Congress. Hamilton in *Federalist* 71 and Madison in *Federalist* 63

remind us that the senators were to serve as custodians of the people's true interests until, through the constant "cool and sedate reflection" of their senators, the
people could be returned to their own sound judgment and good sense. Both
Hamilton and Madison suggest that the people can be coolly and sedately reflective. But the majority, as in democracies past, were inclined toward impetuosity
and intemperance.

How is the people's cool and deliberate sense to be distinguished from its
rash, intemperate, and unreflective sentiments? Hamilton tells us in *Federalist*
71 that "the republican principle demands that the deliberative sense of the
community should govern the conduct of those to whom they intrust the management of their affairs" (1987, 409). Presumably, the representatives of the
people would judge whether the people's view is reflective or impetuous. How
could it be otherwise, when the people were without opportunities to develop
and express that deliberative sense? How could that sense prevail? One way
might be to take the people's collective temperature through national opinion
polls. Then representatives can debate about which opinion is unreflective and
which is deliberative. George Will dreams of a deliberative democracy of this
sort, in which our elected officials do not rush to translate the people's appetites
into governmental action, but, rather, endeavor to control the popular will by
disciplining desires with reasons. Government, then, would remind its citizens
of what it is we ought to want, not help us attain whatever it is we do want. The
conservative overtones here are familiar.

Will's definition of deliberative democracy is straightforward: "A deliberative institution is one in which members reason together about the problems confronting the community and strive to promote policies in the general interest of
the community" (1992, 110-11). Yet he wants to see deliberation restricted to
one institution, one body, a group of elected representatives serving at some
"constitutional distance from the people" (110). Will believes that this distance
is crucial for preventing our representatives from being lured into the people's
impetuosity.

Will is content to leave the deliberations to Congress, and it would be a victory indeed if Congress coolly and sedately deliberated. Yet Will also acknowledges that the ingredients necessary for successful deliberation—thoughtfulness,
persuasion, judgment, and reason—constitute "the noble power possessed by
ordinary people" (115). Then why shouldn't all, on some occasions or in some
forums, exercise their power in public, for the community? Perhaps Will thinks
that our extended republic is simply too vast for that kind of deliberative democracy,[9] but I suspect that the real reason lies in his concern that the people want
more than they ought to want. This calls into question their fitness to rule. When
it comes to one's own impulses and desires, each citizen is unable to curtail or
temper his own desires, though he can curtail or temper the desires of others.

Thus the inability to rule one's self makes each citizen unfit to govern the self of the collectivity.

James Fishkin also acknowledges that the people are capable of deliberation. In his view, however, their deliberations are stymied by the number of citizens and the size of our republic. It is impractical, says Fishkin, "for the entire electorate to be engaged in face-to-face deliberation" (1991, 84).

Fishkin proposes a national, deliberative opinion poll that "brings the face-to-face democracy of the Athenian Assembly or the New England town meeting to the large-scale nation-state" (1991, 4). That is a grandiose claim. As Fishkin admits, it brings deliberation not to the nation-state but to a microcosm. His deliberative opinion poll would consist of 600 randomly selected citizens who would meet at a single site to engage in two or three days of dialogue with presidential candidates.[10] From the deliberations of these few, the many, presuming that citizens would watch the proceedings on television, would learn how better to assess the candidates.

The immediate question is, how are these ideas any improvement over, or any different from, our current political campaigns? Fishkin's scheme gives us, he claims, a statistical representation of "what the electorate would think if it could be immersed in an intensive deliberative process . . . if it could be given an opportunity for extensive reflection and access to information" (1991, 81). While restructuring campaign debates and organizing more Clintonesque "town meetings" might give the electorate more candid questions and answers, as well as longer discussions of particular issues, the learning would still be "filtered through the media rather than resulting from face-to-face interaction with the candidates" (1991, 6).

It is not deliberation Fishkin wants to focus on, but the transmission from these 600 citizens to the rest of the electorate of what to think about these candidates. After all, the great benefit of dialogue is the ability to engage in it, especially face to face. Fishkin's scheme is merely a different form of representative politics. There is nothing participatory except for the 600 who, despite being drawn nationally, are an elite who will tell us what they, and thus we, think. Fishkin insists, of course, that the deliberative opinion poll is not elitist because it is representative of ordinary citizens; the group is drawn from all over the country, from the pool of eligible voters, not from any single segment of society or socioeconomic status. Yet elite also means that a group exercises the major share of authority or influence within a larger organization.

We have no practical political alternative, says Fishkin, to his scheme. Using Dahl's idea of "enlightened understanding," Fishkin argues that enabling each citizen to have adequate and equal opportunities for discovering and validating his or her preferences on a pending political issue is an ideal. It is an ideal and not a viable proposition for political decision making where what is called for is action, or restraint from action. Meeting that ideal might bring us close to something like Habermas's "ideal speech situation," which Fishkin describes as "a situation of free and equal discussion, unlimited in its duration, constrained only by the consensus which would be arrived at by the 'force of the better argument'" (1991, 36). But in politics, when a conflict challenges and possibly disrupts the collectivity, there is some urgency in arriving at the best possible political solution within a given time frame. There is not the luxury, in Fishkin's view, of unrestricted and unlimited discussion.

Habermas's model, and even Braybrooke's stepped-down version—the "logically completed debate"[11]—would be "far out of reach for any actual deliberative body limited by what Dahl calls the 'time permitted by the need for a decision'" (1991, 37). Not that far out of reach. One can permit a free and open discussion for a limited time period, measured in hours and not minutes. Few political issues what we might think appropriate for direct democratic decision making would require an immediate course of action, a point to which I shall recur in the next section.

Fishkin says that "American democracy has been moving in the general direction of sacrificing deliberation to political equality" (1991, 40). Does Fishkin mean that as we included more, and "different," citizens in voting, we moved away from deliberation? But, as I have argued, it seems that American democracy began in some measure with political equality and little deliberation. All property-owning white males, regardless of education or sense, voted equally, though perhaps could not serve equally in government. But where and when was there ever deliberation among voters? Deliberation on or about what? Conducted in what way?

That is Fishkin's problem. He does not address the central irony that among voters there has not been much to deliberate about except which candidate was better, and that has historically been little more than a sharing of opinions (if not gossip) on character. Are these matters for deliberation? It is not as if Fishkinian deliberations will result in an alternative, a synthesis, or a solution to a problem. Rather, his deliberations lead only to a new or reinforced opinion on a candidate—or perhaps an alternative candidate, but not an alternative to the candidates.

According to his own typology, a "Direct, Madisonian" democracy—that is, a democracy in which political decisions are made directly by the citizens but in which certain safeguards against majority tyranny are built in—would involve no deliberation. Deliberation for Fishkin, as for Will, is appropriate only for elected leaders (1991, 45-46), either among themselves or between them and the electors during campaigns.[12]

Although Fishkin never defines or describes what he means by deliberation, I agree with him that "[t]he fact that our present quiescent, disengaged public has not bothered to think enough about politics to have public opinions (rather than political preferences) worthy of the name, does not mean that it might not arrive at more informed and more deliberative opinions under conditions designed to truly engage it" (1991, 58). But will his scheme do any more than our current system to effect informed and deliberative opinions among the public, not just among the 600 polling subjects?

Fishkin and I also agree that more deliberation is necessary in our democratic politics. Yet he thinks that only a representative democracy with rights safeguarded and power delegated by a written constitution can bring deliberation while preserving political equality. On the other hand, and using his own terms, I think that deliberation can be combined with political equality in a system with more, if not greater, direct democratic practices and Madisonian protections. The system would not be direct-majoritarian; the Constitution would still separate, and balance, powers and protect rights. Fishkin and I disagree because the sort of deliberation he is after our democratic system already provides in kind though not for Fishkin sufficient degree: "[W]e get some deliberation among political elites in representative institutions" (1991, 44). All we need to do to improve the system, he says, is provide "an effective hearing to competing political views," views with a "significant following," or, as he defines them, views that generate a movement or an elite (1991, 45).

Fishkin is right that we cannot recapitulate Athenian democracy in the modern nation-state. There are too many citizens to make it feasible for them to meet face to face (1991, 84). But the entire nation-state does not have to meet face to face as a single group. Instead there could be myriad deliberative groups limited only by a realistic assessment of the size needed to accommodate open participation (1991, 93). With the advances in telecommunications, why couldn't there be a network of interactive town meetings, or Jeffersonian wards, with the various candidates spread throughout the country, or in one state, talking to one another via telecommunicative hookup, while being interrogated by citizens and experts in person and via telephone?[13] Granted, not everyone's question, or every question, could be addressed, but two days of such town meetings would provide enough information for well-informed deliberations to ensue. On the third day citizens could meet face to face in their wards or deliberative groups, without candidates or experts, to deliberate among themselves on the issues and candidates. That would be intensive deliberation of a positive sort for all citizens inclined to participate. If deliberation is good for the participants (1991, 83), then let's have deliberation for everyone.

If Fishkin really wants to combine deliberation and political equality, then why not institutionalize a system in which everyone can participate in some democratic deliberations necessary for making some of our public policies? The question then becomes not whether we should do so, but how we could do so: on regional and local issues rather than national? In a system of representative government and participatory referenda? Through various methods of interactive telecommunications? In other words, we ought not to concur that people have the capacities for deliberation but then dismiss deliberative settings for all because theorists can envision no way to institutionalize Athenian democracy in our sizable nation-state. Aristotle argued that a fundamental component of a good human life was deliberation; indeed, it is part of what defines us as human. Therefore, to exercise our humanity and develop those essentially human capacities we need to engage in activities that require deliberation. For Aristotle, as well as for us, that must include politics.

If we agree with Noah Webster that we reach good decisions and create binding legislation only "after attending to the best official information from every quarter, and after a full discussion of the subject in an assembly, where clashing interests conspire to detect error and suggest improvements,"[14] then we ought to pursue this kind of deliberation for everyone, and perhaps not only in strictly political settings. If we conclude that political deliberation is good for everyone, then let us examine exhaustively the issues that preclude its realization rather than pretending that a "deliberative opinion poll" will bring us deliberative democracy.

At the same time, let us remind George Will that while Edmund Burke averred that Parliament was "a deliberative assembly of one nation, with one interest, that of the whole,"[15] he also concluded that when the people act with deliberation, the multitude "is wise, and when time is given to it, as a species it always acts right."[16] Although deliberation solely by representatives might save a step in creating political policy, since they would simply recapitulate, on an extrapolation from Fishkin's reading, how the citizenry would itself deliberate, and while this might eventuate in good policy, such representation excludes the citizens from the (putative) personal benefits of deliberation and from generating even better policy: coming to a deeper understanding of the issues and a deeper commitment to a position on them; expanding one's own, as well as the public's, view; discerning the true interest of the country; expanding fellow feeling and social solidarity; overcoming apathy through feelings of efficacy; and feeling that one is not only guiding one's own life but is also helping to guide the collective life.

Politics of Initiative

What are the appropriate settings for deliberative democracy? Such a question, of course, raises the issue of how we could hope to establish citizenship participation in political decision making in so expansive a nation as ours. Jefferson gave us a clue as to how government could be organized. It would consist of tiers, starting at the local level with Jeffersonian wards, or their equivalent, and progressing up through elective bodies at the city, county, regional, state, and national levels. Deliberative, or dialogic, democracy would thus be a mix, an imbrication, of representative and participatory institutions.

Whatever the mix—and we might follow, for example, the schemes and arguments of two political theorists: Jane Mansbridge (1980) or Benjamin Barber (1984)—deliberation or dialogue must hold a prominent place in the life of the polity. That is so not only because the exercise of deliberation is fundamental, both to autonomy and democracy, but also because there are significant political issues that the people must decide. A society would have to sort out, and decide how to sort out, which tiers would be participatory, and when. Consider Iain McLean's sobering example:

> Suppose the U.K. were broken up into direct-democratic communities of about 2,000 population each. There would be about 30,000 of them. So if they each sent one delegate to the national meeting deciding the balance between energy conservation, coal power, and nuclear power, that meeting could not itself be run on direct-democratic lines, even with the best computing equipment imaginable. So there would have to be a two-stage procedure. Perhaps each commune in Oxfordshire (200 of them) would send a delegate to a county meeting, there select a county delegate and decide how she should vote on every motion on the published agenda for the national meeting. Then she would go to the national meeting with the delegates from each of the other counties. At the national meeting somebody proposes an amendment to a motion on the order paper. The business must stop while each delegate must go on line [via computer] to her county assembly, each county assembly goes on line to its communities and the results are passed back up. Somebody then proposes another amendment. . . . I hope I do not need to go on. (1989, 139)

Such an example illustrates the need for electing Burkean representatives, not delegates, and thus for the mix of representative and participatory levels. One way to do this is to use the wards or neighborhood assemblies not only for deciding local political issues, but also for deliberating on national issues through something like a "politics of initiative."

An initiative is a proposed resolution that is to be acted or voted on by the electorate as a whole. It is proposed in writing and printed, or otherwise copied, and distributed not for initial approval or consideration, but to secure the signatures of some number of fellow citizens who support the bringing of this resolution before the electorate.[17] I have in mind here citizen initiatives, those proposed by citizens themselves.

Initiatives, often considered in conjunction with referenda and recall, have long been part of our political landscape. Since the seventeenth century initiatives have been used in New England town meetings as a means of enabling citizens to exercise their law-making powers by placing on the agenda through petition various proposed ordinances to be discussed and voted on. A look at the literature, however, reveals almost no emphasis on deliberation in the politics of initiative.[18] As it is now conceived, a politics of initiative is insufficient as a forum for the public exercise of autonomy; that is, as a deliberative democratic forum. It is not enough simply to be able to cast a ballot on behalf of or in opposition to a particular initiative. We need the interaction of citizens in forums of deliberation or deliberational dialogue.[19] By including dialogue, a politics of initiative could provide a crucial form of deliberative democracy.

As currently constituted, an initiative, once sanctioned and accepted, must be publicized so that the electorate knows that it is on the ballot and is to be decided. Depending on the nature of the issue to be decided, hearings of experts should be conducted on television by representatives or disinterested bodies (such as panels of Fishkinian citizens or even of political theorists). This will provide background and informed perspectives for the citizens to use in their deliberations, but would not substitute for deliberation itself. Call-in hearings would also allow citizens some participation. The hearings could be conducted in a "town-meeting" atmosphere, with a live audience of citizens or even of conflicting special interests.

With transcriptions and recordings of the hearings widely circulated, printed in newspapers and placed on audio- and videocassettes made available, like periodicals, in local libraries (at government expense), citizens would meet in their wards or neighborhood assemblies[20] for deliberation on the initiative, one initiative at a time. Some set number of days might be set aside for hearings and public discussions; some set number of hours might be set aside for ward deliberation. Citizens should not be locked into a choice of either/or.[21] Voters should be asked to consider and vote for two, or at most a few, options.

How the resolution is decided is itself a political issue, but a majority vote would on the surface seem acceptable. This would be a majority vote of all the participants, not just of each ward. Depending on the level at which the initiative appears, perhaps the chief executive (president, governor, or mayor) would have veto power over the vote, a veto that would require the electorate to vote on the measure a second time.[22] Courts would have the same authority to review successful initiatives as they do to review legislation; after all, the judiciary holds the power to declare laws unconstitutional or otherwise to mitigate their purposes, applications, or consequences. The legislative assembly, of the states or of the federal government, could review the initiative for possible amendments, which would have to be approved by the people. Some limits should be placed on how often and when a defeated initiative could be reopened or resubmitted.

As implied above, initiatives could be statewide, regional, or national. The United States is one of the few nations never to have had a national initiative or referendum.[23] Thomas Cronin opposes the idea of a national initiative because the process "would involve making national laws based on general public opinion at a particular moment" (1989, 194). By general public opinion Cronin means "simple" public opinion—citizens vote their preferences or prejudices and may or may not be informed well or at all. In our scheme, however, information and deliberation are essential components. "[I]nitiative processes divorced from innovative programs for public talk and deliberation fall easy victims to plebiscitary abuses and to the manipulation by money and elites of popular prejudice" (Barber, 1984, 263). Cronin does say that initiative democracy stimulates educational debate, but his version of such debate is of a pallid kind: "[P]ublic officials, newspapers, radio and television stations, and various interest groups often take a stand and trigger at least limited public discussion" (1989, 226). Again, in this view, citizens are mostly left watching discussions. Deliberation must be active, must be active political talk, to use Barber's phrase. Observing is an exiguous form of participation.

A politics of initiative as proposed here is not the same as plebiscitary democracy. A plebiscite is a direct vote in which citizens are asked to accept or reject the proposal initiated by a person or group. While my version of direct democracy contains a plebiscite, that vote is to be preceded with testimony by and examination of experts and then by deliberation among citizens. Additionally, a politics of initiative could use the multichoice ballot. This format provides a range of options that runs from simple "yes, I strongly support the initiative," through support for the initiative but with reservations or even calls for reformulation, to outright opposition to it. As Barber points out (1984, 287), "the multichoice format discourages purely private choices and encourages voters to have public reasons for what public acts." Deliberation among citizens demands of participants some airing of their views and, more important, their reasons for holding those views.

Nor would a politics of initiative necessarily diminish political leadership, for our representatives, at whatever level, should lead the way in presenting cogent arguments in favor of or in opposition to various proposals. They might well be part of the expert testimony, as witnesses or as questioners of witnesses.

Would people participate? That seems the wrong question to ask, for on one level we want to institute democratic procedures in which citizens *can* participate in making political decisions important to them. Certainly few if any citizens would participate on every initiative; that would be overwhelmingly time-consuming. They will participate when they think that the issues are central to their lives. As Delos Wilcox pointed out in 1912:

Popular indifference to politics becomes more and more inconceivable as the people's intimate dependence upon cooperation for the rendering of necessary services increases. What can be more interesting than the character of the roads we use, the amount of the taxes we have to pay, the efficiency of the schools where our children are educated, the purity and abundance of the water supply, the quality and price of gas and of the electric and telephone services, the removal of garbage from our doors, the convenience of . . . transportation, the reliability and promptness of the postal service, the maintenance of adequate fire and police protection, the prevention and cure of disease by the health department, and other things like these? (252)

Initiatives are thought to stimulate greater interest and participation in the political process. "In fact, in the 23 states with initiatives on the ballot, turnout has been much higher than in states without initiatives on the ballot" (Hahn and Kamieniecki, 1987, 18). In 1991 the state of Washington had a euthanasia initiative on the ballot, which brought out over 68 percent of the electorate, far larger than the state electorate's turnout in the 1992 presidential election. In several western states more citizens vote on the ballot measures than vote in state legislative races. In Oregon in 1986 "voters paid more attention to a controversial 'right-to-work' referendum than to the hotly contested U.S. Senate and gubernatorial races" (Cronin, 1989, 67-68).

I am not suggesting that all citizens will participate in deliberations on all initiatives. Oscar Wilde's quip about socialism taking too many evenings would then pertain to democracy as well. Instead, I am suggesting that when citizens have some personal interest, and even a stake, in an initiative proposal, then they will participate. How many initiatives that might be I cannot predict, but surely if participation is counted in days and hours per initiative, then citizens can handle several per year.

What issues might appear on our national initiatives? A balanced budget amendment, the equal rights amendment, gun control, congressional pay raises, affirmative action, the volunteer army, campaign reform, prayer in public schools, right-to-work laws, term limits for members of Congress, English as the official national language, termination of tobacco and dairy subsidies, capital punishment, euthanasia, and hate speech are all issues that might appear. It is difficult to imagine that autonomous citizens would ignore participation that exercises autonomy, that makes a citizen more autonomous by enabling him to help make decisions on issues that affect his life.

In large groups, in national elections, one participant has virtually no effect on the outcome. But in small groups the opposite is true. In a neighborhood assembly one's participation could have a decisive effect. Any single participant's contribution could significantly alter the outcome, as individual arguments prove to be persuasive. But the ward serves only as a forum for deliberation. In the end, after testimony and deliberation among fellow citizens, each voter votes his/her conscience.

Does any citizen's vote have any greater impact with the introduction of deliberation? Obviously, no. Yet the crucial point of participation is the exercise of autonomy, which includes a chance to have an effect on creating with others good policy—that is, to participate in a democratic decision-making procedure that enables all participants to contribute their perspectives, to have those perspectives heard, and to hear the perspectives of others. In this way, one can come to accept the outcome of the procedure even when that outcome is not the one a participant sought.

Perhaps of all the reasons for participation, this is the most fundamental, and impressive: deliberation aims to arrive at agreement on the content of a proposal. That is so because the procedure demands that each participant offer the reasons why a participant holds a certain view. This is the accountability one expects from any person who is autonomous, and it is the accountability that the democratic procedure demands from any citizen who participates. The purpose of the procedure is to find reasons that all participants will find persuasive. It is to find reasons that can make the proposal, or its defeat, acceptable to others.[24] It will happen, however, that all do not agree, that all are not satisfied or persuaded. But regardless of the outcome, the group, having been through the procedure and having had the opportunity of presenting their positions and reasons for them, as well as hearing those of others, are more likely to acknowledge the legitimacy of the result.

If deliberative democracy is impracticable in large societies, and yet liberalism promotes the exercise of autonomy as part of the good life, then either liberals must settle for the traditional setting of autonomous action—the private sphere—or else deliberative participation must also be available in the public sphere. In a large society the appropriate public sphere would be a politics of initiative—county, state, region, nation—as well as local politics.

Yet in the private sphere the exercise of autonomy is less demanding. If I do not care whether my choices are autonomous, then I can retreat to my inner citadel and remain isolated from the opinions or deliberations of others. The perspective that I have been developing here is that liberals want to exercise autonomy; they want to define, author, and control their own lives; and most want to do so with full knowledge that they are *self*-determining and *self*-ruled. In a pluralistic culture they want to explain to others the reasons they live as they do and hold the values, goals, and ideas that they do. Moreover, they want to hear about the lives, goals, values, and ideas of others. In short, they want to persuade and want to be persuaded.

Therefore liberals, as persons and citizens, are continually looking for venues for exercising autonomy: for making self-reflective, rational choices and for adducing the reasons for doing so. According to this theory, many liberals, if they could, would extend into the private sphere the public, democratic procedures in which the exercise of autonomy is required. Here any group or association of which one is a member, including workplaces, would institute democratic procedures so that decisions for that group or association could be made through "public" arguments and the adducement of reasons.

I am not suggesting by this that the presence of democratic—that is, deliberative—procedures indicates that a group or association becomes a site for government intervention. Liberalism must still respect the need for the public/private boundary that separates the state from the affairs that are properly the citizen's own business. Otherwise, it is possible for restive and malignant democratic majorities to tyrannize through their decisions segments of the citizenry. That liberals need and respect the public/private boundary goes without saying. It must be kept in mind, however, that where that boundary is drawn is itself a political question.

The point I am making here is different. Democracy is at bottom a way of making collective decisions and of resolving or temporarily settling political conflicts. Political conflicts arise whenever there is a disagreement or dispute between the two parties. Whenever such a conflict arises, it ought to be settled through a dialogic democratic procedure, for this process provides for the hearing and evaluating of different perspectives and can lead to compromises or solutions that parties, because of the nature of their participation, might more readily accept. That procedure is, of course, the "public" exercise of autonomy. In other words, the political conflict creates from the relationship of the individual, or group, and the collectivity involved in the dispute "a public." No matter how small the collectivity or how private its operations—workplace, family, school, hospital, union, occupational association—once the public is created—which occurs out of a political need (a conflict erupts or a collective decision must be made)—then dialogic democracy ensues. No conflict could be ended, therefore, without the public presentation and discussion of arguments—reasons and evidence—related to the dispute. Resolution or settlement occurs only through deliberation, persuasion, and attempted agreement.

Once again, I am not suggesting widening the sphere that we call the "public" sphere—those areas of life administered by or that are the purview of the state. Rather, I am suggesting that even within the legitimate private sphere—within, that is, civil society—there are political conflicts that ought to be resolved democratically. Liberal democrats, recognizing the political aspects of all social settings—including the family, social clubs, workplaces, philanthropic organizations, professional associations, and the like—might well press for democratic procedures in those settings when political conflicts arise.

Whom would these liberal democrats press? The state? We can imagine an overzealous liberal democrat proposing "democratic courts" or "state arbitrators" who would referee disputes. Imagine further that a domineering husband makes all the decisions in a family: what cars to buy, what food to eat, what colors to paint the house, what schedules family members should be on. Would the wife who resents this domination seek redress through a democratic court? Would the husband deign to participate? Would the state intercede and make him participate or else hold him legally liable? But this is not a case for state intervention. This is a private dispute between husband and wife/family. Our liberal democrat might try to persuade them to deliberate about their relationship, just as he might try to convince his bridge club to introduce democratic procedures for their decision making. But persuasion is the only recourse. State intervention is not an option.[25]

A multicultural society that is also a participatory democracy will necessarily include, avers Nancy Fraser, "many different publics, including at least one public in which participants can deliberate as peers across lines of difference about policy that concerns them all" (1990, 70). Who is included in all? A political conflict in a group can become an issue for that "private public." In such a case only members of this group can participate in the resolution of the conflict. The proper political sphere is the private public. Political matters that are public affairs pertain to all citizens, whether the matter is local, regional, statewide, or national. Thus all citizens would be eligible to participate in Public matters—about, say, whether one has a right to do X, Y, or Z where those might stand for "have an abortion," "medically assist in someone's suicide," or "publicize pornographic material for sale."

More narrowly, residents of a specific neighborhood could participate in an effort to close a topless nightclub, while residents of certain western states could participate in the resolution of a dispute about diverting water from the Colorado River. Only workers in a factory, however, could participate to require the factory to cease unsafe labor practices. Once again, it is important to point out that who participates can itself be an issue of political conflict. Who is to decide whether that factory, located in Scranton, Pennsylvania, should close so that its manufacturing can be done in Taiwan?

The standard line of participatory democrats used to be that what affects all should be decided by all (*Omnes Tangit Ab Omnibus Approbitur*). When a political issue directly and significantly affects your life, you should be able to help make decisions about that issue. Yet the terms "directly and significantly affect" are ambiguous, equivalent to the ambiguity of Mill's notion of harm. Contemporary issues such as environmental pollution, depletion of the ozone layer, and the epidemiological scourge of AIDS defy political boundaries. What happens to the justification for participatory democracy when the political issue is a global one cutting across political boundaries? Can we say to the Canadians that they have no right to participate in our decisions on what to do about acid rain? What do we say to consumers who may be affected by the product lines of a manufacturer? They, too, are directly and significantly affected. Yet the definition of "participant" cannot rest on whether one's vote on the issue places a burden on or removes a burden from oneself. That pertains as well to those affected by the outcome who may live in other, foreign political jurisdictions. The only way to restrict participation is to recognize that participants can only be those who have been defined or designated as members of the collectivity in the dispute. Such definitions or designations are themselves open to political conflict and thus to resolution through democratic procedures.

Regardless of who participates, mutual respect and the importance of difference is required of participants in dialogic, or deliberative, forums. When citizens participate, they must take into account when making a collective decision the different, and differing, views and proposals offered. This taking and giving an account is what I mean by mutual respect, and the mechanism for operating in this way, for maintaining mutual respect and acknowledging difference, is built into the democratic process itself.[26] It is not a required virtue brought by each citizen to the process. The Framers got this right: the political system should strive to make virtue superfluous as a prerequisite of participation. Instead, the democratic procedure should be a device that can take and work through citizens as they are. What conditions should be built in? They are, to review, some of the conditions of autonomy:

1. Free inquiry requiring freedom of thought and expression;
2. Tolerance of diverse and divergent views, but, more important;
3. Openness, the seeking out and soliciting of differences and the taking up and consideration of different perspectives as if they were one's own; and
4. Reasonableness and common sense, the undogmatic use of one's rational abilities.[27] *See Chap. 4*

Citizens come with their own interests and prejudices, but participation will demand that they move, at least temporarily, beyond those interests and prejudices. They must think inclusively, not exclusively; comprehensively, not parochially; reflectively, not instinctively. They can continue to hold to group perspectives, but they must recognize that other groups different from theirs have their own perspectives that deserve to be taken into account. Taking them into account, even when the perspectives are despicable or outrageous, does not mean that these positions have to be adopted uncritically. Taking up a perspective is to treat that perspective as if it were one's own. That is, one should consider it seriously, and that means, furthermore, that the perspective—its assumptions, evidence, and consequences—will be critically examined. In other words, participants cannot simply assert their positions and opinions. They must be willing and able to adduce arguments as to why their perspective is right, just, proper, and the like.[28]

Openness to other perspectives and a willingness, indeed, a requirement, to hold those perspectives reflectively and to consider them seriously, which includes critique, is to pay a compliment to difference. As I said earlier, this is a sign of respect, even of dignity.[29]

This is not a gargantuan demand. We expect and demand proper behavior even today when citizens participate in the system. Education, let alone the state, cannot guarantee that all citizens will manifest the traits of or will understand mutual respect and openness. But citizens can learn how to act and can understand what is required in democratic procedures.

But this might be an egregious demand of groups and individuals unprepared for the democratic procedures, those who have been on the margins or previously excluded from participation. What of them? Why should deliberative democracy prevail and not the specific behavior or rules of conduct of marginalized groups? Because these procedures are thought to be the best way to treat all persons and groups and even different ways of life with equal respect. The reader should not need to be reminded that I am describing a *liberal* democracy, and values central to liberalism will appear to be favored. But not all liberals, clearly, will subscribe to my definition and description of liberalism. Classical liberals will not, nor will those who favor individualism, strong neutrality, and politics as the aggregation of particular interests, with the winner taking all.

Democracy as Collective Autonomy

It is difficult, but not impossible, to see how a person could think of himself as autonomous, could think that his actions and his life were indeed his own, if the political sphere were beyond his direct participation. An entire, and fundamentally significant, portion of his life would be out of bounds. Then, again, politics may touch none of a person's good life; he might decide autonomously not to participate. Yet the question is not so much whether one will participate, but whether one can participate: can one who seeks to be self-ruling be *fully* autonomous if she cannot be self-governing; that is, cannot participate in making those decisions that affect not only her own life, but also her life as it intersects with the collectivity? Philosopher Richard Norman comments:

> It is an entirely pertinent psychological fact that [there] are matters about which people feel helpless, at the mercy of forces which they cannot control, and hence singularly lacking in autonomy. And the only way in which they could have any degree of effective control over them would be through democratic institutions in

which they could feel themselves to be playing a direct and active part. . . . [T]he individual who has no access to the process of collective debate may thereby have less rational control over his or her own life. (1992, 49)

Full autonomy does not mean that one must have critically examined every choice. It means that an autonomous person could critically examine *any* choice and could give reasons for why she made that choice. This condition seems exiguous. But, furthermore, a fully autonomous person would be one who is self-determining in all those aspects of her life plan and its activities that she thinks (self-reflectively, of course) to be vital to her living a good life. It is difficult to imagine that such aspects would not include work and family and some political issues.

How reflective does one have to be? In truth, the procedures I envision are not much different from a discussion in a classroom. Essential to such a discussion are freedom of thought and expression, openness, tolerance, reasonableness, and respect for the personhood of others. Above all, it is the desire to participate, rather than talent for expressing one's views in discussion, that is paramount. This, comments Eva Brann, makes the intention to participate "potentially universal" (*Paradoxes of Education in a Republic,* 1979, 106). One need not be highly articulate or deeply philosophical to participate.

The keystone of a classroom discussion and of the democratic procedures that I envision, and built into both, is the recognition that participants are there to collaborate. The intention among all participants, therefore, should be to hear, review, and examine all perspectives as possible enrichments of one's own perspective and of the perspective of the group or collectivity. If such a position vis-à-vis a particular perspective is not possible—to wit, if someone's view is daft or wrong—then the flaws should be pointed out as carefully and cogently and respectfully as possible. In short, participants are expected to be civil to one another, and it is no accident that *civil* and *civility* derive from the Latin *civilitas,* which was originally used to translate the Greek *politike* or civil government.

Is it required that citizens come to deliberative democratic procedures with certain prescribed character traits or values? It is not. Yet they ought to come with certain habits of mind, for that will enable them to participate more readily, and perhaps heartily. But certain habits of mind are not a prerequisite of participation either. At the same time, liberals will want to cultivate those habits of mind that enable persons to be effectively autonomous. It is no accident that the conditions built into the democratic procedures are those of autonomy, for in a liberal democracy it is evident that such conditions are the best way to treat all citizens fairly and equally.

Must citizens be autonomous to participate? Is the liberal democratic state going to demand that all citizens be autonomous? What does this say to those who resist autonomy?

What I have suggested is that democratic dialogue is built upon the same elements that autonomous choice is built upon. One might be able to participate easily, deliberate widely, and reflect deeply without self-critically distancing oneself from the values, ends, and practices central to one's *individual* life. Democracy as the public exercise of autonomy is *collective* self-direction, and that must entail a self-critical distancing, at some point in the deliberations, from the values, ends, and practices of the polity itself to scrutinize those values, ends, and practices.

This definition reflects the Greek understanding of autonomy as independence of the city from control by foreign powers. Citizens in Athens were responsible for what the city did, how it behaved, and what it became. Just so in liberal democracy the citizens are responsible for what the polity does, how it behaves, and what it becomes. Herein the requirement, as a collectivity, is for self-critical distance. Therefore democracy is collective autonomy, for it is not just what *I* choose, but what *we* choose. The procedures for political decision making will require capacities for reflection and deliberation. They include and build upon the same capacities and the same procedure that liberals as individuals use to exercise autonomy. Although no citizen will be required to turn those capacities on herself and her way of life, "critical distance . . . is likely to result" (Galston, 1991, 255).

Amy Gutmann raises the issue of whether self-reflection can be separated from critical reflection: "The skills of political reflection cannot be neatly differentiated from the skills of evaluating one's own way of life" (1995, 578). The key term here is "neatly." As Macedo suggests, there will be spillover into other areas of one's life when the habits of critical reflection are fostered through education (2000, 139, 179), and surely many students who are reflecting critically may turn those reflections onto their own deeply held beliefs. My point is that teachers cannot *require* students to do self-reflection without overstepping liberal authority and possibly harming the students in the process. I take up this issue again in chapter 5.

The liberal polity cannot demand that its citizens or its students be autonomous; nor can it demand that they participate. The best political decisions, however, will be made by reflective individuals engaged in deliberative dialogue, internally and intersubjectively, and therefore the polity can demand of its citizens, as they demand of themselves, that they be prepared to operate politically by equipping themselves intellectually with the skills of thoughtfulness. That requires the polity to commit to an education in deliberation. This is not an education *in* autonomy or *of* autonomy; it is at best an education that may prepare one to be autonomous, to be able to exercise autonomy. One is not forced by this education to be autonomous in public or private. One can be deeply reflective on or about an issue without being required by the state or state officials to be *self-*

reflective. The state, the school, and individual teachers cannot force any student to use the skills of thoughtfulness in a self-reflective way. It may be unimaginable that any student with those skills will refrain from doing so. But that in itself is, or could be, an autonomous choice and is not the business of public education. Liberal individuals, cherishing the individual excellences of self-responsibility or autonomy, will, however, want to do so.

Which ought to come first, education in deliberation or the deliberative procedures in participatory settings? Should deliberative democratic forums be delayed until the society has established education in deliberation as its public-school agenda? In this way those who are unprepared for democratic participation will not be disadvantaged and suffer de facto disenfranchisement. Or should the participatory structures be put into place—in public and/or private—while or even before the educational agenda is set?

These are the two ways to move our polity toward greater public dialogue and deliberative democracy. In the first way we would press for a widened use of such practices as a politics of initiative and the extension of democratic procedures in private as well as public settings. In the second we would take seriously what many social commentators, political theorists, media pundits, and citizens already believe to be the case: our democratic system requires a well-informed, highly motivated citizenry capable of independent, critical judgment and deliberative decision making, and so we educate them to develop those skills. But in our current system, we certainly don't need this as long as we can produce a well-informed, well-educated elite. Then the people can continue to vote on "character," not issues. Preparing all citizens for dialogic democracy would change that.

Ideally, we should push for both ways. Since my focus is on education in deliberation, I advocate the second way in this book. Yet educating in deliberation could well result in generating autonomous adults who will demand a democracy in which they can be self-governing as well as self-ruling.

Thus pushing one way—an education in deliberation—could result in a push the other way—the call for deliberative democracy—as citizens demand autonomy's full exercise. This harkens back to Tocqueville's speech in 1848 before the Chamber of Deputies: spreading among the people, he said, are "opinions and ideas which are not concerned just with overthrowing this or that law, this or that administration, even this or that government, but society itself, shaking the foundations on which it now rests" (1969, 752). This was not because the propertyless masses were demanding social and political transformation; it was, instead, the educated as well as the workers who called for more democracy. It may be the same in our own time. Jefferson, whom Tocqueville called "the most powerful apostle of democracy there has ever been,"[30] reminded us of something similar. Jefferson advocated "a little rebellion now and then" to warn the rulers that the people were serious about preserving their liberties. The people may also become serious about exercising their liberties as rulers.

Notes

1. See Held, 1987, chapter 9.

2. For an argument that takes on those critics who see autonomy as reinforcing self-sufficiency, see Crittenden, 1993.

3. Eamonn Callan calls this the "multiplicity of perspectives" (Callan, 1997, 176) and argues public schools need to engender its appreciation within a context of dialogue (197). I discuss Callan's view in a subsequent chapter.

4. Kateb's parenthetical phrase "guided, *in some way"* suggests that perhaps he does not quite accept his own position. Emphasis added.

5. My friend and colleague Richard Dagger asks why such choices cannot serve as directing and authoring our own lives. "If I choose my physician, lawyer, stockbroker, etc., with care," he asks, "reflecting rationally on my aims and considering various conceptions of the good life, am I not acting autonomously?" Under such circumstances, one surely is acting autonomously. No one surrenders autonomy, pace Robert Paul Wolff, when he chooses someone to represent him. As I said, this is an autonomous act. But we defer to the expertise and judgment of such professionals as Dagger mentions in the light of our own lack of information and experience. As I argued in chapter 2 and as I shall argue in this chapter, many political issues, especially where they touch us personally, are not beyond our ken or experience and thus to defer to elected representatives in those cases is to surrender autonomy or to settle for less than full self-rule.

6. I have elsewhere (1992) elaborated on a set of decision-making procedures—called the "generative procedures"—that can yield, or generate, decisions that redound to the benefit of both participants and the collectivity. That is, participation in these procedures results in the development and expression of certain personal qualities, while at the same time producing a possible political solution or policy on which there is a good possibility all participants can agree. I refer to the outcomes of these procedures as a compound common good, which is not discovered by participants but is made or constructed by them. While my emphasis here seems to be on the procedures themselves rather than the outcomes, it should be noted that the compound common good is created out of the myriad, and often conflicting, contributions offered by participants. These contributions serve as the common pool of perspectives from which will be drawn the content of policies and decisions. I shall have more to say about these procedures in chapter 6.

7. "[A] deliberative perspective . . . cannot reach those who refuse to press their public claims in terms accessible to their fellow citizens" (Gutmann and Thompson, 1996, 55). See also 82-84.

8. From *de*, "down to the bottom or the dregs, (hence) completely or thoroughly" and *librare*, "weight'; from *libra,* meaning "scales." See *The Oxford Dictionary of English Etymology,* 1979, 246, 253.

9. Will argues that today we have "direct democracy." This democracy is not direct in the historical participatory sense. Rather, it is "the immediate and emphatic response of government to the public's will" (1992, 108).

10. Until funding fell short, this was the plan for a "National Caucus," to be held at the University of Texas and broadcast by the Public Broadcasting Service (PBS) over the weekend of January 17-19, 1992. A version of this caucus was funded for and was broadcast during the presidential campaign in 1996. Also, two or three such polls have been conducted in Britain, although not with candidates. Thanks to Richard Dagger for this information.

11. See David Braybrooke, "Changes of Rules, Issue-Circumscription and Issue Processing"; listed by Fishkin (1991, 109, n. 15) as "forthcoming."

12. At the same time, Fishkin describes direct Madisonian democracy as "a crazy proposal," because it combines "a two-way cable television system set up for voting in the home" with the notion of "unanimous direct democracy" as proposed by Robert Paul Wolff (49). He is right; this is a crazy proposal. But it is the product of insufficient political imagination (or an overwrought political imagination), because it seems completely sensible to suggest a democratic system of direct democratic decision making on some, not all, set(s) of political issues, provided that the results are in keeping with the Constitution and the fundamental rights protected therein. What this system reposes on, what prevents it from lapsing into either Wolffian unanimity or the Rubik's "Qube" of politics, is the requirement of deliberation. I see no reason, and none is offered, why Wolff's unanimity requirement would be an element in Direct, Madisonian democracy, unless it is that that is the *only* way to have such a democracy that is also nondeliberative. While this proposal rounds out the eight extremes in Fishkin's scheme, it seems the least plausible, since it would be unattractive to everyone, including Wolff himself. (See figure 1 in Fishkin, 1991, and Wolff, 1970.) Nor am I persuaded that, as Fishkin concludes, "only a direct-majoritarian vision of democracy is considered legitimate in the public eye" (1991, 67). He does not argue why this is so, except to say, without substantial evidence, that American electoral politics is headed in this direction; nor does he say why other visions are not and would not be considered legitimate.

13. See Iain McLean, *Technology and Democracy* (1989) and Ian Budge, in Held, 1993 (*Prospects for Democracy*).

14. Noah Webster, "Government," *American Magazine* 1 (1787-88): 206; quoted in Wood, 1972, 380.

15. "Speech to the Electors of Bristol at the Conclusion of the Poll" (3 November 1774); quoted in *Representation,* ed. Hanna Fenichel Pitkin (New York: Atherton Press, 1969), 175.

16. "Reform and Representation in the House of Commons" (1782); quoted in G. Sabine and T. L. Thorson, *A History of Political Theory* (Hinsdale, Ill.: Dryden Press, 1973), 539.

17. North Dakota, for example, requires 10,000 signatures for an initiative and 20,000 for a state constitutional amendment. Most states require signatures from roughly 8 percent of those who voted in the previous gubernatorial election. For the kind of national initiatives that I am proposing, the figures would vary, of course, from state to state, depending on the size of the electorate and their territorial distribution. A national initiative might require something like 3,000,000 total signatures divided proportionately among the states, similar to a measure proposed in the 1970s by Senators James Abourzek (Democrat, South Dakota), and James Jones (Democrat, Oklahoma). To avoid undue influence, if not domination, by regional interests, there might be a requirement that a specific number of signatures must come from 20 to 25 states. If the number of required signatures is set too high, say, for 10 percent of eligible voters, then the danger is that proposing initiatives could be taken out of the hands of "ordinary" citizens and monopolized by the well organized and well financed. See Tallian, 1977, 80-82.

18. See, for example, Wilcox, 1912; Tallian, 1977; Hahn and Kamieniecki, 1987; Cronin, 1989; and David Schmidt, 1989.

19. David Schmidt claims that initiatives raise "lively public debate" (1989, 27), but this can only be construed as informal debates among voters, candidate debates on the issues raised by the initiatives, and media coverage of the campaigns and of the issues.

20. See Benjamin Barber's excellent discussion (1984, 267-73) of the role of neighborhood assemblies in institutionalizing deliberation, or what he calls "strong democratic talk," among citizens.

21. Barber also discusses televised town meetings and civic communication (273-78), a national initiative and referendum process (281-85), and, most important of all, a multichoice format on the ballot in lieu of the yea/nay ballot (286-88).

22. Wilcox, 1912, 31, and Barber, 1984, "Two Readings," 288-89.

23. See Hahn and Kamieniecki, 1987, 2; see also Cronin, 1989, introduction. One proponent of a politics of initiative argues that if the United States in 1861 had had a national initiative on the issue of slavery, the Civil War might have been averted (Tallian, 1977, 7). Tallian invokes the name of my great, great uncle, Senator John Jordan Crittenden from Kentucky, who on January 3, 1861, offered a resolution in the Senate "that provision ought to be made by law without delay for taking the sense of the people and submitting to their vote the following [constitutional amendments to solve the slavery question by compromise] as a basis for final and permanent settlement." Alas, even if Senator Crittenden's resolution had passed and a national initiative on slavery had been presented to the people, I'm sorry to say that he obviously failed to offer a deliberative aspect to his proposal. Taking the sense of the people is nothing other than taking an opinion poll, though if the people had been opposed to slavery and if the initiative had been binding, then much bloodshed and suffering might have been avoided.

24. See Joshua Cohen, "Deliberation and Democratic Legitimacy" (1989) for an excellent discussion of this point.

25. Nancy Fraser comments that where there is "only a single comprehensive public sphere," which, on her account, both Habermas and liberal theorists stress (1990, 66), there will be "no arenas for deliberation among" subordinate or minority groups about their needs, objectives, and strategies (66). Any deliberation, then, would have to happen in the single public sphere under the supervision of the dominant groups. Why can't, and don't, these subordinate groups generate their own "public" arenas, their own private public in which participation is limited to members of the group? They do. Fraser calls these arenas "subaltern counterpublics" (69). So where's the rub? It lies in the forced separation between the single public realm and the counterpublics, who wish to make their case "publicly." Yet to avoid having the state interfere with these counterpublics or to avoid having a majority tyrannize over them, why isn't it beneficial for the counterpublics to keep to the private side? They can play a broader role by serving as arenas or "bases," as Fraser calls them, "for agitational activities directed toward wider publics" (68).

26. Gutmann and Thompson argue that mutual respect must be a prerequisite of democratic deliberation (1990, 126). Participants must proceed along lines of mutual respect, and they must understand this before they enter the procedures. I agree completely, provided Gutmann and Thompson are not suggesting that citizens manifest a pre-procedural characterological disposition toward mutual respect. Rather, the procedures should demand that they honor the perspectives of others when they participate. It is part of the process, not necessarily brought to the process as part of one's makeup.

27. Again, I shall discuss these conditions in some detail when I lay out my version of democratic discussions in chapter 4.

28. In a different context, Harry Brighouse criticizes Amy Gutmann for inculcating in their democratic education "a substantive value, civic [or mutual] respect, which requires that we take the conflicting ways of life of others seriously, and this genuinely conflicts with the teachings of many religious parents" (2000, 108). I think that Brighouse misunderstands Gutmann. To examine and explore other ways of life critically requires taking them seriously. That does not mean that we necessarily come to honor those other ways of life.

29. This is similar to Habermas's notion of communicative ethics in a dialogue that is unconstrained and uncoerced: where participants can say whatever they want, but where what they say can be openly challenged. Habermas, 1990, 89.

30. 1966, Volume 1, 261. Tocqueville also referred to Jefferson as "the greatest democrat ever to spring from American democracy" (203).

Chapter Four

Civic Education

Democracy literally means "people power" or "people rule." The people's power to rule themselves, in my view, rests on their capacity to think self-reflectively and to act on that thinking; to wit, autonomy. As persons we want to define, direct, author, and own our lives; as citizens we want to meet, deliberate, and decide collectively political issues important to those lives. Democracy is a process for collectively making reasoned choices, especially when faced with conflicting values or goals or policies. Deliberative democracy, like autonomy, is a process of self-reflective choosing where the self under examination is the collectivity and where the decision made should have a collective benefit.

Before turning to how we should actually structure an education in deliberation, I want to consider in this chapter how such an education fits in and compares with certain other theories of democratic, or civic, education. In particular I want to establish within the context of a current debate among political theorists my distinction between critical reflection, which ought to form the democratic curriculum, and critical self-reflection, which is the heart of autonomy and is beyond the purview of public officials.

When Hamilton wrote in *Federalist* 23 that the federal government ought to be granted "an unconfined authority in respect to all those objects which are intrusted to its management" (1987, 187), he underscored the need of the newly organized central government for, in Sheldon Wolin's words, "a new type of citizen . . . one who would accept the attenuated relationship with power implied if voting and elections were to serve as the main link between citizens and those in power."[1] Schools were entrusted to develop this new type of citizen.

It is commonplace, therefore, to find among those who examine the interstices of democracy and education views much like Franklin Delano Roosevelt's: "That the schools make worthy citizens is the most important responsibility placed on them." If voting and elections are the main activities of citizenship, then what kind of civic education is warranted for worthy citizens? Future citizens might be required to know how our system works—the functions of the different branches, the purpose and procedures of elections, the history of our government and governmental institutions—and to know the rights and obligations of citizenship. This is, of course, the content of much civic education today, and, to be honest, given the nature of our system, this is about all that it should be. We might prefer that our citizens know how to deliberate, but we don't require that they do, because our democratic system does not require much of it. Indeed, to continue with this line of thought, our system does not really require much civic education. No extensive knowledge and no particular skill beyond being able to read the ballot and sign one's name are required. As I have argued previously, the Founders designed the system that way: "Who are to be the electors of the federal representatives? Not the rich, more than the poor; not the learned, more than the ignorant; not the haughty heirs of distinguished names more than the humble sons of obscurity and unpropitious fortune. The electors are to be the great body of the people of the United States."[2] Regardless of the individual citizen's level of knowledge, formal education, occupation, or status, all citizens voted equally, with no one's vote counting for more or less, and no one's vote doing any damage. No damage can be done, because the representative system is such that virtually every vote is constrained to fall within the choices that appear on the ballot.

If little education is necessary for citizenship, why, then, has there been throughout our history and continuing today an outcry for better, and more, civic education?[3] One can only suspect, it seems to me, that those raising the cry and making demands believe, because they have observed, that many citizens are failing to understand, take seriously, and fulfill their obligations as citizens.

I do not think, as Chantal Mouffe does,[4] that it is the liberal conception of citizenship, with its emphasis on rights, that has reduced citizenship to merely a legal status. Rather, it is the structure and concomitant demands of modern democracies that have rendered citizenship ineffective and inactive, and, indeed, the liberal conception of citizens as rights-bearers is the perfect conception for deliberative democracy. Citizens, guaranteed their voices and protected in their various identities and ways of life by constitutional rights, can decide autonomously when to participate. They will no doubt decide to participate when the issue is judged to be important to their identities or ways of life. When citizens are able to help make actual decisions on political issues, participation may also be presupposed. It is only when citizens are denied such power that commentators cry "Crisis!" and must then seek out ways to bolster a neorepublican conception of citizenship that encourages, if it does not mandate, active forms of participation in a democratic system where the people's relation to power is remote.

There must be some doubt about whether educating students for citizenship in our current representative democracies requires educating them in the arts or skills of deliberation. To educate them, as Aristotle said, to fit the present democratic systems would seem to make them better viewers, not discussants; better spectators, not actors; better consumers, not necessarily even better readers, since so much of politics today rests on images.[5] The first open election in South Africa was identical to ours, with two exceptions. First, people waited in long lines for hours in order to exercise their newly acquired right to vote;[6] second, ballots carried the pictures of the candidates, a concession to illiterate voters. If free and fair democratic elections can be held in which problems of illiteracy can be handled by ballots with pictures, then what is the argument that representative democracy needs a literate, let alone a deliberating, citizenry?

If we wish to prepare our future citizens to participate in our current democratic systems, then we can continue with the kinds of civic education that they now receive: minimal basic skills in reading, writing, and mathematics; short class periods with lots of gimmicks and gadgets—not unfamiliar to those who watch television;[7] and even some willingness, for financial reasons, to accept a certain level of illiteracy among high school graduates. In short, it doesn't really matter what we teach them if the goal is to prepare them simply to follow campaigns and to vote. We might want to improve on how citizens follow campaigns and why they vote by focusing more of our curricula on issue analysis. That might even encourage citizens and future citizens to pressure candidates to focus on issues during their debates and campaigns.[8]

If, however, we wish to prepare future citizens for deliberative democracy, then we need, as I shall argue below, a different focus in our civic education. Such an education is precisely what Amy Gutmann proposes as our democratic education. Her arguments are worth looking at in some detail.

Deliberation in Gutmann's Democratic Education

Gutmann points out that any democratic society has a significant stake in the education of its children, for they will grow up to be democratic citizens. At the very least, then, society has the responsibility for educating all children for citizenship. Because democratic societies have this responsibility, we cannot leave the education of future citizens, argues Gutmann, to the will or whim of parents. This central insight leads Gutmann to rule out certain exclusive suzerainties of power over educational theory and policy. Those suzerainties are of three sorts. First is "the family state" in which all children are educated into the sole good life identified and fortified by the state. Such education cultivates "a level of like-mindedness and camaraderie among citizens" that most persons find only in families.[9] Only the state can be entrusted with the authority to mandate and carry out an education of such magnitude that all will learn to desire this one particular good life over all others.

Next is "the state of families" that rests on the impulse of families to per-petuate their values through their children. This state "places educational author-ity exclusively in the hands of parents, thereby permitting parents to predispose their children, through education, to choose a way of life consistent with their familial heritage" (28).

Finally, Gutmann argues against "the state of individuals," which is based on a notion of liberal neutrality in which both parents and the state look to educa-tional experts to make certain that no way of life is neglected or discriminated against. The desire here is to avoid controversy, and to avoid teaching virtues, in a climate of social pluralism. Yet, as Gutmann points out, any educational policy is itself a choice that will shape our children's character. Choosing to educate for freedom rather than for virtue is still insinuating an influential choice.

In the light of these three theories that fail to provide an adequate foundation for educational authority, Gutmann proposes "a democratic state of education." This state recognizes that educational authority must be shared among parents, citizens, and educational professionals, because each has a legitimate interest in each child and the child's future. Whatever our aim of education, whatever kind of education these authorities argue for, it will not be, it cannot be, neutral. What we need is an educational aim that is inclusive. Gutmann settles on our inclusive commitment, as democratic citizens, "to collectively re-creating the society we share" (39); that is, citizens must be prepared to share in "conscious social re-production" (14 and passim) or the self-conscious shaping of the structures of society. To actuate this commitment we as a society "must educate all educable children to be capable of participating in collectively shaping their society" (14).

But is this the only aim of education? What about shaping one's private con-cerns? Or will the skills that encourage citizen participation also be those neces-sary for personal decision making? If not, then Gutmann is offering a justifica-tion for, at best, a truncated education; if so, then Gutmann is describing the skills that constitute autonomy. For Gutmann, it is the latter. She says: "[M]any if not all of the capacities necessary for choice among good lives are also neces-sary for choice among good societies" (40). She goes even further: "a good life and a good society for self-reflective people require (respectively) individual and collective freedom of choice" (40). This is precisely the language, if not the description—self-reflective choice—that I have been using to discuss and de-velop the grounds for an education for autonomy. Here Gutmann is stipulating that to have conscious social reproduction citizens must have the opportunity—the freedom and, in her view of freedom, the capacities—to exercise autonomy, or self-reflective choice.

Gutmann clearly recognizes the virtues of and need for developing in chil-dren the capacities for examining and evaluating competing conceptions of the good life and the good society and for precluding the inculcation "in children [of the] uncritical acceptance of any particular way or ways of [personal and political] life" (44). This is the crux of her democratic education. For this reason, she argues forcefully that children must learn to exercise critical deliberation among good lives and, presumably, good societies. To assure that they can do so, limits must be set to when and where parents and the state can interfere. Guidelines must be introduced that limit the political authority of the state and the parental authority of families. One limit is nonrepression, which assures that neither the state nor any group within it can "restrict rational deliberation of competing conceptions of the good life and the good society" (44). In this way, adults cannot use their freedom to deliberate to prohibit the future deliberative freedom of children. Furthermore, claims Gutmann, nonrepression requires schools to support "the intellectual and emotional preconditions for democratic deliberation among future generations of citizens" (76).

The second limit is nondiscrimination, which prevents the state or groups within the state from excluding anyone or any group from an education in deliberation. Thus, as Gutmann says, "all educable children must be educated" (45).

Gutmann's point is not that the state has a greater interest than parents do in the education of our children. Instead, her point is that the citizens of the state have a common interest in educating future citizens. Therefore, while parents should have a say in the education of their children, the state should have a say as well. Yet neither should have the final, or a monopolistic, say. Indeed, these two interested parties should also cede some of their educational authority to educational experts. There is, therefore, a collective interest in schooling, which is why she finds parental choice and voucher programs unacceptable.

The first question to ask of Gutmann is, of course, what the purpose is of an education in deliberation, given our representative system. Given the requirements of that system, given what citizens are asked to do, an information-centered, standardized-test educational format seems adequate.

But how could an education in deliberation hurt? The first answer is, if we follow the perspective that I have been developing, that it can only help us push toward deliberative forums. One would like to hear something from Gutmann on that, if only to avoid accusations of hypocrisy, since through an education in deliberation citizens have been prepared for a democracy different from the one they shall find in their polities. It is surprising, and disappointing, therefore, to find Gutmann stating that she will not "defend fully the conception of democracy that coincides with the ideal of democratic education" discussed in the book (xi). The good news is that she may have in mind a conception of democracy that comes close to deliberative, or dialogic, democracy.[10] But any such conception is undefended and underdeveloped. To say, as she does, that her conception is of democracy as both a political process and a political ideal fails to move us forward, for it tells us precious little about what it means, in her words, "to share in ruling" (xi).

Gutmann seems aware of this problem, as she says early on that since politics itself is a form of education, then "a more robust democratic politics . . . would render the concerns of democratic education not less but more important" (18). Clearly having more political deliberation among citizens, as discussed previously, would constitute a more robust form of democracy, and an education in deliberation could push us toward it. Yet in Gutmann's view, deliberation might mean private deliberation, where individual citizens weigh the evidence in private and then bring their individual conclusions to the public arena to be aggregated. Indeed, it seems that without dialogic or deliberative democratic forums, or something like them, then that is all that deliberation could mean. This reinforces, rather than diminishes, the notion of democratic politics as consumer choosing: voting is a private affair in which we register our preferences, even if determined through reflective deliberation, much the way the ideal consumer amasses information on cars and stereos before shopping or buying. The kinds of alternatives deliberated about in this situation are exiguous. If campaigns have become more and more missions to sell candidates, no different from selling any other product to willing and unwilling consumers, then what catches the public's eye is more often image than substance.

Gutmann herself may not accept any such conception of democracy, having in her mind a different one. But some who read her might interpret "deliberative education" to be just what the system needs in order to encourage better private judgments as a way to enhance individual, self-sufficient, atomistic behavior. Democratic politics, in this view, becomes another arena for aggregating private, consumer-like interests.

Sheldon Wolin observed that the Framers of the United States Constitution "hoped to combine the principle of rule by a republican elite with the principle of popular consent: real politics for the few, formal participation by the many" (1989, 48). Gutmann may be buying unwittingly into this combination, for although she wishes to have citizens consciously reproduce society, she makes few allowances for the virtual absence of any democratic politics where the populace can do so.

Thus, those who do deliberate may opt out of the political system. In being good citizens, and in weighing the evidence related to the representative democratic system itself, citizens could, and logically should, conclude that their individual votes do not mean anything, that voting is ineffectual and irrational. Therefore, lacking the means to influence, or reproduce, the system, they should not vote or otherwise participate.

Public schools receive public funds because they serve a public function. That function is to prepare the youth for participation as adults in the collective or social life. Not all of that life can be captured by the term "citizenship." Public schooling ought not to be thought of as only preparing students for life as citizens. Gutmann acknowledges that, inadvertently, when she argues for an education in deliberation in a political context that does not require it. Because our current democracies do not call for public deliberation, the deliberation Gutmann has in mind either pertains to a different form of democracy, as said, or describes part of the process of autonomous choice most salient in private.[11] If the latter, then her recommended education might more accurately be called *liberal* education rather than *democratic* education.

In addition to the problems surrounding the purpose of deliberation, there is a problem with how Gutmann proposes to apply deliberation. She may place herself in a position in which she violates her own principle of nonrepression.

Because the state is interested in the education of future citizens, all children must develop those capacities necessary for choice among good societies; this is simply what Gutmann means by being able to participate in conscious social reproduction. Yet such capacities enable persons to scrutinize the ways of life they have inherited. Thus, Gutmann concludes, it is illegitimate for any parent to impose a particular way of life on anyone else, even on his/her own child, for this would deprive the child of the capacities necessary for citizenship as well as for choosing a good life.

But some parents are not interested in autonomy and having their children choose ways of life. They believe that the way of life that they currently follow is not simply best for them but is best *simpliciter*. To introduce choice is simply to confuse the children and the issue. If you know the true way to live, is it best to let your children wade among diverse ways of life until they can possibly get it right? Or should you socialize the children into the right way of life as soon and as quickly as possible?

Yet what about the obligations parents, as citizens, and children as future citizens, owe the state? How can children be prepared to participate in collectively shaping society if they have not received an education in deliberation? To this parents could respond that they are not particularly interested in having their children focus on participation, or perhaps on anything secular. What they appreciate about liberal democracy is that there is a clear, and firm, separation between public and private, and they seek to focus exclusively on the private. Citizenship offers protections of the law, and it does not require participation. Liberal democracy certainly will not *force* one to participate.

Gutmann's position is that government can and must force one to participate in an education for citizenship. Children must be exposed to ways of life different from their parents and must embrace certain values such as mutual respect. On this last point Gutmann is insistent. She argues that choice is not meaningful, for anyone, unless persons choosing have "the intellectual skills necessary to evaluate ways of life different from that of their parents." Without the teaching of such skills as a central component of education, children will not be taught "mutual respect among persons" (30-31). "Teaching mutual respect is instrumental to assuring all children the freedom to choose in the future. . . . [S]ocial diversity enriches our lives by expanding our understanding of differing ways of life. To reap the benefits of social diversity, children must be exposed to ways of life different from their parents and—in the course of their exposure—must embrace certain values, such as mutual respect among persons" (32-33).

Yet what Gutmann suggests goes beyond seeing diversity as enrichment. She suggests that children not simply tolerate ways of life divergent from their own, but that they actually respect them. She is careful to say "mutual respect among persons," which can only mean that neo-Nazis, while advocating an execrable way of life, must be respected as persons, though their way of life should be condemned. Perhaps this is a subtlety that Gutmann intended, but William Galston, for one, has come away thinking that Gutmann advocates forcing children to confront their own ways of life as they simultaneously show respect for neo-Nazis.

In our representative system, argues Galston, citizens need to develop "the capacity to evaluate the talents, character, and performance of public officials" (1989, 93). This, he rightly recognizes, is what our democratic system demands from citizens. Thus he disagrees with Gutmann, so much so that he says, "It is at best a partial truth to characterize the United States as a democracy in Gutmann's sense" (94). We do not require deliberation among our citizens, says Galston, because "representative institutions replace direct self-government for many purposes" (94). Civic education, therefore, should not be about teaching the skills and virtues of deliberation, but, instead, about teaching "the virtues and competences needed to select representatives wisely, to relate to them appropriately, and to evaluate their performance in office soberly" (94).

Because civic education is limited in scope to what Galston outlines above, students will not be expected, and will not be taught, to evaluate their own ways of life. Persons must be able to lead the kinds of lives they find valuable, without fear that they will be coerced into believing or acting or thinking contrary to their values, including being led to question those ways of life that they have inherited. As Galston points out, "[c]ivic tolerance of deep differences is perfectly compatible with unswerving belief in the correctness of one's own way of life" (99). We should not be surprised, of course, that tolerance is at the heart of liberal values precisely because it shows this compatibility.

To continue with Galston's views for the moment, it is also the case, he says, that many liberals will think that "the unexamined life is an unworthy life" (99). But pace Galston and given all that we have already established, liberals ought to think that. This does not mean, however, that liberals are suspicious of or would suspend the right to live an unexamined life. To a liberal the unexamined life is not worth living, for it cannot be autonomously evaluated and maintained. It is, however, within one's rights to live such a life. Thus, in Galston's view, parents who object to autonomy and rational inquiry and even deliberation can opt out of those classes and curricula, and even those schools, that reflect and build upon such values. They can school their children in private, provided they meet the minimum educational standards of providing instruction in the basic mental skills.

Galston goes further than I am willing to go with the notion that the unexamined life can be worth living. Although persons can flourish, for example, in religious ways of life that do not brook scrutiny of basic assumptions and beliefs, an overall avoidance of the skills of rational, critical inquiry, an avoidance that Galston would accept, denies the very nature of democracy. Even if one is referring only to the deliberations among elected representatives, the basis of democracy is the resolution of conflicts through reasoned dialogue; that, through argument. Those unwilling, or unable, to use rational, critical inquiry will surely have a difficult time arguing against countervailing views when their only defense is, "That's not what we believe." Few citizens, and probably few relatives, are going to accept as a good reason for holding a position that "I like it."

Indeed, the necessity of critical examination and argument for all citizens, present and future, may prove too much for those who live inherited lives. They will be discouraged from participating.

Such persons will be casualties of liberal democratic politics. Yet those who live inherited lives still hold the right to participate, whether they exercise it or avoid it. Some may participate by critically examining the positions of others without introspecting or reflecting critically on their own beliefs and values. Better simply to eschew the entire process. Still others may be able to examine their inherited life, find compelling reasons to live it, and thereby establish a commitment to that way of life. Yet this is to make a distinction, which Galston does not make, between an inherited life and an unexamined life. Is it within the bounds of liberalism—indeed, it is perhaps a liberal tenet—that inherited ways of life can be defended cogently, but only if examined. Is it not the case that a worthwhile way of life evolves and continues to have adherents because the reasons that undergird its customs and practices and values have withstood scrutiny and the test of time? It does not necessarily follow from self-examination that one will only find or will be swayed only by the disadvantages of an inherited way of life. If that is so, isn't it thus advantageous to reject that way of life? The point is that none of this is possible unless students learn to reflect rationally and critically.

In Gutmann's view, because children are members of the state, they must have this kind of education, an education in deliberation. Even in private (and home) schools where parents have prevailing educational authority, the state still has an interest in the education of future democrats. Therefore, all schools must meet a minimum standard of education. What constitutes, in Gutmann's view, minimum standards? They must "provide [all] members with an education adequate to participating in democratic politics and choosing among (a limited range of) good lives" (42). Two questions follow from this: first, what is an adequate education; second, why a limited range of good lives, limited to what and by whom?[12]

Adequate Education. What is an education adequate as preparation for participation in democratic politics? It is an education that accounts for the interests of three legitimate educational authorities: parental education that they may perpetuate particular conceptions of the good; a state education that enables children to evaluate and appreciate goods and ways of life different from their parents'; and a political education that "predisposes children to accept those ways of life that are consistent with sharing the rights and responsibilities of citizenship in a democratic society" (42).

Of course, these authoritative views conflict, if they do not contradict one another. The perpetuation of particular conceptions of the good is only compatible with evaluation of ways of life and goods different from one's parents' if those ways of life and goods are welcome to evaluation. Where an inherited way of life does not welcome or tolerate scrutiny, such evaluations will be considered an imposition and deleterious.

In *Pierce v. Society of Sisters* the Supreme Court ruled that the state of Oregon could not require parents to send their children to a public school because that unduly restricted their liberty to guide their children's education. To ensure an adequate democratic education, Gutmann would stand, I think, as I would, with those who favored the Oregon law and believed that the state had a justifiable right to compel all future citizens to receive appropriate public preparation for their responsibilities as citizens. The exception for Gutmann would be if there were assurances that the minimum democratic standards—in my terms, an education in deliberation—could be met in private schools.

Similarly, in *Wisconsin v. Yoder* Chief Justice Warren Burger wrote that the Amish "object to the high school and higher education generally, because the values they teach are in marked variance with Amish values and the Amish way of life; they view secondary school education as an impermissible exposure of their children to a 'worldly' influence in conflict with their beliefs." Whereas high schools emphasize intellectual accomplishments, competition, worldly success, and social life, the Amish, as we have already seen, build their life around "goodness" rather than intellect, wisdom based on the Bible and life in harmony with nature rather than technical knowledge, community welfare rather than competition, and separation from worldly influences rather than the embrace of such influences. High school values alienate "man from God." In short, high school takes the Amish away from their way of life and places them in an environment hostile to it.

The Amish do permit public schooling through the eighth grade, because up to that level the public schools, in the Amish view, teach "basic reading, writing, and elementary mathematics," skills that can then be refined by and applied to hands-on community work and life. Such basic skills would also seem to be adequate to what is necessary for good citizenship in our representative democracy. The Court held that the state of Wisconsin had failed to make an adequate showing that its interests should override the defendant's right to act freely in accordance with her/his religious beliefs. Gutmann, I think, would fail as well. Why?

Including democratic education or education in deliberation as part of the minimum educational standards forces students to participate in practices that could jeopardize their living an inherited way of life, and it does not further the children's capacities for participation in a representative democracy. Mandating democratic education for everyone, on the grounds that children once past compulsory-school age can then decide for themselves, may already foreclose for some the option of accepting the inherited way of life. Would an Amish child exempted from high school be *unable* to reflect critically on his inherited way of life? Would he be unable, because unprepared, to participate in democracy?

Neither of these seems to be true. Some Amish have left their communities; some undoubtedly have renewed their faith in that way of life after critical reflection. But if an education in deliberation in high school, which seems unjustified from the point of view of what democracy today asks of its citizens because it does not add appreciably to what citizens are asked or required to do politically, destroys the faith in that way of life so that an Amish child would not choose it, then the argument must be to exempt that child from public school but not from *all* school after the eighth grade.

In short, the liberal state, and Gutmann, cannot use, it seems to me, an argument for an education in deliberation as the basis for prohibiting religious parents from opting out of public education, given the requirements of current representative systems. To succeed in doing so the state would have to demonstrate that deliberation was necessary for active political participation.[13]

Shelley Burtt reminds us that "[I]f children are truly to have the choice of a strong religious faith, their early contact with the pluralistic and secular values of a modern society must be guarded and carefully supervised" (1994, 67). Burtt's position does not seem far from Galston's on inherited ways of life. People can live rich, fulfilling lives—religious or secular—even when they are inherited, unexamined, and unchosen. So, when can a way of life or a religious faith be subjected to critical inquiry? Adherents to that way of life might think that this is the wrong question. Those who live an inherited way of life are capable of scrutinizing other ways of life and religious faiths. They simply do not scrutinize their own. Such a way of life relieves them from the pressure to choose continuously how they are to live.

But the question is precisely the right one to ask, because the fear is that children will not be capable of scrutinizing any ways of life or religious faiths if they are deprived of public education; that is, education for deliberation. Religious parents, in wishing to avoid the children's examination of their own way of life, may refrain, when given the educational authority, from schooling their children in rational inquiry. This is why Gutmann insists on deliberation as part of the minimum educational standards, to be enforced even in private and home schools.

Her point is a good one, if we keep in mind the distinction I have made between critical reflection and critical self-reflection. Public schools and the state have no right to force students to examine their own ways of life; public school teachers cannot demand that students think self-reflectively about their deeply held beliefs. That is, students can, should, and must learn the skills central to critical inquiry so that even religious students, who may well grow up to be religious parents, can scrutinize other ways of life when confronted by them. But they cannot be required to turn those skills onto themselves.[14]

The strength of this argument rests on seeing the value of using, if not the need to use, rational inquiry in private and not just in public life. This is, clearly, a position that Gutmann acknowledges, but she needs to emphasize, once again, the importance for the liberal state in preparing students for autonomy.

The skills of critical, intellectual inquiry are especially important, of course, to citizens where there are deliberative arenas in the democracy. Even when citizens prefer not to participate in that kind of democracy, the state has an obligation to prepare them to be able to do so. But because democracy today is not deliberative, Gutmann seems to have little argument from the perspective of citizenship for requiring students to deliberate or for enforcing deliberation in private schools.

Gutmann wisely points out that a democratic state must defend some set of values, while criticizing others; no democratic state, and thus no system of public education within that state, can be neutral among all competing values. Which values should a democratic state promote? In "Undemocratic Education" (1989) Gutmann presents two, which coordinate with what she says in *Democratic Education*: (1) mutual respect for reasonable differences of opinion and (2) rational deliberation among differing ways of life.

We can see how fundamentalist Christian parents might well object to the second of those, finding both the method and the content detrimental to their religious ways of life. In fact, from a political point of view, one might question whether either of Gutmann's values is democratic at all. Our democratic system could be interpreted as an adversarial one, in which participants are really those officeholders who try to smear their opponents and ridicule opposing ways of life. This is not as we wish it, but as it is. Preparation for participation, then, might be more efficacious if students were taught propaganda techniques, not deliberation; and were taught competitive debate tactics, as practiced by courtroom attorneys, not cooperation.

Do we find ample instances of the need to exercise mutual respect and deliberation? I am not asking whether we can exercise these or whether we should, but whether the system demands or even encourages such exercise. If not, then what is the harm of religious parents seeking to exempt their children from certain classes or assignments? Should there be, why should there be, any enforceable minimum democratic standards, since one of the rights of citizens is not to participate?

It depends on what those minimum democratic standards are. Gutmann's, as I have suggested, are too stringent. If her "conception of democracy" were dialogic democracy, then I would agree with her that public education should be an education in deliberation. Parents may opt their children out of certain classes and assignments and may even opt them out of the public schools. What they cannot opt out of is the development of those mental abilities associated with deliberation: reading, writing, mathematics, analytical thinking, summarizing, differentiating fact from opinion, identifying and marshalling evidence, and so on; in short, all those skills and tasks involved in critical thinking—in forming, advancing, and criticizing arguments. These are the skills that a modern liberal democrat thinks will assure a citizen that he can effectively negotiate any way of life he chooses or is found in. In this way, society also assures that this citizen can give back to and can participate in society, even when that participation is not political.

Gutmann claims that citizenship is so intellectually demanding "that we cannot assume that the absence of any set of skills renders an adult incapable of exercising her democratic rights and responsibilities" (278). What about the skills of deliberation? Though she is less than clear on what, precisely, those skills are—and perhaps, for the sake of consistency, she is vague because there is no single set—nevertheless she leaves hints in the text. Deliberation is about "arguing, negotiating, and compromising with people who have conflicting commitments" (239). The relationship of deliberation, in this definition, to democracy is itself clear in theory but fuzzy in practice. But we can agree with Gutmann on this much: citizens can easily participate in today's democratic system and democratic culture without the skills of deliberation.

Rather than being too demanding, citizenship today is not demanding enough. What intellectual skills are actually necessary for persons to participate? They are not necessarily, as Gutmann herself points out, the skills of literacy. One could work on a campaign without being literate. One can keep abreast of political issues through television (CNN, C-SPAN, and so on) and can convey one's views to her representatives over the phone. Besides, illiterates can surely deliberate; they can surely engage in debate and dialogue about political issues.

If the minimum purpose of education is to foster literacy, then education is not necessary for citizenship in our representative democracy or for participating in the common life of the culture. Why, then, educate for literacy? Literacy may not be essential for citizenship, but it makes one's participation in public as well as in private life better. It is an enhancement, not a necessity, and it is important because it leads to more effective social and political participation. We believe, as parents and as students and as citizens, that an education that at a minimum fosters literacy gives us a better chance to live a worthwhile and fulfilling life; that such an education enables us more easily to live, if not to do well, in this society. Otherwise, we can make do, but the lack of education and the presence of illiteracy make life extremely tough and limit social, and not simply political, efficacy.

Because we recognize the dignity of all persons, literate or illiterate, we treat them as autonomous beings. We assume until shown otherwise that adults are autonomous and thus are sovereign citizens. Autonomy does not necessarily follow from education, nor is schooling always necessary for autonomy. Education, however, can provide a foundation for autonomy and can be an accelerator to it for a democratic population. We recognize that "wholesale" autonomy is enhanced through education in which future citizens learn and can practice the skills of deliberation and democratic participation. Those skills, when democracy has practices that are deliberative and direct, are identical with the skills of autonomy. Schools, therefore, are the principal institution for educating future citizens in and for the independence of life and interdependence of citizenship and deliberative democracy. Where such an education is not offered or where political opportunities to exercise or practice such independence on real issues are limited, developing autonomy as self-ruling is left to chance and opportunities for self-governing are nugatory.

In other words, citizenship and autonomy do not rest on education, but the absence of education for autonomy, for independence (in this context), would be detrimental. It is difficult to imagine how a population without this education could achieve the skills required of participatory democracy and could avoid sliding into a political system of wholesale manipulation more overt than, say, Tocqueville's friendly despotism.[15]

If citizenship and autonomy do not rest on education, then what is the argument for compulsory schooling? Compulsory schooling arose, first, as a way to thwart the exploitation of child labor and, second, as a way to circumvent those parents who were either hostile or indifferent to sending their children to school.[16] Yet, as we have seen, there are good reasons to be hostile to sending one's children to school. Compulsory schooling can be justified only where school provides an education that is an enhancement to learning, not a hindrance. In terms of politics, a lack of education can be a hindrance, as it correlates with inhibition of political action: "Lower levels of education are associated with lower interest in politics, fewer opinions, less frequent political discussion, greater ignorance of what choices would be in one's own interest, and less confidence to deal with the political environment."[17] Thus the very people most likely to eschew education if it were noncompulsory are the most likely to be hurt politically, which would be even more severe if the democratic system were in part deliberative.

This assumes, however, that a lack of schooling is the same as a lack of education. Children can certainly gain an education by being taught at home, if there are assurances that the minimum standards are met. Those standards are, first, the standards of literacy. We must require of all children that they learn to read, write, compute, and communicate, not simply because these skills will be important to them, but also because their having those skills will be important to us as fellow deliberative citizens.[18] As citizenship becomes more demanding, as we move into deliberative forums like a politics of initiative, and if we wish to use education to press for such democratic forms, then there is greater warrant for compulsory schooling and for more stringent educational standards. I shall say more about educational standards in the next two chapters, but consider, as an example, that children at home are less likely to engage in the kinds of talking, listening, recapitulating, and analyzing that deliberative democracy, at all levels, requires. There is a need, therefore, to require that all future participants have ample opportunities to develop and to exercise the deliberative capacities, which is one of the principal points of democratic schools (chapter 6). Those who are articulate and highly verbal will always have an advantage in deliberations. Others need experience in how to deal with loquacious types and in how to feel comfortable participating. Schools that offer an education in deliberation will offer such experience as part of the curriculum.

The capacity to deliberate can arise in persons who have not been schooled, or have been schooled at home, but if deliberation is to be the heart of democracy, and I have obviously gone well past Gutmann here, then we cannot rest on its spontaneous unfolding. Even less spontaneous would be the proclivity to deliberate collectively, to address problems by reasoning with others. Tocqueville observed that persons in a democracy such as ours will withdraw into individualism, into an isolated circle of family and friends distant from society at large. As we move toward deliberative democracy, this temptation is a current against which we must assiduously struggle. Compulsory public schooling, in which we show students the benefit of reasoning together and in which reason will rule, can aid in that struggle.

For those parents who must opt out, let there be something potent for them to opt out of. Let them see the advantages that their children can miss by opting out of education in deliberation. Yet this is an adequate education when we presuppose some movement toward greater participatory democratic procedures. This is not an adequate education, as Gutmann suggests, if we take, and leave, the representative system as it is.

Limited Range. It is possible, as Galston maintains, that one can flourish within an inherited, and unexamined, way of life. Yet Gutmann is right that no liberal could think that or could do so, because a good life must be lived from the inside, by accepting and identifying it as one's own. Indeed, no life of any sort can be committed to unless it has been examined self-reflectively; unless, that is, it is an autonomous choice. Once an inherited life is scrutinized, however, it might lose its force and its meaning. That is the danger. Yet in examining it, one may also come to see and appreciate its force and meaning. Then one brings oneself to that way of life; one can even find oneself in and identify with that life, whereas before, when it was simply inherited and unexamined, that way of life merely embedded the person and kept its boundaries and assumptions hidden.

Gutmann wants to teach future citizens not only the skills necessary to participate, but also certain appreciations and predispositions. She wants predispositions not only in favor of democracy, but also against certain ways of life. "A democratic state of education constrains choices among good lives . . . out of a concern for civic virtue" (42). If a democratic state of education must constrain choices among good lives, must limit the range, then how strong is that civic virtue? How effective is the capacity to deliberate, which Gutmann herself proclaims the core democratic virtue (46, 52)? She must not think that it is effective enough, or at all, against those ways of life that must be ruled out. Why else must children be predisposed "toward some ways of life and away from others" (43)? Why not offer them full-blown choice, without limitation, among different ways of life? Because such choice may lead some to renounce democracy itself and those institutions and dispositions that undergird it? But if democracy represents or supports good, if not the best, ways of life, then is it not defensible on grounds firmer than simply asseverating that most of us prefer it? Indeed, I think that it is; democracy provides the means whereby we can live out the good life among myriad and competing conceptions of the good life.

Gutmann, I think, has doubts about this. She sticks to the formalities of citizenship and the closed range of good lives because, in the end, she seems suspicious of people's abilities to judge. "Children," she says, "first become the kind of people who are repelled by bigotry, and then they feel the force of the reasons for their repulsion" (43). This may simply be an empirical claim, that this is how children react to bigotry. Yet Gutmann offers no evidence that this is so.

On the other hand, she may be making a normative claim: socialize children first to be repulsed by bigotry and later provide the reasons for why they should be repulsed. Yet why should children, why should anyone, be repulsed by bigotry? Because bigots do not treat other people as equals. But under Gutmann's scheme are bigots treated as equals? Would she say that bigots are equals, but bigotry is to be loathed? Do children who have been socialized first to be repelled by bigotry make such distinctions? Do they loathe bigotry but respect the bigots' personhood as equal to their own? And how will Gutmann teach the distinction once the repulsion is inculcated?

Gutmann's argument hints at the skepticism underneath her own democratic education: "[C]hildren are not taught that bigotry is bad by offering it as one among many conceptions of the good life, then subjecting it to criticism on grounds that bigots do not admit that other people's conceptions of the good are 'equally' good" (43). Instead, she intimates, children should learn to rationalize a learned response. We shape character by first inculcating values, and then we learn to justify what has already been inculcated. If children need first to be' taught that bigotry is repulsive, then they might well be "learning" about ways of life at too early an age, when they are not yet able to deliberate or reflect critically. If so, then what Gutmann is offering is less an education in deliberation and more a catechism.

If it is not too early, then why is it not equally valid, and I would say better, to teach that bigoted ways of life are aspects of lives swirling "among many conceptions of the good life"—which they are—"and then [subject them] to criticism"? It is not the way to educate because this approach is "the basis of an education that strives for neutrality among ways of life." I think that Gutmann is simply wrong here. There need be no striving for neutrality. Instead, the alternative is to live up to her own approach: to teach deliberation, to strive to develop students or children who can think, who can make connections and discern differences—perhaps not immediately or not in all cases or in these cases—who have been taught the techniques for doing so, and who learn when and how to apply those techniques.

I think that the difference between us is more than one of emphasis. Whereas Gutmann wants to "cultivate in children the character that *feels the force* of right reason" (43, emphasis added), I want education to cultivate reason first and let that reason in part determine or lead character. Her method is to instill not a knowledge of what is bad, or a way to judge what is bad, but a *feeling* that *this* is bad. Only then will students learn why it is bad. I think it is better to present the case of what a way of life is and what it represents and, then, through criticism, why it is bad. Can it be said that both methods permit and encourage children to make up their own minds, when in one case feelings, character traits or dispositions, and even prejudices have already, and before thought, been inculcated?

Although Gutmann sees it as negligent in her democratic state of education to inculcate in children an "uncritical acceptance of any particular way or ways of life" (44), it appears that it is desirable to inculcate in children first an uncritical rejection of certain untoward ways of life to which are then added reasons for the rejection. Critical appraisal is reserved for deliberation among a range of good lives and good societies from which those deemed unsavory have been expunged. It is ironic, if not cynical, that Gutmann emphasizes the virtue of deliberation and yet is willing to suspend or deny discussion of those beliefs, values, ideas, and ways of life that run counter to democratic virtues, that ideas, and ways of life that run counter to democratic virtues, that "appear to threaten the foundational ideals of democratic sovereignty."[19] Thus, teachers can predispose students toward the virtue of patriotism (63), but why should they have to do so? If the values associated with democracy are solid, able to withstand critical scrutiny, will they not survive the deliberations central to democratic participation and advocated by Gutmann as democracy's principal virtue and education's primary aim?

Should children be predisposed toward egalitarianism and away from sexism? Gutmann says yes. But shouldn't there first be open discussion, for example, of those religious denominations or traditional ways of life that argue that a woman's proper and most fulfilling role is within the home? Shouldn't there be deliberations about whether a practice that restricts women to the nurturing of children and the creating of a stable home life, from the perspective that the virtues exercised and acquired there can lead women to happiness and peace, has the same basis and moral standing as the view that women belong anywhere they choose to belong? Surely there is some educational merit in evaluating the different ways that sexist perspectives have been justified.

Gutmann argues that children should be predisposed to see sexism, irrespective of its basis, as reprehensible. Then they should be taught the grounds for thinking so. In this way the democratic character can be shaped. Children may need to be exposed to ways of life different from their parents', but if they are members of a religious group that holds divergent views—for example, sexist views—they will have to suffer the condemnation of the teacher and the predispositive censure of their classmates as those students come to be repulsed by sexism.

Gutmann also argues that "parents and citizens may legitimately *partially* prejudic[e] the choices of children by their familial and political heritages" (43, emphasis in original). On what grounds? On the grounds "that some ways of life are better than others *for us and our children* because these orientations impart meaning to and enrich the internal life of family and society" (43, emphasis in original). All Gutmann has done here is expand the circle of concern from the family to the family-cum-society. That does extend the boundaries and does generate more freedom within those boundaries. Nevertheless, Gutmann here adduces in support of her democratic state of education the same argument that she rejects in the "state of families" for parental control and exclusivity. In short, Gutmann rules out certain ways of life and methods of education because they will undermine family and society. Yet those ways of life and methods are precisely the ones that children as students need to examine because, as she says herself, it is essential to meaningful and free choice that children appreciate and evaluate "ways of life other than those favored by their families" (42). Why is that same position invalid once we include the phrase "the politics of their society" (43)?

It is invalid because "the good of children includes not just freedom of choice, but also identification with and participation in the good of their family and the politics of their society" (43). But the good of the family is precisely what is in question, and what if their identification rests not with the politics of their society but in questioning and debunking the politics?

The principle of nonrepression requires schools to support "the intellectual and emotional preconditions for democratic deliberation among future generations of citizens" (76). Thus schools cannot limit students' capacities for deliberation. But doesn't Gutmann violate that principle when she constrains deliberation to a limited range of ways of life? Gutmann does limit or restrict democratic deliberation, but perhaps she does not consider this a restriction of students' capacities for deliberation. Regardless of the distinction, Gutmann has a problem.

She argues that book banning is illegitimate because it violates the principle of nonrepression. Yet it would be legitimate if two conditions were met: first, if the banning were the outcome of "deliberative democratic procedures" and, second, if the ban covered "only those books that served, either by their intent or their effect on students, to glorify an abhorrent way of life" (99). But who defines an abhorrent way of life? The school board? The teachers? Do they judge the author's intent? Is a way of life abhorrent if the student, upon hearing about it, makes a face? Why is abhorrence a central criterion?

As to the first condition, a democratic decision to ban books is legitimate, because it affords the community "the right to be wrong." The U.S. Constitution, through the Bill of Rights, protects persons with a minority view. There are no such protections here. Book banning is not simply denying the use of a particular book in the classroom. It is, instead, the removal of the book from the school. Why should this be the outcome rather than establishing special permission to read it? Book banning is a clear violation of nonrepression.

Moreover, Gutmann insists that "decisions concerning what theories are taught in the classroom are a matter of professional, not democratic, authority" (101). If so, then why isn't book banning also a professional, not a democratic, matter? Why, if teachers have standards for making such decisions, don't librarians? Or why are decisions about what theories to teach not also a matter of democratic authority?

Critical Reflection versus Self-Reflection

So it looks as if Gutmann wants future citizens, having already absorbed certain perspectives and having generated certain feelings, to learn to understand and evaluate competing conceptions from within a range of options constrained by the democratic state of education. If that is not Gutmann's point, then I have misread her. Regardless of the outcome of that issue, she and I still have one intramural dispute: would she say that within her scheme of democratic education educators are authorized to force students to be self-reflective, not simply to hear about and scrutinize different conceptions of the good life and the good society, but also to evaluate those conceptions as they relate to the students' own lives and conceptions? That is, would she force students to be autonomous?

Engle and Ochoa argue that students, "[a]s they reach the time when rational thought is possible, certainly by the time they are in middle school . . . should be encouraged and helped to develop the intellectual capacity for independence of thought, social criticism, and problem solving?" (*Education for Democratic Citizenship*, 1988, 12). I, and Gutmann might agree, want to take Engle and Ochoa at their word and accept a distinction between requiring students to question their ways of life, which I have called an education *in* autonomy, and helping them to develop the intellectual *capacity* to do so, which is an education *for* autonomy or *in* deliberation. Having the capacity does not necessarily mean that one has applied or must apply that capacity to one's own way of life. When, however, a person claims to be following a *chosen* way of life, then he should be able to provide, as part of autonomy, substantive reasons for that choice and its attendant beliefs.[20] I am not suggesting that students should not question various assumptions, practices, values, and histories. They should. Too much is taken for granted and passed along without reflection. But critical reflection is not necessarily self-reflection. It is not the place of the state, and therefore of public school teachers, to require students to examine their own personal beliefs on all subjects or relate directly to their personal lives what is being examined. A student, for example, might be asked to reflect on reasons and possible remedies for homelessness. A student cannot be asked, however, to reflect on how his personal way of life possibly affects the state of homelessness. A student may raise that on her own; her classmates may raise that issue. If they choose to do so, they should not necessarily be discouraged. It is their own choice. But self-reflection cannot be a course requirement; teachers, as public servants, should eschew such temptations.

Perhaps this distinction between requiring students to question their ways of life and helping them to develop the intellectual capacity to do so is too fine, and impractical, a line to draw. Yet it seems that a compromise is needed between Galston, who argues that there can be value and flourishing in unexamined lives, and Gutmann, who sees the need for self-reflective citizens. Gutmann might well accept such a distinction, for although she says that "equipping children with the intellectual skills necessary to evaluate ways of life different from that of their parents" (30) is required of democratic citizenship, she does not say that children must apply those skills to evaluate critically their parents' way of life.

This issue, of whether to teach students to be autonomous, has been the subject of some debate recently among political theorists and educational philosophers writing on liberalism and civic education. Stephen Macedo (2000), for example, argues that the mission of the public schools is to teach students the capacities needed to function as citizens in our liberal democracy. School is to bring together "children from different normative perspectives" so that they might "discover that their differences do not preclude cooperation and mutual respect as participants in a shared political order" (194). Macedo asks, reasonably, it seems to me, the following question: "[H]ow can tolerance be taught, how can children from different religions and cultural backgrounds come to understand each other and recognize their shared civic identity, without exposing them to the religious diversity that constitutes the nation's history?" (160). Where else, we might ask of fundamentalist parents, will their children be exposed to diversity?

Fundamentalist parents who cannot countenance any thinking beyond the boundaries of biblical authority, for to do so is to be guilty of impiety, might even object to readings of the Bible that run counter to theirs. Their children, then, would not even be exposed to the diversity within Christian denominations. Such narrow instruction is not just deferring to the parents; it is also what Eamonn Callan calls "ethical servility," even servitude.

Isn't mere exposure to diversity a means of undermining fundamentalist belief by leading students to self-reflect? It might be, but it does not have to be, as Judge Lively pointed out in *Mozert v. Hawkins*. Students do not necessarily apply those diverse views to their own lives, though we may think it nearly inconceivable that they would not. More to my point, the state, or its agents—to wit, teachers—cannot require students to do so. When teachers require students to examine their own lives, there appears to be an element of coercion, which seems to undercut the very value of autonomy that teachers would be after. Autonomy is *self*-investigation, not only on the self, but also undertaken by the self, by the person himself or herself.

Macedo, I think, would agree with the distinction between demanding that students investigate alternative ways of life and investigating their own ways of life. As liberals, he says, "we should insist that all children are provided with the basic intellectual tools needed to perform the duties of citizenship and to fashion responsible, productive lives for themselves . . . and yet," he continues, "we must honor the limits of liberal political authority" (2000, 138).

Such a limit is to be noncoercive when dealing with people's own deeply held beliefs. Macedo says as much: "Public schoolteachers and authors of materials for public schools should avoid advancing the notion that children need to think about their religious beliefs critically for the sake of better understanding of religious truths" (239). Yet he also says that a basic aim of civic education "should be to impart to all children the ability to reflect critically on their personal and public commitments" (239). How does Macedo reconcile these two positions? He does not say, but we can do so if we hold in mind the distinction between teaching the *ability* to reflect critically on convictions—that is, teaching the skills of critical thinking—and the *requirement* in public schools to exercise that ability as self-reflection—that is, the requirement to apply those skills to one's own deepest beliefs.

Macedo goes on to say that "[a]ll children should be made aware of the ethnic, racial, and religious diversity that constitutes our society so that they can think as citizens and so that they will not live in a mental straitjacket at odds with freedom" (240). That mental straitjacket is Callan's "ethical servility," and on this view Macedo and I agree: children must be exposed to the diversity of society so that they can understand the kind of society, and world, they live in.

There seems to be general agreement among theorists of liberalism and civic education that students ought to be exposed to alternative ways of life. Harry Brighouse (*School Choice and Social Justice,* 2000) writes, for example, that such exposure must be undertaken by teachers "in a controlled and non-pressured way" (75). I interpret that way to mean that teachers cannot force students to examine alternatives by requiring them to compare one way of life with their own. Brighouse describes his version of civic education as an "autonomy-facilitating" curriculum. For him that means teaching the "basic methods of rational evaluation" (69), but it does not mean requiring students to be autonomous or inculcating the disposition to exercise autonomy. "The education does not try to ensure that students employ autonomy in their lives, any more than Latin classes are aimed at ensuring that students employ Latin in their lives. Rather it aims to enable them to live autonomously should they wish to, rather as we enable them to criticize poetry, do algebra, etc. without trying to ensure that they do so" (80).

One theorist who disagrees with Brighouse's, and presumably my, approach to civic education is Eamonn Callan (*Creating Citizens,* 1997). Callan argues that creating good liberal democratic citizens must entail teaching autonomy. Autonomy "signifies not merely the ability to subject received ideas to critical scrutiny; it also refers to the motivational and affective propensities that guide the exercise of the ability in securing a self-directed life" (227, n. 8). When Callan then describes "an education directed towards autonomy," he does not mean what I mean—an education in critical thinking that is a preparation for autonomy. He means an education that will nourish these propensities. Although he and I, and Macedo and Brighouse, agree that the critical thinking or "deliberative capacities" (227) are essential to this civic education, we disagree on whether to develop the character traits that will induce students to exercise autonomy.[21]

The basic issue separating Callan and me comes to this: is requiring critical thinking among our students sufficient for enabling them to escape from the forms of parental "ethical servility"—the attempts by parents to enclose their children in a worldview impervious to outside influences, attempts that violate liberal freedom and, as Macedo says, that might undermine our citizen's shared commitment to liberal democracy? No one would disagree that a curriculum based on teaching the skills of critical thinking provides the enabling conditions for such an escape. But isn't more required?

Brighouse claims that inculcating the habit or character of autonomy can have deleterious effects. "There are other, more affective, facets of personality which are relevant to learning how to live well, which may be undermined by trying to alter the characters of those whose constitutions are such that they cannot become fully, or habitually, autonomous" (2000, 82). Callan all but concedes Brighouse's point, as he cautions against an education that "wrenches [children] abruptly away from all that gives meaning to their lives outside of school" (1997, 132).

No doubt students need to be exposed critically and sympathetically, as Callan suggests (133), to beliefs and ways of life different from one's own. Yet how far should schools go in presenting ways of life at odds with a student's own? Should students be exposed to totalitarian, unpatriotic, immoral, and racist ways of life? Should state agents be probing students' lives? Callan himself is concerned about this: "[A]ggressive educational intervention for the sake of autonomy may incur prohibitive moral costs by inflicting pain and humiliation that either obstruct its achievements or outweigh its benefits" (2000, 151).

Callan's concession strengthens the position that Brighouse and I are laying out for a public education that only facilitates but does not require autonomy. But our point is not so easily won. For Callan makes what I think is an equally strong claim. "Nonautonomous belief and preference formation often, perhaps characteristically, works not merely by blocking the acquisition of knowledge or skill. Instead, affect and desire are shaped so that even if the knowledge and skill is later acquired, these will not be used to correct the results of the original process" (2000, 146). Therefore, knowledge of alternative careers and ways of life might do nothing to shake off the belief of a child raised to believe that "I must be a housewife when I grow up."

Such a child is clearly an example of Callan's "ethical servility." An education for autonomy may be necessary for establishing that child's ethical freedom, but only an education in autonomy is sufficient, on Callan's view, for combating such servility.

Both Brighouse and Callan are making empirical claims, in support of their normative claims, for which no evidence is offered. In fact, both may be true. Requiring all students to be autonomous—to critically self-reflect—may come at a cost to some students that outweigh the benefits. But failing to require autonomy of students may condemn some to lives of ethical servility. I am willing to scrutinize the empirical data, if any, and adjust my own position accord-

quote

ingly. For now, I come down on the side of providing an education for, but not in, autonomy, thinking that a habit of thoughtfulness will indeed, as Gutmann and Macedo say, spill over into one's way of life. Plus, I maintain that there is an important distinction between one who can scrutinize her way of life but won't from one who simply cannot.

Finally, I return to Callan's own concern about the deleterious effects of autonomy. "The younger the child, the higher those risks are likely to be" (1997, 158). The risks can even occur among adolescents, who can be left "merely confused, demeaned, or frightened" (158) by their critical self-reflection. When adolescents are trying to establish ego boundaries and identity, when their ethical convictions are not yet established, then real harm, as Callan says, can be done. Far better to let adolescents pass the threshold of high school before "Who am I?" becomes a focal point of the curriculum.

Therefore, let critical self-reflection come at a time when rational thought, when formal operational thinking, is usually fully established—the college years or late adolescence. Prior to that, schools ought to develop the capacity for self-reflection, the tools or skills of critical thinking that can be applied to introspection, but should limit its use. In this regard, I would modify Engle and Ochoa's "challenge to democratic education." A reasonable accommodation is necessary, as they say, between socialization of youth and the development of their critical capabilities. Yet so, too, is an additional accommodation required between that development and its application to examining one's own way of life.

Judgment and the Habit of Thoughtfulness

My last concern about Gutmann's education in deliberation has to do with the nature of deliberation. As we have seen, she describes deliberation as "arguing, negotiating, and compromising with people who have conflicting commitments" (239). To deliberate about these conflicting commitments—different conceptions of the good life and the good society—claims Gutmann, requires as a foundation certain character traits—for example, honesty, religious toleration (only religious?), and mutual respect (44). This requirement, I believe, creates a fundamental problem for Gutmann, as it simultaneously points to a weakness in her argument, a weakness that she and William Galston share.

Galston distinguishes between civic education and philosophical education. Civic education shapes future citizens; philosophical education establishes the disposition in persons to pursue the truth through the conduct of rational inquiry. "[P]hilosophical education can have corrosive consequences for political communities in which it is allowed to take place. The pursuit of truth . . . can undermine structures of unexamined but socially central belief" (1991, 242).

In a liberal democracy it seems that civic education and philosophical education come together, for are there any central but unexamined beliefs in a liberal democracy, even in the liberal polity as described by Galston? When politics emphasizes rational inquiry, rational empathy, and public discourse within a context of multiple conceptions of the good, society's basic assumptions, values, practices, and goals will be open and susceptible to inspection, especially by those who disagree respectfully with them. Liberals can agree, as we have seen, that some unexamined lives are well worth living, but in a liberal democracy no unexamined public beliefs are worth holding. Certainly autonomous citizens won't think so.

What seems ironic is that Galston believes that "few individuals will come to embrace the core commitments of liberal society through a process of rational inquiry" (243). This seems odd, given Galston's views on rationality (175-76) and rational empathy (79), and especially in light of the similarities between philosophical reasoning and political deliberation. Both require "a process of scrutinizing opinions in order to arrive at descriptions (of what is the right thing to do or say) that have withstood every test that we can devise and which are therefore candidates for informed agreement" (35).

Here Galston and Gutmann come together. Gutmann argues that the aim of primary education is to instill in future citizens the virtue of deliberation. Galston admits that "[p]hilosophy, like deliberation, is the collective effort of preparing ourselves to recognize what is worthy of our assent" (35). Civic education in a liberal democracy is, indeed, Galston's philosophical education. We want our citizens to pursue the truth of matters through rational inquiry, while understanding that the truth will rest upon the evidence and arguments advanced in support of differing propositions. Civic education is to shape "individuals who can effectively conduct their lives within, and support, their political community" (243). That conduct and support in a deliberative democracy presupposes and requires critical inquiry, which itself is instilled through philosophical education. Thus it is the method or path of rational scrutiny and deliberation that unites civic and philosophical education.

Because Galston does not think that individuals will embrace liberal tenets through rational inquiry, he, like Gutmann, argues for character formation. His argument is, in part, that citizens will need to have their characters shaped in order to participate. But such shaping may only be necessary because participation is undemanding and unimportant. Character formation would instill in future citizens those traits that predispose them toward participation. Thus, the danger of philosophical education is not simply that it will fail to lead citizens toward participation.[22] The danger is also that philosophical education will undercut participation and perhaps the system itself. Civic education, on the other hand, fulfills "the task of fitting pedagogical practices to existing communities" (246) and, we might add, existing political institutions.

Galston's position and arguments are reminiscent of Aristotle's distinction between the good man and the good citizen. The task of civic education would be to assure that the citizens fit the constitution of their state (*Politics*, 1337a). Yet for Aristotle democratic Athens required civic education toward, if not in, *phronesis* or deliberation, which is part of Galston's philosophical education. Galston clearly sees rational inquiry as part of philosophical, not civic, education (1989, 89). Since rational inquiry is essential to the pursuit of the truth, which, in turn, is the point of philosophical education, then it is to play little part in civic education since the pursuit of truth can undermine the unexamined but significant beliefs of some citizens.

Civic education, on the other hand, is concerned with "formation of individuals who can effectively conduct their lives within, and support, their political community" (1989, 90). Nothing in that education can undermine faith in the political institutions or undermine the desire to participate. As citizens, Galston declaims, we share "something important in common—a set of political institutions and of principles that underlie them" (93). We share as well the values underlying and reinforcing those institutions. We need to teach those values, Galston argues; we need to teach future citizens to be willing to fight for one's country and to obey the law (93). Yet why is the proper virtue fighting for one's country rather than protesting injustice or rallying against military intervention? It would seem far more suitable, for a democracy, to have citizens who could judge when to fight and when to protest. Yet this seems to involve judging and *phronesis,* which gets us back to Galston's distinction between philosophical and civic education.

When specific virtues such as patriotism are advocated as essential to citizenship, it is imperative to define them carefully so as to distinguish between the indoctrination of a feeling of exaltation for the nation, whatever its actions and motives, and an ability and willingness to examine the nation's principles and practices to see whether those practices are in harmony with those principles. The first requires loyalty; the other, judgment. We teach one through "pledges of allegiance, salutes to the flag, loyalty oaths . . . a loyalty to 'my country, right or wrong'"[23]; we teach the other by teaching critical inquiry.

The weakness in the argument is not that Galston favors indoctrination over education, but that he does not tell us how to avoid indoctrination in a civic education that seeks to suit future citizens to the existing political practices and institutions. The conclusion is that this cannot be avoided. Gutmann, who argues for an education in deliberation, seems able to avoid the problem of indoctrination. Yet because she, too, insists on character formation, the establishing of certain character traits, she may be guilty of a similar weakness. Behind her arguments for education in deliberation, as behind Galston's civic education, lurks the specter of duress. In both theories civic education is not simply to prepare future citizens to participate in politics. It is to encourage future citizens to participate. Civic education is effective when citizens participate, even in democratic procedures where there is little chance to deliberate and little power to make decisions.

When future citizens have the proper predispositions and character traits, then, as good citizens, they will want to participate. The character traits to educate for are those that conduce to democratic participation: cooperation, honesty, toleration, respect. These aren't surprising or improper; they are some of the values that I have discussed as liberal values.

A cynic might well conclude that inculcating, or trying to inculcate, a democratic character of honesty, toleration, cooperation, and respect where there is little public requirement for such traits in democratic participation is a way to perpetuate and expand middle-class values under the guise of democratic citizenship. It could be another form of oppression, like the poll tax. If we were to say to people that in order to be citizens they had to demonstrate that they were honest, tolerant, cooperative, and respectful of others, who would be the judge? Who would establish the criteria of successful demonstration?

Political or electoral participation is a right of citizenship. It might be preferable to have citizens of a certain character, but should we insist on that? Would we then test for character? And how would we test? For what character traits? What would we do if someone were to fail our test? In lieu of this intrusive, divisive, and vexatious entanglement, we should insist only that those who participate in democratic procedures behave as required.[24] What if they misbehave? Short of disruptive behavior, we would exercise our liberal virtues of tolerance and mutual respect as we attempted to cooperate honestly with them.

The point of democratic education, as Gutmann persuasively argues, is to prepare future citizens to participate in politics. That is done by developing in future citizens the skills necessary for effective participation. Depending on how one conceives of democracy, those might be the skills of deliberation. How much character is required in deliberation? Certainly there are participatory virtues, and these should be taught by example. Rather than telling students how to behave, for example, we ought to make those behaviors come alive. "Students learn much from the way a school is run," comments Theodore Sizer, "and the best way to teach values is when the school is a living example of the values to be taught" (1984, 120, 122). That is, schools should be run as democratically as is reasonable. At the least, it must be recognized that the school is one of the students' most salient environments, if not communities. Therefore, certain aspects of how the school operates (not classroom instruction, not the overall curriculum, not hiring and firing, and not wages and salaries) should be open to control by the community at large; that is, by all members of it, as with any private public. I shall have much more to say about this in the chapter on demo-cratic schools.

Will establishing democratic schools produce moral character in students and citizens? It may, for, as John Dewey pointed out, practices influence character.[25] Dewey appears to be following Aristotle's recommendations for generating habits.

To Aristotle, the capacity to make judgments and the will to put those judgments into action constituted the virtue of *phronesis*. This virtue of judgment or practical wisdom was central to character, according to Aristotle, for "in the case of those virtues which entitle a man to be called good in an unqualified sense . . . as soon as he possesses this single virtue of practical wisdom, he will also possess all the rest."[26]

Phronesis is judgment in practice: when to compromise, when to draw the line between doing and not doing something. That judgment is developed through practice. To both Plato and Aristotle, institutions form character, because repeated behaviors in them lead to the formation of habits, which themselves are moral virtues. So if we want to be brave, we must undertake brave acts. If we want to be deliberative, we should undertake deliberative acts. That is, we should practice deliberation. We learn, therefore, by doing; we develop habits by practicing the required virtuous behaviors.

As Philip Brook Manville tells us about Athenian citizenship, it was not so much the hearts of men that stabilized and gave strength to the polis. Rather, it was the codification and publication of the laws, the carrying out of social reforms, and the establishment of political structures and institutions.[27] It was Aristotle's view, on Stephen Salkever's reading of him, that democracy ought to aim "at institutionalizing a certain kind of political interaction" (1990, 247). The habit of interacting in this certain way is what Aristotle means by "ruling and being ruled"[28]; it is the habit of deliberation and prudent judgment.

Deliberating and judging are also the practice of the habit of thoughtfulness, which Eva Brann (1979, 106) tells us is the point of liberal education. This habit of thoughtfulness is not about learning to follow specific rules or commandments; it is about seeing conflicts as puzzles requiring perspective, thought, the weighing of evidence, and judgment.

This single habit, thoughtfulness or judgment (or *phronesis)* is the master virtue that I am after, that I want to see schools cultivate. This habit would be the basis of character education within an education in deliberation. Flowing from the exercise of that master virtue should be the reinforcement of those additional virtues essential to the active exercise of thoughtfulness; that is, those virtues listed by Gutmann and described above as liberal: honesty, cooperation, tolerance, and mutual respect. Civic education, then, would focus on repeated practice in thoughtfulness.

One might infer that I am inculcating habits and thereby contradicting my own view of a critical or reflective education. It is true that habits are simply repeated practices performed without necessary evaluation. In that sense they are

inculcated. But one would and should expect that within the curriculum on critical thinking these habits themselves will come under scrutiny. I am not suggesting, therefore, as Gutmann and Galston do, that there are any values or habits
that are themselves exempt from critical scrutiny, including the values, habits,
practice, and theory of critical thinking itself.[29]

It is of course important to recognize that our schools, as socializing institutions that at least mirror society's predominant norms and values, are already reinforcing certain values and behaviors. The structure of the school, its daily operations, the decorum in the classroom, all demand certain repeated behaviors
from students that will become habits. Educators will demand of their students,
and thereby reinforce the importance of, such values as sitting in their seats,
raising their hands before speaking, handing in assignments on time, punctually
changing classes, displaying good sportsmanship on the athletic field, trying to
do one's best, and the like. The teacher's commands, demands, manner of interacting with students, and own conformity to the regulations of the school establish an ethos of behavior—a way of conducting oneself within that institution.

Obviously in teaching thoughtfulness and the skills required of critical
thought and deliberation, values will be taught. In the quotidian operations of the
schools, as suggested, certain values are prominent. Students are asked to be
punctual, civil, orderly; in the democratic decision making within the schools
they will also need to be tolerant, cooperative, honest, and respectful.

Therefore, in following Aristotle, we arrive at a method of imparting democratic character. Democratic education, from school through adult participation
in deliberative procedures, focuses on the exercise of practices that become habits. But I am not suggesting that those who do not develop or who forsake these
habits will be excluded from deliberative participation. Education is an enhancement, not a prerequisite; it is to help make future citizens more familiar
and comfortable with, and effective in, the requirements of democratic deliberation.

In a liberal democracy all citizens have equal rights, including the right to
participate in politics. It is a truism that rights cannot exist without responsibilities, for I neither exercise some of my rights nor have them assured unless you
refrain, or are restrained, from interfering with that exercise. All rights carry that
responsibility. Yet in the context I am establishing, more is involved. Rights are
enabling conditions. They represent, they are, those conditions necessary for me
to live out my life as I see fit. At the same time, rights are themselves bounded
by responsibilities, which are those conditions necessary for society as a whole
to coalesce, function, and continue. Rights as conditions for living the good life
have little meaning when responsibilities or conditions for social continuation
are absent. Autonomy, clearly, is central to the rights, if it is not itself the principal right,[30] of liberal democratic citizens. Likewise, central to the responsibilities

of liberal democratic citizens is the duty to behave democratically when participating politically.

Notice, however, that I did not say that citizens had the duty to participate.
While it is true that liberal democracies could not continue if no citizens partici-
pated, we have abundant evidence that many citizens will even participate in a
democratic system where it is not rational for them individually to do so and
where their decision-making power is reduced to periodic voting for governmental representatives. The duty or responsibility of participation should rest, therefore, with how citizens must behave within the democratic processes, however
those processes are presented. It does not rest with whether they participate.

The assurance that we as citizens want is that our future fellow democrats
have knowledge and judgment sufficient to make informed decisions and the
thoughtfulness or critical-thinking skills to deliberate politically. Beyond that,
the state needs to guarantee that students have ample opportunities within the
schools for deliberating and judging. That is part of, that is, the heart of, democratic education. Once students become citizens, whether they choose to partake
of the political opportunities available to them is itself a matter of autonomous
choice and not a characterological, if not programmed, predisposition.

The problem, however, with arguments for civic education like Galston's
and Gutmann's is that they read as if persons must be shaped into democratic
participants who *will* choose to participate. Otherwise, citizens will not fulfill
their civic duty.

Yet that seems so only because citizens have been engineered or inveigled
into participating, because they do not see that participation brings benefits,
whether practice or moral or psychological. If participation were truly about
making decisions important in one's life, individually and collectively, then in
terms of civic education would we need to educate beyond developing the habit,
or virtue, of thoughtfulness and its attendant virtues?

I applaud Gutmann's call for an education in deliberation, but I disagree with
some aspects of it. But that rendering points up one important fact: there may be
no crisis in civic education; there may be, if anything, a crisis in democracy.
Many citizens, and perhaps it is more and more citizens, are deciding not to participate. The cry has been, as we have seen, to motivate them to do so through
revamped civic education. Yet this seems to me to miss the fundamental political motivations of citizens. They avoid participation because democratic politics
is not meaningful enough to them. This, as the Framers pointed out, is the fundamental problem: citizens are thinking in terms of their self-interests and not in
terms of the public good. As long as they think in terms of self-interests, they
will not participate. The purpose of civic education, therefore, is to inculcate not
only a willingness, if not a desire to participate, but also those traits that will encourage them to put aside or transcend their self-interests for the sake of the
common good.

This is one reason why Richard Battistoni, for example, argues against a curriculum in "critical education" or "critical rationality." It overlooks or denigrates affective content that can engender or increase "feelings of solidarity with fellow citizens." When that is missing from the curriculum, students are left "without attachments or common purposes." In fact, each person may be left without meaning or purpose in life (1985, 157).

If affection among citizens is not developed through civic education, then, says Battistoni, "the affective bonds necessary to the continued success of democratic politics will not develop" (159). Here I agree with Battistoni. Our current representative democracy cannot survive without affective ties. While he nowhere makes an argument that democracy needs such ties for its "continued success," one can agree that an education in thoughtfulness or critical rationality might well lead students, and future citizens, to find fault with, and thereby undermine, our representative system. Missing from that system, of course, are deliberative opportunities in which the people can exercise the power to decide, which is democratic power. Having received an education in the skills of critical thinking, often helpful to decision making, these future citizens are empowered to shape and direct their own lives. "Why," they might ask, "should we be denied that power in democratic politics?"

This is precisely what Battistoni deplores. It is evident that such questions evince a decided lack of those affective ties necessary for our representative democracy's continued success. He does acknowledge, however, that a method of instruction based on deliberation and dialogue, in which students "come together to share experiences and deliberate about common concerns," would meet both cognitive and affective goals. On this he and I also agree. Yet it is possible, if not likely, that students meeting together will come to loathe some of their fellow future citizens. It is not the affective ties that bring citizens together and keep them coming back; it is not affective ties that enable them to collaborate and accept an outcome even when it goes against them. Students can do this even with those they loathe. Citizens keep coming back, or would keep coming back, to deliberative democracy because through the deliberative democratic procedures they can participate in making decisions important, if not central, to their lives, individual and collective. They would keep coming back because even though a decision made today goes against them, one made tomorrow could favor them, or because they can accept both of these decisions, since they judge the democratic procedures to be open and fair.

Notes

1. 1989, 189. Ironically, as Wolin points out, the power implied—which is "remote, abstract, and virtually unseen"—"bore certain unfortunate resemblances to the kind of power which the colonists had rejected less than two decades earlier when they had rebelled against the authority of the British Crown" (189).

2. *Federalist* 57, 371.

3. For some indication of how prevalent the outcry is, see *The Civic Arts Review,* whose raison d'etre is to call attention to the need for, and to promote, civic education and political participation.

4. Liberalism's version of citizenship, Mouffe writes, "reduced citizenship to a mere legal status, setting out the rights that the individual holds against the state" (1992, 5, 227).

5. Michael Walzer comments: "Citizenship . . . is today a passive role: citizens are spectators who vote" (1992, 99).

6. It seems the case that while voting is immensely significant when a nation is democratizing, which implies that the people have been deprived of the right to vote, its significance diminishes in a democracy where citizens are to rule but instead only vote periodically for representatives who make the rules. As Benjamin Barber observes: "For while the election of representatives requires some periodic activity from citizens, it is a political act whose purpose is to terminate political action, for all but the elected delegates. It achieves accountability by alienating responsibility, and leaves elected politicians as the only real citizens of the state" (1989, 64). This view, of course, echoes Rousseau.

7. See Neil Postman, *Amusing Ourselves to Death* (New York: Viking, 1985).

8. The effect of this might well be similar to what I have argued about the effects of an education in deliberation: to wit, to push the democratic system in a different direction. Indeed, a curriculum based on issue analysis will involve, it seems to me, many of the same elements of critical thinking that an education in deliberation requires, though without the need for democratic schools. The absence of that need would explain why an issue-analysis curriculum will not have as dramatic an effect on the democratic system as an education in deliberation might. In short, an issue-analysis curriculum might push us toward a new focus or emphasis within representative democracy, while an education in deliberation might push us toward deliberative democratic forums.

9. Gutmann, 1987, 23. In this section of the chapter, all page numbers in parentheses, unless otherwise specified, are from that text.

10. Articles written after *Democratic Education* indicate that indeed Gutmann does have in mind a version of deliberative democracy, though she has not yet spelled it out. See 1993b, 1995, and, with Dennis Thompson, 1990 and 1996.

11. For a discussion of how autonomy can avoid reinforcing atomism, see Crittenden, 1992 and 1993.

12. Limiting the range of choices is a way of restricting, if not negating, autonomy, which might not bother Gutmann, who sees autonomy not as process but as a substantive end among other such ends. See Crittenden, 1992, 74-77.

13. Shelley Burtt claims that "religious parents and secular schools share the end of an education in the basic skills and virtues of liberal democracy" (1994, 62). Such a claim would mean that there should be no clash between religious parents and the state over minimum educational standards. But is she right? What most religious parents object to, Burtt continues, is the lack in public education of the preservation of some sense of the transcendent in our lives and of the provision of resources necessary to live a righteous life (63). If public schools offered both of these, then such parents would not object to teaching the skills of "critical rationality." Yet a focus on critical rationality must be at least partly responsible for undercutting a sense of the transcendent, as that is currently understood and taught in the West, and for increased skepticism about the composition, if not the concept, of a righteous life.

Burtt seems to acknowledge this: "What seems to us instruction in critical rationality can seem to some parents an education that might undermine their child's growth in grace" (64). Burtt's position, then, can instruct us as to why religious parents object to public schooling. Religious parents do not necessarily show a "reflexive intolerance to the presentation of other views"; instead, they may "not want their child corrupted by a premature or improperly mediated introduction to 'other' forms of religion" (64). But the consequences of that objection bring us to the same conclusion: religious parents object to a curriculum based on critical rationality. That being so, such parents do not share the same ends as those who support secular education or education in deliberation. As long as "growth in grace," however understood, is the educational end, then rational inquiry is not an acceptable educational approach, irrespective of content.

14. There is some support from developmental psychology for those religious groups, like the Amish, who wish to exempt their children from public education after elementary school. Piaget found that before adolescence students by and large lacked the structures of formal operational thinking that enabled them to think abstractly and concretely. Thus, elementary school students can generalize, but only from specific evidence. They can follow abstractions in a concrete way, say, reading a map or building a model, but they cannot readily create a mental framework for relating abstractions analytically. Thus their level of rational inquiry, in comparison to the possibilities opened up with formal operational thinking, is truly elementary. (See Barbel Inhelder and Jean Piaget, *The Growth of Logical Thinking from Childhood to Adolescence* [New York: Basic Books, 1958].) Thus elementary school children would not be as susceptible to the self-scrutiny that would lead them to compare and question an inherited way of life. Learning about other ways of life would not necessarily interfere with their living their own religious life. Of course, a possible rejoinder is that knowledge learned today is available tomorrow.

Piaget, however, did have to acknowledge that the unfolding of formal operational thinking is relative. Moreover, he admitted that the performance of various cognitive operations also depends on the experiences of the child. The greater the opportunities to grapple with problems demanding reasoning, one can surmise, the quicker the child can think analytically. Charlotte Crabtree found that first-graders could hypothesize and evaluate their hypotheses if guided properly. That guidance marks, of course, a significant difference and certainly has a significant role to play in self-reflectivity, if that can even be entertained at an early age. Also, the presence of formal operational thinking does not mean that one uses it to reflect on oneself. The Crabtree study is cited in Cleary, 1971, 89.

15. Shoshana Zuboff adduces a decidedly late twentieth-century reason for the importance of compulsory schooling. She observes that new technologies of information gathering, organizing, storing, and delivering—computers, telecommunications, and the like—decentralize information access, retrieval, and use and may thereby generate "social amnesia" that destroys value perspectives. Therefore, in this information age, education is even more crucial "to remind students of the classical themes in human experience, create a sense of kinship between present and past, and heighten understandings of the continuities in the human condition." "Smart Machines and Learning People," an interview with Shoshana Zuboff, *Harvard Magazine* (November-December 1988): 60. See also Zuboff, 1988.

16. Butts, 1989, 96.

17. Thompson, 1970, 169. For the evidence Thompson relies upon, see his chapter 3, notes 47-49, 204, and chapter 5, note 64.

18. For an argument that schools should focus exclusively on the skills of literacy, see Patricia Alberg Graham, 1981. Benjamin Barber points out that rampant illiteracy, especially among the young, "is our own, reflected back at us with embarrassing force. We honor ambition, we reward greed, we celebrate materialism, we worship acquisitiveness, we commercialize art, we cherish success. . . . The kids know that if we really valued learning, we would pay teachers what we pay lawyers and stockbrokers" (1992, 220). Ironically, Barber reduces value to money, which places his point within the same hypocrisy. To reduce the solution to paying teachers more is to succumb to the view that money is the only means of valuing learning or valuing anything. Unfortunately, this seems so in our culture.

19. For a detailed discussion of this point, see Brighouse, 1998.

20. Engle and Ochoa intimate something like this in their argument that social studies, whose concern is exclusively with educating citizens (13), should be both socializing and counter-socializing. In the counter-socializing phase, when students are instructed in and encouraged to undertake "independent critical thinking" (a subject I take up in detail in chapter 6), students question propositions and truth claims and look for alternative evidence, explanations, and conclusions without necessarily turning such scrutiny onto their personal lives. They are examining the content of their social studies course, which may not highlight, use, or suggest personal experiences. Self-reflective scrutiny ought to be reserved for post-secondary education.

21. Even though Callan implies that he is after "an education that could conduce to autonomy" (60), a position with which I agree. I think that his book makes clear, as does his response (2000) to Brighouse, that he is after something well beyond that.

22. Gutmann herself suggests that one of the participatory democratic virtues that ought to be cultivated is "a desire to participate in politics" (91).

23. Butts, 1989, 103, 123.

24. See chapter 6.

25. See Dewey, 1948, especially 147 and passim.

26. *Nichomachean Ethics*, book 6, chapter 13.

27. Manville points out, using Plutarch's story about Solon and the Skythian prince, Anarcharsis, that the written laws and political institutions of Solon were a foundation for Athens as a political community firmer than many, including Anarcharsis, had imagined. One important reason why these institutions resisted destruction at the hands of the greedy, the unjust, the rich, and the powerful is that political business was conducted in open dialogue in the agora (Manville, 1990, 150-55).

28. See Nussbaum, 1990, 233.

29. For a full discussion of this problem for Gutmann and Galston, from the perspective of liberal legitimacy, see Brighouse, 1998.

30. See Crittenden, 1992, chapter 6, and Dagger, 1997.

1) too much rests on the distinction between teaching a capacity for self-reflection and requiring self-reflection. Who will be satisfied by this distinction among interested parties? Is there a moral imperative to self-reflect?

2) Crittenden tries to split the difference between Brighouse and Callan, while avoiding the lack of clarity in Gutmann + Macedo.

3) w/o imperative to self-reflect, is deliberative capacity here rhetoric (in the worst sense)?

Chapter Five

Critical Thinking:
The Core across the Curriculum

As I have argued elsewhere, and as Gutmann and Thompson point out (1996) "the point of dialogue, of 'public' presentation, is to show one's claims to be grounded in reason(s) that others can accept as reasons even when they disagree" (Crittenden, 1992, 165). This means that one who disagrees must, when in public dialogue, disagree through reasons and evidence. The qualities of one's reason and evidence justify holding to a certain position. These qualities will be tested, validated, or refuted intersubjectively; that is, through reasoned, public dialogue. This is not only a liberal claim, but it is a democratic claim as well.

Which values, then, should schools transmit? They should transmit those values that underlie, and underscore, our liberal democratic institutions. When fully practiced in listening to and even soliciting dialogue, weighing evidence and reasons, drawing inferences, defending and clarifying positions, addressing divergent views, and the like—when, that is, students have been educated in deliberation—then citizens as participants will not only feel comfortable and confident in the procedures, but they may also develop abiding commitments to the values inherent in those procedures.

The democratic mission of liberal education is to prepare students for a common political life while encouraging the maintenance and expression of the multicultural backgrounds that make these students distinct. The core to this education follows from the approach John Dewey called "active thinking."[1] It is the judgment behind moral values and actions that we must educate. To do so, we must teach the skills of critical thinking, which serve as both the skills of deliberation and the foundation of autonomy. Critical thinking is therefore the subject of this chapter.

Why Can't Johnny Think?

At the beginning of a new century and a new millennium, we are dismayed to find in the most powerful democracy in the world high school graduates who cannot read. We ask, "Why can't Johnny read?" But even when Johnny can read, we find that Johnny can't think. That does not mean that Johnny has no thoughts. It means that he cannot argue for beliefs, values, ideas, and goals; he cannot separate reasons from opinions, assumptions from conclusions, facts from preferences; he cannot differentiate a challenge to his thoughts from an attack on his person; he thinks that every view or opinion is as good as and therefore is equal to every other view or opinion; he cannot follow arguments or attend to a lecture; he cannot in a sustained and systematic way explain why he thinks what he does. In short, Johnny has thoughts, but he cannot think critically.[2]

Critical thinking is another way to describe deliberation. If we are ever to introduce dialogic democratic procedures, let alone sustain them, then we must have citizens who can think critically, who can deliberate. In "The Challenge of Multiculturalism in Political Ethics" (1993a) Amy Gutmann reasons that if citizens are to deliberate "in a way that actually invites people to engage in the give and take of argument, where reasonable positions are well-considered, and the best arguments on all sides are brought to light" (200), then certain background conditions must obtain. Education in critical thinking—which is not only the skills of deliberation or those background conditions, but is also the foundation of autonomy—is essential.

Our schools can teach children how to sort out choices, how to examine options and explore the implications for or consequences of choosing one over others. Schools can teach them to seek out and to voice reasons for choosing one option over another. Schools can teach students how to weigh evidence and reasons; how to form, advance, and challenge arguments; how to articulate reasonable positions; and how to engage with others in the give-and-take of discussion. Schools can teach all of that, but often they don't.[3] Instead they too often teach to standardized tests.

These tests are multiple-choice exams that require students within a short time span to search for the correct answers to problems and issues that may well be of little interest to them. There is no need for students to give reasons for these answers. As a result, comments John Goodlad, "the majority of teachers do not regularly employ methods that encourage thinking in their students; rather, most teachers invite students to merely recall information. Teacher talk comprises [sic] 70% of classroom instruction, yet invited, open requests for student reasoning and opinion comprise only 1% of teacher talk."[4]

Why do schools operate this way? One reason is that critical thinking is demanding, for both teachers and students. Indeed, in some schools the students seem unable, intellectually and motivationally, to learn to think critically. In

'reasonable': these's that word again

some schools the student-teacher ratio is too high, or there is a paucity of resources, or the teachers are inadequately trained. As a result, comments Daniel Resnick, the expectations that we hold today for our students are little different from the expectations held almost five centuries ago. Our model of reading and writing and thinking resembles "the Reformation pattern," which Resnick associates with education "believers, not thinkers." In other words, he claims, we are providing an education not for autonomy but for "catechism-dependent students," one in which "texts [are] assumed to be authoritative, teachers . . . know all the answers, and repetition . . . passes as learning" (1990, 17).

Such a model is not geared toward developing independent thinking, for catechism controls not only what is read, but also how it is interpreted (18). We need not agree with Resnick's account of Reformation religions to take his point that too often students today are taught to answer designed questions by giving formulaic answers. No emphasis is placed on questioning or generating ideas or arguing about the value or truth of claims. Why not? Resnick argues that the roots of our expectations lie in the emergence of the comprehensive high school in the early twentieth century. The explosion of our population and the concomitant expansion of public schooling made it impossible to transfer the rigorous academic programs of the elite secondary—predominantly boarding—schools to the public schools. To accommodate the diverse student population in the most efficacious way meant the collection into one building of nearly incompatible programs: academic, general, and vocational programs. This became the only way to address the disparity among students' interests, abilities, and preparation (20-21).

When we raise expectations, however, students meet them.[5] It is time to raise expectations to the level where all students are expected to learn how to think critically. Critical thinking is crucial to the development of persons both as private individuals and as citizens. Autonomy, as I have developed that idea in this book, is central to both, and thus the skills developed in critical thinking are those central to autonomy: the skills of deliberation in making judgments, decisions, or choices.

What Is Critical Thinking?

What exactly is critical thinking or deliberation? Can it be taught? How is it best taught? Should it be part, let alone the core, of a curriculum? These are not new inquiries. Indeed, there has appeared over the past fifteen years an impressive array of works devoted to the subject. Richard Paul points out that a computer search a few years ago turned up 1,849 articles over a span of seven years with critical thinking as the major descriptor (1990a, 102).

With so much attention devoted to the subject, we should assume that by now the educational community has a solid understanding of what the term "critical thinking" entails, as well as how to teach it. This, unfortunately, is not the case. As John McPeck comments, the term "critical thinking" is "both overworked and under-analyzed" (1981a, 2). I want, therefore, to consider first how the three most prominent educational philosophers of critical thinking understand that process. Doing so will place my own view in context and will serve as a useful perspective for understanding why I think that critical thinking should be taught through writing. Such consideration may also indicate why the intramural debates among proponents of critical thinking stymie widespread movements to introduce the teaching of critical thinking to our schools.

Harvey Siegel

A critical thinker, in Harvey Siegel's view, is one who is able to use reasons to justify and criticize various viewpoints, including one's own. This makes a critical thinker a rational person, because she believes and acts on the basis of reasons; she can "act, assess claims, and make judgments on the basis of reasons."[6]

But this cannot be all there is to it. To say, "I swung the cat by its tail because the cat looked at me" is to give, and to act on the basis of, a reason. Yet one should hardly consider that an adequate justification. For a critical thinker the reasons offered must be good reasons, not just any reasons. Siegel acknowledges this in an oblique way when he says that a critical thinker is one who is "*appropriately* moved by reasons" (1988, 2, 23, 32, and passim; my emphasis). These will be, or must be, good reasons (149, n. 5). So what does Siegel mean by good reasons? He begs the question. Good reasons are those "which actually have convicting [convincing?] force and which warrant conviction" (149). Yes, but what kinds of reasons are those?

Reasons, Siegel reminds us, are expressions or signifiers of principles, which are general rules applied consistently when making decisions or judgments. Principles determine the strength and relevance of reasons. Principles, and therefore good reasons, are the opposite of arbitrariness. Thus swinging the cat by its tail because she looked at me is not critical thinking, because it is not principled thinking; the reason is arbitrary, unless the person so swings all cats that looked at him (in which case he is not rational but is insane). Critical thinking presupposes standards by which principles are grounded and by which judgments following from those principles are made.

Siegel argues that there are two types of principles used when we assess reasons. First are "subject-specific principles" that enable us to assess specific reasons used in specific fields; second are "subject-neutral principles" that transcend or cut across fields and contexts. This second type refers to "all those principles typically regarded as 'logical,' both formal and informal" (1988, 34). An example of the first type would be principles governing the proper interpretation of X rays; an example of the second type would be principles regarding proper inductive inference. Both are important to the assessment of reasons; that is, of whether a reason is a good reason.

The ability to assess claims, make judgments, and act on the basis of good reasons is for Siegel necessary but not sufficient to qualify a person as a critical thinker. One must also have "an appropriate attitude" (1988, 38), a "critical spirit" (1988, 39). One must not only be able to think critically, one must also be disposed to do so (1988, 7, 39, 41). To think critically one must have "the propensity or disposition to believe and act in accordance with reasons" (1988, 23). It is not enough, therefore, simply to use the skills of critical thinking, or analytical thinking or logical thinking or reasoning; one must show a tendency or disposition to do so. Such a thinker is not, then, simply convinced or moved by reasons; she is also moved to reason.

Why is that so? Again, Siegel does not say. What does he mean when he says that critical thinkers are those who "habitually seek reasons and evidence"? He wants to distinguish between those persons who have the skills to think critically but do not use them, and those who have both the skills and the inclination to use them. If by this Siegel means that in our schools we ought to demand that students practice, practice, practice critical thinking such that it may, and probably will, become a habit, then he and I agree. But he goes on to say that "a person who is to be a critical thinker must be, to the greatest extent possible, emotionally secure, self-confident, and capable of distinguishing between having faulty beliefs and having a faulty character" (1988, 41). He must have a "positive self-image" (1988, 41). Without such psychological traits a thinker may face "practice obstacles to the execution of critical thinking" (1988, 41). What obstacles? We may know immensely talented academicians who are skillful critical thinkers and prone to think critically, but who are also immensely insecure, with large and yet fragile egos and terrible self-images. No matter how much they publish or how well received their work, they see only the flaws, in their work and in themselves. Or they manifest insecurity in the opposite way— a vast arrogance that masks it.

As far as critical thinking goes, such characterological concerns seem beside the point. Is an emphasis on disposition as outlined by Siegel not in itself a strong reason why public schools might shy away from teaching critical thinking? Is Siegel suggesting that educators should evaluate students not simply according to the academic skills learned and mastered at particular levels, but also according to whether each one's character is outstanding, acceptable, unacceptable, faulty, or in need of work? Will teachers, in judging the character if not "personhood" of students, be able, and willing, to recommend that character can prohibit students from advancing to the next grade?

As I have argued, schools should develop in students the habit of thoughtfulness and the values, or even virtues, that attend it. But Siegel has not told us why persons must have such character traits as a "positive self-image" or emotional security. He has not said why having the skills alone is not sufficient. Note, for example, in the following statement by Israel Scheffler, quoted with admiration by Siegel (1988, 45-46), that there is no mention of character dispositions and ostensibly no need to mention them:

> To teach . . . is at some points at least to submit oneself to the understanding and independent judgment of the pupil, to his demand for reasons, to his sense of what constitutes an adequate explanation. To teach someone that such and such is the case is not merely to try to get him to believe it: deception, for example, is not a method or a mode of teaching. Teaching involves further that, if we try to get the student to believe that such and such is the case, we try also to get him to believe it for reasons that, within the limits of his capacity to grasp, are *our* reasons. Teaching, in this way, requires us to reveal our reasons to the student and, by so doing, to submit them to his evaluation and criticism. . . . To teach is thus to acknowledge the 'reason' of the pupil, i.e., his demand for and judgment of reasons. (Scheffler, *The Language of Education* [Springfield, Ill.: Charles C. Thomas, 1960], 57, emphasis in the original)

Teaching, therefore, is putting students in positions where they must make arguments—either for their own positions or against those of others. At every step, whether in primary school or university, the student struggles to explain, define, defend, and refute by using reasons and evidence "within the limits of his capacity to grasp." It is that capacity that changes, but the nature of what he is asked to do—that is, to argue—remains constant. As for his character, that may change as his capacity changes, but there is no necessary causal relationship between them.

Richard Paul

Richard Paul thinks that learning to think critically is essential to a person's everyday life. Such thinking is crucial in confronting and solving those "political, social, and personal issues which most concern us and students."[7] As examples that concern us Paul offers abortion, nuclear energy, poverty, social injustice, socialized medicine, government regulation, sexism, racism, rights to private property, and rights to world resources. Surely many of these issues are ones that we as citizens today see and that our future citizens of tomorrow will see as significant for our individual lives and collective life. If critical thinking is needed to confront and solve such issues, then we can see the benefits of critical thinking to deliberative democracy and personal autonomy.

Paul describes the reasoning central to critical thinking as "dialectical reasoning," and it dovetails nicely with ideas that I have already presented on deliberation in democracy. (See Paul, 1990a, 414.) Dialectical reasoning is "thinking critically and reciprocally within opposing points of view." It is "the ability to move up and back between contradictory lines of reasoning" (94). Given the connections with Marx and Hegel, "dialectical" is a loaded term. As Paul uses it, the term is interchangeable with "dialogical." By both he simply means argument and counterargument. Critical thinking involves dialogue, or the exchange of perspectives, that moves in a dialectical way: back and forth.

This sort of dialogical or dialectical thinking is the only way that our personal and political concerns can be resolved. Because there is no Archimedean point from which to observe objectively the many frames of reference, including one's own, in play in any single conflict or discussion, we can step outside our own frames of reference only by stepping into the frames of others. To do so, one has to be able to reproduce those frames of reference accurately; to identify both their strengths and their weaknesses; to assess the evidence, data, or reasons adduced in support of or as a challenge to the frames; and to evaluate the implications and consequences of acting according to these frames of reference. Such skills, Paul says, are how we gain command over the elements of thought (1990a, 34).

To gain such command students need practice in questioning—in framing questions and in pursuing adequate answers to them—in the context of what Paul calls "argument networks." These networks are made up of arguments and counterarguments in which contesting points of view are brought into rational conflict (1990a, 371). As Paul points out, contesting perspectives are rarely refuted by simply identifying logical fallacies within them. Such identification is merely an intellectual move within the larger context of an argument exchange. It is a dialogue between opposing perspectives, rather than a series of individual intellectual moves, that resolves issues or conflicts.

It will come as no great surprise to learn that Paul finds this kind of approach largely absent in our schools today. He depicts a typical classroom in the following way:

> Blank faces are taught barren conclusions in dreary drills. There is nothing sharp, nothing poignant, no exciting twist or turn of mind or thought, nothing fearless, nothing modest, no struggle, no conflict, no rational give and take, no intellectual excitement or discipline, no pulsation in the heart or mind. Students are not expected to ask for reasons to justify what is presented to them. They do not question what they see, hear, or read, nor are they encouraged to do so. They do not demand that subject matter "make logical sense" to them. They do not challenge the thinking of other students nor expect their thinking to be challenged by others. . . . They mechanically repeat back what they were told, or what they think they were told, with little sense of the logicalness or illogicalness of what they are saying. (xvii)

While Paul's depiction may seem overstated, we can probably recall for every class different from this description at least two classrooms just like it. I am confident of this, because the source of such classroom decorum, if it can be called that, is the teacher, most of whom have been schooled in just this way and trained to accept and adopt pedagogical methods that they themselves rarely question. Paul comments that teaching in this country has historically been a low-prestige, low-paying job. Early in our history teachers were those who could read, write, and figure and who had no other job. They were not expected to demonstrate reasoning ability. "At no point along the way, even to this day, were, or are, prospective teachers expected to demonstrate their ability to lead a discussion Socratically, so that, for example, students explore the evidence that can be advanced for or against beliefs, note the assumptions upon which they are based, their implications for, or consistency with, other espoused beliefs" (1990a, 5). Given that the purpose of mass education has historically been to inculcate routines and not to question assumptions, this should not be surprising either.

Paul does not stop with his proposal of argument networks, where students will ask questions, define issues, and challenge norms and claims. He also proposes that students challenge their own worldviews. If such challenges are not repeatedly made, then a student may become a critical thinker, but only a "weak" critical thinker.

Paul differentiates between a "weak" and a "strong" conception of critical thinking. The weak conception, which is really not a conception but a "sense," refers to those persons who have the skills to think critically but who lack the empathy to examine accurately or fairly the perspectives of those with whom they disagree or who use the skills "selectively and self-deceptively to foster and serve their vested interests" (1990a, 570 and passim). The "strong sense," on the other hand, refers to those who use their critical thinking skills to examine their own values, ideas, and assumptions and who can accurately reconstruct the perspectives of others.

In other words, the strong critical thinkers are persons who are autonomous. From Paul's perspective, therefore, what I have proposed as an education for autonomy calls for teaching critical thinking only in the weak sense; that is, teaching students the skills associated with critical thinking but not the habit of self-reflectivity, the habit of turning these skills onto themselves. If we hold aside Paul's derogatory comments on the lack of empathy and on the self-serving nature of weak critical thinkers, comments which Paul reserves by and large for the glossary of his book but which also appear haphazardly in the text, then I agree that the mission of public schools is to cultivate weak critical thinkers, though this is itself a derogatory and wholly unnecessary description.

The description is unnecessary because to think critically or rationally does not require that we exercise self-reflectivity. To argue that this is precisely what strong critical thinkers must do, Paul is forced by his own logic to issue statements such as the following: "Only if we experientially contest our inevitable egocentric and sociocentric habits of thought can we hope to genuinely think rationally" (1990a, 217, chapter 6). Leaving aside why our habits of thought are inevitably egocentric and sociocentric, Paul avers that only if we think self-reflectively can we think rationally. Yet we know from our own experience that this is patently false. We can think critically about causes of World War I or about why the Founding Fathers introduced the idea of the separation of powers without needing to contest experientially our egocentric habits of thought. This can be genuine rational thought and does not require examining first our own habits of thought. To think that we can be rational only by being self-reflective seems to heighten, ironically, our own egocentrism.

Paul must sense this himself. He provides several examples of questions that require reflective but not necessarily self-reflective thinking: "Was the American Revolution justified? Should the colonists have used violence to achieve their ends? What is the meaning of this story? What would a true friend do in this situation? Is money the root of all evil? What are America's real values? Should the big Billy Goat have killed the Troll" [in "Billy Goat's Gruff"] (1990a, 250)? The point of such questions is to argue based on evidence and reason for one perspective, or some perspectives, over others.

Paul, I think, clarifies his own position in his chapter on "Teaching Critical Thinking in the Strong Sense." Here he places self-reflective critical thinking in the context of university-level students:

> Students studying critical thinking at the university level have highly developed belief systems buttressed by deep-seated uncritical, egocentric, and sociocentric habits of thought by which they interpret and process their experiences, whether academic or not, and place them into some larger perspective. Consequently, most students find it easy to question simply, and *only*, those beliefs, assumptions, and inferences they have already "rejected," and very difficult, often traumatic, to question those in which they have a personal, egocentric investment. (1990a, 370; emphasis in the original)

College or university is the site par excellence for self-reflective, or autonomous, thinking. It is often an environment of persons from diverse backgrounds and with diverse interests who interact daily, and often intimately, for some years. Because of this environment—some workplaces and the armed services are also such environments—and because students are reaching the age of intellectual maturity (in a developmental sense), they are ready for the exercise of, rather than merely an education for, autonomy. Paul is correct, therefore, that at the post secondary level "students need experience in seriously questioning previously held beliefs and assumptions and in identifying contradictions and inconsistencies in personal and social life" (1990a, 370-71).[8] Self-reflective thinking, work in partnership with scholars, and preparation for a life of scholarship or for certain careers are what a college education should be about. Otherwise, much of the work that post secondary education now undertakes, and accomplishes, would already be met by an education in deliberation, thus making college for many students redundant.

As with Harvey Siegel, a central issue for Paul is whether we need to develop critical persons instead of persons who can think critically. This is Paul's distinction between strong and weak critical thinkers. Critical persons, or strong critical thinkers, are those who have the skills to think critically and the dispositions or traits to use those skills (1990a, 378). Indeed more than just this, those who are weak critical thinkers are those who use critical thinking narrowly and selfishly. Yet if weak thinkers are those who "shore up their beliefs" (1990a, 570) without examining those beliefs, then one wonders whether they think critically at all. Isn't Paul here describing rationalization and not rationality? It is one thing to say that weak thinkers do not, or do not often, apply the procedures of critical thinking metacognitively; it is another to suggest that they do not do so because they will not or cannot.

My point, again, is that it is beyond the purview of the public schools, and public school teachers, to enforce self-reflective thinking. In his method of teaching critical thinking, Richard Paul gives a central place to autonomy. Yet he uses autonomy in two senses. On the one hand, it is a student learning for herself and being able to do so independent of the teacher; on the other, it is a student learning about and questioning herself. I think that public secondary school education should cover only the former sense, not the latter.

I agree with Paul that there is good critical thinking and bad critical thinking, but those are defined by the procedures of critical thinking. Critical thinking can be used to ride roughshod over another's argument. If one exaggerates or distorts that person's argument in order to destroy it (1990a, 402), then one may be following the proper procedures, but may be doing so badly or poorly. Such thinking may be critical thinking, but unacceptable errors were made. Students of critical thinking would be able to identify those errors.

Paul wants critical thinkers to be able to "proceed empathically and fair-mindedly." What does he have in mind? Participants should be able to reproduce a speaker's position to that speaker's satisfaction—that is, to mirror a speaker's position. When no position can be summarily dismissed without good reasons or evidence, then participants will listen to and treat others' views carefully and fairly. When such a position is not so dismissed, then participants will need to treat that position with empathy in order to take it seriously, if not to make it their own. It is the specific challenge of the speakers before us, and our own experiences with critical thinking, that leads us to appreciate Paul's following observations:

> When we read or listen as critical thinkers . . . [w]e recognize the difficulty of entering into and appreciating the thoughts, the experiences, the point of view of others. We recognize the need to engage in a dialogue with the text we are reading or the person to whom we are listening. . . . We recognize the need to read

and listen actively to enter into the mind of another. . . . We immediately recognize the difficulty of re-creating in our own mind the thoughts of others based simply on hearing their words. Knowing the elements universally present in all thinking, we know, however, how to begin; we know what to look for, and how to look for it. We know how to question the structure of other people's thought, how to probe for their points of view, how to look into their reasons, their experiences, the evidence that underlies their ideas, beliefs, and conclusions. We know how to clarify and draw out their thought, how to generate examples which may make their thinking more concrete, how to dig for their assumptions and underlying ideas and values. We know how to identify possible problems or objections that might be raised to their thinking, and how to contrast their thinking with other thinking. We know, in short, how to actively engage in the give-and-take of intellectual exchange. (1990a, 405)

I agree that this is precisely how we think critically. Notice, however, that there is nothing within the procedure indicating the need to think self-reflectively. So one element in Paul's "strong sense" is unnecessary. To teach the skills of critical thinking as described above through continual practice can generate and inculcate the habit of thoughtfulness, which is also a way to develop the kinds of "critical persons" whom Paul is after.

We can see in this review of Siegel and Paul how different emphases in what critical thinking is and how to teach it might lead to impasses in what to implement in our classrooms and how to implement it. Teaching critical thinking wholesale, as the architectonic of a curriculum, is therefore postponed as philosophers of education debate what critical thinking really is. Another aspect of such debate currently centers on the differences between those like Siegel and Paul who think that critical thinking is a generalizable skill that can and should be taught through separate courses and those like John McPeck who see critical thinking as field-specific and thus embedded in each field or discipline.

John McPeck

McPeck argues that there is no discrete skill of critical thinking; we are always thinking about something. Therefore, he claims, "it makes no sense to talk about critical thinking as a distinct subject" (1981a, 5). To say, "I teach critical thinking, simpliciter, is vacuous because there is no generalizable skill properly called critical thinking."[9]

The upshot of this view is that McPeck argues against teaching critical thinking through separate courses in thinking or logic. Because the things we reason—or think critically—about are of such variety, no set of skills, let alone any single skill, enables us to be competent reasoners in all of them.

At first blush, this seems to fly in the face of our intuitions. There clearly seem to be patterns of thought that cross disciplines or that transcend subjects and that we apply to different disciplines and subjects. Logic would be one. Yet McPeck says that the connection between logic and critical thinking is overblown. The thinking behind this notion is that since logic is fundamentally related to reasoning, learning logic will help one learn to reason better. While logic is necessary for critical thinking, it is hardly sufficient, because, in McPeck's view, the major requirement for making good arguments is epistemological, not logical. In other words, to make good arguments reasoners need to learn what constitutes good reasons within the fields or disciplines within which one is reasoning. Also needed, therefore, is knowledge of and experience in the norms, standards, techniques, and terms of specific fields. This is so because, according to McPeck, critical thinking is field- or subject-dependent.

Courses in logic or thinking focus on the form of arguments, not their content. "Typically," McPeck suggests, "we are in a quandary less about the logical validity of an argument than about the truth of the putative evidence . . . whether the evidence is good or not" (1981a, 28). Assessing reasons most often depends upon knowing what counts as good reasons in a particular field or area. Because what constitutes good reasons in one area or field can differ from what constitutes good reasons in another, there can be no generalizable ability to reason that transcends or cuts across disciplines.

The idea that critical thinking is generalizable will lead us toward teaching critical thinking courses and workshops, such as Siegel and Paul propose. That can lead to teaching merely the subset of thinking that deals with logical reasoning: fallacy recognition, syllogisms, statistics, quantitative analysis, symbolic logic, informal and formal logic, and the like. This subset, to McPeck, is not only small, but also less important than coming to understand the kinds of reasons involved in the meanings of field-specific and field-dependent concepts. "In a proposition, for example, which is expressed as 'P—Q,' it is far more important and complex to understand what 'P' and 'Q' mean than it is to understand the syntactic relation between 'P' and 'Q'" (1981a, 22).

McPeck is not simply concerned with the emphasis in logic courses on formal relationships and on the validity of arguments. He argues that one cannot be a critical thinker unless one has substantive knowledge of a discipline so that one can know what counts as a good reason in that discipline and can thereby judge the hard cases. Within every substantive area are different conceptions of and approaches to critical thinking corresponding to the sorts of justifications used in that area.

Perhaps the only generalizable characteristic of critical thinking, or the only one that is notable, is the requirement of "reflective skepticism" (1981a, 6-7). This requires that one consider alternative hypotheses and possibilities. McPeck refers to this as "reflective" skepticism because it is not simply skepticism per se or skepticism applied willy-nilly. "Not just any question will do. . . . Learning to think critically is in large measure learning to know when to question something, and what sorts of questions to ask" (1981a, 7). This brings us back to the necessity of knowledge of and experience in a specific field. For McPeck the condign skepticism is that which enables us to question procedures, beliefs, and assumptions in a specific field once we suspect that the normal operations in that field are inadequate (1990, 42). Being skeptical, therefore, requires substantial knowledge of the content and procedures in a field.

In McPeck's view one can be skeptical only when one has sufficient knowledge of the field to be suspicious. Yet McPeck has still not argued why a person able to think critically, or skeptically, in one field cannot do so in another. "[W]e may say of someone that he is a critical thinker about X if he has the propensity and skill to engage in X (be it mathematics, politics or mountain climbing) with reflective skepticism."[10] Why don't the skills transfer? Can a critical thinker in mathematics not think critically in politics? If she can do so, McPeck might rejoin, it is only because she also has the propensity and skill required in political thinking. But if she cannot, then is McPeck not pointing out a massive incommensurability problem?

Yet we ask students all the time on national standardized exams, for example, to read and respond to—to reflect on—excerpts out of context, often out of their experience, and certainly out of their expertise. McPeck might suggest that such exams are worth little for this very reason. Well, isn't it possible that the content about which one thinks is the thinking process itself? Wouldn't that content cross over fields and disciplines? Here McPeck would surely point out that there can be no such content, for any thinking about thinking must be thinking about thinking about something. Yes, but thinking processes are themselves something. Moreover, are there only discipline-specific norms for argument or reasoning? How are field boundaries determined? Aren't many of them artificial? McPeck does not say.

He does give us discipline-specific examples. "[C]ritical thinking about an historical question requires, first and foremost, the skills of an historian; similarly, critical thinking about a scientific question requires the knowledge and skills of a scientist" (1990, 9). Yet it seems equally, perhaps more, plausible that there is a mode of reasoning that can be applied across disciplines. While the mode of reasoning is the same, the reasons, or content of that reasoning, change. Are there scientific questions and scientific skills that cross the field boundaries of various sciences? If such questions and skills pertain to all of science, why not to all scholarship or to all critical thinking?

Perhaps we can understand why logic is not the appropriate universal here. There are different kinds of logic, and logic is often concerned solely with the relationships among, not the meaning of, propositions. Yet McPeck agrees that logic is necessary but not sufficient. What McPeck has done is helped us clarify what we are after in chasing the meaning of critical thinking: the mode of reasoning (or logic) that is universal and the content or what constitutes reasons, especially good reasons, that is field-specific. So while there is not universal skill that can be called critical thinking, there is an essential universal component: a mode of reasoning we can call logic. Additionally, what is needed to think critically is content that varies from field to field, content that we might refer to as "reasons." After all, no one who advocates the teaching of critical thinking, including logicians, argues that reasoning procedures should replace the content of different fields: biology, chemistry, history, law, math, Spanish, and so on.

More mystifying is McPeck's assertion that "to do philosophy is to engage in critical thought" (1990, 63). If philosophy is critical thinking, and philosophy is its own discipline (63), then what are we to make of philosophy of science, of political philosophy, of philosophical anthropology, and the like? It would seem that each of these recognizes an approach to a discipline that is a generalizable approach, one that, if McPeck is correct, engages in critical thought across disciplines but that also recognizes varying contents.

Yet perhaps the clearest sign of contradiction in McPeck's work lies in the forward to *Teaching Critical Thinking*. There Michael Scriven points out that McPeck is doing in that volume precisely what he says cannot be done; namely, "analysis that depends on refined use of the vocabulary of reasoning without deep entry into substantive subject matter" (1990, x).

When we look for empirical evidence in the sciences and for rational justifications and interpretations in arts and humanities, aren't we undertaking the *same* epistemological steps in assessing the evidence and reasons even though the fields are distinct? Don't we look to separate fact from opinion, argument from assertion, conclusion from assumption in all these disciplines? Don't we reason about knowledge in these fields in similar, if not in the same, ways, notwithstanding the differences in the sources of knowledge?

McPeck says that we do not. While it is fashionable to think of reasoning as the "fourth R," after reading, 'riting, and 'rithmetic, this is simply "a seductive linguistic confusion" (1990, 38). Just because there is a single word *reading* to describe a single process that corresponds to all acts of "reading" does not mean, McPeck says, that this is true as well for reasoning. All cases of "mending" share a common property of fixing something. But "to mend a fence, an auto engine, or a sock require [sic] very different skills" (38). This, however, is not an argument, for McPeck does not tell us why reasoning is more like mending than it is like reading or writing.

Indeed, it seems to me that McPeck's own illustrations undermine his position. Writing is the same in all cases involving writing. What we write about is different; our audience may be different; but *how* we write is not (as I shall argue below). This appears to be precisely the case with reasoning. How we reason remains the same, despite what we are reasoning about. When McPeck then invokes Wittgenstein's connection between thought and language, he makes this point even stronger: To improve one's capacity for thought you must improve that person's capacity to use language (35). Writing and reading, as well as speaking and listening, are obvious ways to improve one's capacity to use language. These processes, so McPeck tells us, are the same, regardless of the context in which they are used. Therefore, when one writes and reads one improves one's capacity to think, by which McPeck means to reason. Why does our improvement in reasoning depend on what we are reasoning about, whereas our reading and writing improve regardless of what we read and write? McPeck would say "because reasoning is discipline-specific." That is to beg the question.

It seems much more likely that the process of reading and writing, regardless of context or content, improves thinking or reasoning because the process of thinking or reasoning or language use that constitutes reading and writing is itself the same regardless of context or content. If reading is a single skill and writing is a single skill, why should we think that reasoning, intimately tied to reading and writing, is not itself a single skill? McPeck does not tell us.[11]

He does say that in reasoning, as with reading and writing, one must understand what one is thinking about. "Once specific background knowledge is required as part of a skill, however, the generality of that skill is seriously restricted" (39-40). This is just the point. Sometimes specific background knowledge is required to make sense of an article. But that is not required as part of the skill of reading or writing or reasoning. One can do all of those, and do them well, with an article that responds to critiques or prior articles never read. One reads the article, writes about what one has learned, and notes those ideas or areas about which one is in the dark because she lacks the background knowledge to comment on them. The reading, writing, and reasoning are restricted only in the sense that what is read, written, and reasoned about would be different—though not necessarily better—if one did have the specific background knowledge. That knowledge, or foundation, would change one's focus in reading and would change the content about which one wrote and reasoned. Would it change *how* one read and wrote and reasoned? More information or knowledge does not necessarily make the reading, writing, and reasoning better, unless one were to stipulate that the purpose of the reading, writing, and reasoning was to comment on the article in light of the earlier critiques or articles. But that stipulation speaks to intentions, not to skills.

Richard Paul comments that McPeck, to be consistent, would have to argue that general composition courses, like courses in critical thinking *simpliciter,* are worthless because there can be no such thing as simple "writing." We must always write about something. That something defines how we write, and thus general writing skills do not exist (Paul, 1990a, 103). The strangeness of, if not the flaw in, McPeck's thought is evident through Paul's analogy. Specific content defines what we write about, but not fundamentally how we write—that is, how we employ the universal principles of English syntax and grammar when we write in English. McPeck responds that writing is a concept "entirely different" from thinking (1990, 117). This statement is curious, especially given McPeck's obeisance to Wittgenstein on language.

Another confusion is that McPeck talks about "the language of disciplines" (40). Disciplines have their own terms or concepts and vocabulary. Those, however, with the possible exception of mathematics, do not constitute their own language. The language of English enables us to express, create, and understand the disciplines. Not only can we learn the terms and vocabulary of the disciplines because they are, or can be, expressed in English, but we also learn to order our thinking about, or in, those disciplines through English. Because we can think in English, and can read and write English, we can understand the various disciplines without needing to learn a new language, except in the colloquial sense in which new terms are a new language. We use new vocabulary and concepts, but we still think in English.[12]

To teach critical thinking, since there is no generalizable skill, McPeck wants schools to abandon separate courses in critical thought and logic and to concentrate instead on presenting critical thinking "as an integral part of other subjects" (1981a, 18). The evidence is in, argues McPeck; students who take separate critical thinking courses do not become better critical thinkers. What makes one a good critical thinker in one discipline does not transfer and make the same student a good critical thinker in another discipline.

We do not need to accept McPeck's premise to agree with his conclusion. Students taking separate critical thinking courses often do not become better critical thinkers. Yet that does not mean that critical thinking is not a generalizable skill. Mortimer Adler points out that the logic courses required of freshmen at most colleges at the turn of the century were discontinued because they failed to produce students who could think critically. As McPeck pointed out, they could identify fallacies, but they could not apply them; as Adler discovered, students could achieve high grades in logic, but could not analyze or "discuss thoughtfully" subjects in their other courses (1986, 28). This is not the case because critical thinking is not generalizable; it is usually the case because separate courses devoted to critical thinking involve students in work that is routine and boring. "It is not hard to see," observes Francis Schrag, how fallacy identification, for example, "could be incorporated into fairly mindless homework [or in-class] assignments and objective tests with correct and incorrect answers" (1988, 155). Students are asked to find in specific passages the emotionally laden terms, hasty generalizations, or ad hominem arguments. This in itself can undermine reflection by emphasizing formulaic patterns.

When the arcana of logic courses—identification of fallacies, modes of inference, and so on—are stripped away, we find that what lies beneath logic is "simply the vocabulary of the careful user of the native tongue" (McPeck, 1990, x). More is involved than mere vocabulary. What lies beneath logic is the thinking of the careful user of language. The key is to recognize that all that is found in special courses in critical thinking—in good courses in logic—is also found in the careful, and thus the thoughtful, use of one's language. Michael Scriven suggests, therefore, that we stop looking to "the language of logic" as if it is separate, and separable, from "the logic of language."

Nor does this view necessarily support McPeck's contention that critical thinking is not a separable, generalizable skill. Indeed, to some who look to the logic of language to teach good reasoning, critical thinking is generalizable but not separable. The Yeats scholar T. R. Henn worked with science students at Cambridge University to improve their writing. His work shows "how what the biologist does is comparable to what the poet does, how close looking in the lab is like close reading of a complex poem."[13]

Scientists, of course, write up their research, as all scholars do. Scholarly writing is not *like* scientific research; it *is* part of that research. All scholarly writing, irrespective of the discipline, has the same elements: a search for evidence; the presentation of cases and arguments; the preparation and execution of experiments, hypotheticals, or oppositions; and the articulation of interpretations. What is writing in this situation but thinking critically on paper by using the logic of language?

"What I discovered," reports Ann Berthoff, "from talking with art historians, microbiologists, literary historians, archaeologists, chemists, and poets . . . is that we all teach rhetoric whenever we present ideas in context—where they came from and how we use them; we all teach rhetoric whenever we attend to discovering topics, points of departure for the exploration of ideas, the art of invention; we all teach rhetoric when we consider the development of ideas, the organization of statements, the art of *disposition*" (1981, 117). What is rhetoric but the study of how words work? Defining terms, placing ideas in context, discovering topics, exploring cases, organizing statements, seeing and establishing relationships among parts and among parts and wholes is critical thinking. This same thinking applies to all disciplines.

William Zinsser, who spent his professional life writing, editing, and teaching writing, discovered that no ideas, however abstruse the subject or field, "are so specialized that I couldn't grasp them by writing about them or by editing someone else's writing about them: by breaking the ideas down into logical units, called sentences, and putting one sentence after another" (1988, 11).

There is nothing more logical than good writing: sentence C follows clearly from sentence B, which follows clearly from sentence A. Yet perhaps McPeck would object that writing is about thinking systematically, about applying order to thoughts, but that writing is not necessarily about critical thinking. To think critically one must then move from generalizable writing ability to field-specific and field-dependent concepts that are the basis of the different disciplines.

Of course, McPeck is correct to say that to understand the concepts central to a discipline one must learn that discipline's vocabulary, even "language." Yet his move at best shifts only the content of the writing, not how the subject is written about. We do need the reasons and concepts, the terms and idioms, of specific disciplines; we need to think about, to write about, something. But when we write English we order or structure those thoughts or content; we think about those thoughts in the same way.

Berthoff and Zinsser are telling us that the best way to learn a subject is to write about it; Henn reminds us that students and scholars alike think critically about and express what they have learned, and are learning, by writing about it, by using the logic of language. John Dewey observed that reflective thought "involves not simply a sequence of ideas, but a consequence—a consecutive ordering in such a way that each determines the next as its proper outcome, while each in turn leans back on its predecessors." This is precisely why writing is such an excellent way to practice and reinforce reflective thinking: "Each term [read: sentence] leaves a deposit which is utilized in the next term [sentence]. The stream or flow becomes a train, chain, or thread."[14]

 Whenever we write, especially expositorily, we order our thinking in the same way, regardless of the subject we are writing about. What way? The way of the language in which we write. We follow the general rules of English grammar and syntax; we follow the logic of that language. Writing in English is thinking—and learning to think—in English. These thinking skills are generalizable and transferable. So if we wish to teach students how to think critically, then we can do no better than to teach them to write clearly, read carefully, listen attentively, and speak directly. These four activities or skills constitute a language arts focus that arches the entire curriculum, kindergarten through twelfth grade (K-12). The keystone in that arch is writing.[15]

Critical Thinking through Writing

McPeck claims, echoing Wittgenstein, that "to improve people's capacity for thought, you must improve their capacity to use language" (1990, 35). The main business of education must be "to teach the process of thought and the operation of the symbol systems in which we think—language and number" (Mitchell, 1979, 111). If language use is the focus, why is writing and not speaking the keystone? It would seem far easier, as well as more accommodating of pluralist perspectives and multicultural backgrounds, to focus on oral communication. This view carries two assumptions, only the second of which I shall discuss in this chapter: one, that multiculturalism might be undercut if students are required to conform their writing, and thinking, to the conventions of Standard English (see chapter 6); two, to if clear thinking is the goal of education, then clear language should be education's focus. Writing and speaking exercise our language use; reading and listening expand it. Language, in this case English, is the instrument of deliberation. It is the means by which we argue our case and challenge those of others. To inquire into any subject; to interrogate any person or position; and to challenge, promote, or alter an argument, including one's own, require the ability to use language in critical—which means both analytical and creative—ways.

Thus, it is the use of language that is central to democratic dialogue. To prepare citizens, that communication is the foremost purpose of writing.

Richard Mitchell provides a direct answer to why writing is the centerpiece: "The words we write demand far more attention than those we speak. The habit of writing exposes us to that demand, and skill in writing makes us able to pay logical and thoughtful attention. Having done so, we can come to understand what before we could only recite."[16] Now able to pay logical and thoughtful attention to their thinking, students can apply that attention to listening and speaking and reading as well.

Writing permits, and pushes, us to more complex ideas. "Just as you can add 2 + 3 in your head, but cannot add 1,827 + 9,369 without paper and pencil, so you can think 'what should I have for dinner?' in your head, but not 'what factors combined to create the conditions for the onset of World War II?'" (Horton, 1982, 2). Writing enables us to handle more complex ideas because it makes a permanent record.

> To analyze and abstract, the mind must be able to return to a subject over and over, for review and reevaluation. The eye must see exactly what it saw the time before. . . . The reader [or writer] can go over the same sentence time and time again, puzzling out its meaning, analyzing its structure, teasing from it every nuance of meaning. . . . Reading and writing provide the key exercise for the literate mind, allowing a critical eye to be turned to everyday experience. (Sanders, 1994, 19)

Permanence is why, as Mitchell says, writing demands more attention; the words will not go away. They can be a permanent testament to one's thoughtfulness or thoughtlessness.[17] The fact that our written words do not disappear permits us to go off to explore different ideas, to discover, perhaps, that they are merely tangents, and then to return to the main idea without having lost—and, indeed, having gained—much in the process. Writing does not simply leave behind traces of ideas, like footprints; it leaves behind the actual body of one's thoughts, to which one can return.

Because writing is permanent, it can freeze thoughts so that the writer can rethink and revise the words, the ideas. Its permanence lets the writer see what she is thinking. "It is a way of holding thought still enough to examine its structure, its flaws."[18] This revisability permits and encourages reflection and deliberation. Writing is also developed within a context of content, as McPeck might say of critical thinking, and thus it is an especially good way to think deeply about such content.[19]

Writing per se, however, is not always a good way to think deeply about content. It is possible to write superficially, to remain on the surface and merely skim the content, and to register only one's emotional reactions to or feelings about a subject. To develop deeper thinking than this, students would need assignments that required them to think critically: to support their perspectives

with reasons and evidence, to provide explanations and interpretations, to analyze texts, and to defend their views with reasons.

So the issue is not simply to have students write more. Instead, students must
be challenged to think and to write critically or reflectively. We can say, then,
that writing promotes critical thinking when students are asked open-ended
questions—that is, questions for which there are no obvious right or wrong answers—when students are asked to order their arguments for or against the subject; when they need to be clear and explicit in their writing, and thinking; when
they are required to compare and contrast or explore connections between ideas
from one context to ideas in another; when they can, and should, investigate the
implications of their conclusions; and, last, when they are required to revise their
writing over an extended period of time.

Students of all ages are largely uncomfortable with such writing assignments, because they signify hard work. Unless the assignment calls for the re-
gurgitation of information read in a text or heard in a lecture, the hard work is
the thinking: what to say and how to say it. After an address, when accosted by a
member of the audience with the scolding query: "Why don't you write any better?" Alfred North Whitehead is alleged to have responded, "because I don't
think any better."

While students and teachers can fool themselves, for a time, that lessons are
learned during lectures, all doubt is removed when the papers come in. Why is
writing so difficult and discomfiting? Unlike delivering a lecture, where our
audiences will often make allowances for our gaps and gaffes, or unlike listening to a lecture, where most of the thinking is done for us, writing is highly organized and structured. It must be so, because the reader can always stop and
zero in on one idea or construction. At the same time, the writing is meant to
take the reader systematically through a thought process that begins at one point,
proceeds through twists and turns, sometimes acute, to arrive at another, often
an altogether different, point.

When students are required to write discursively—that is, when they are required to write essays that form, advance, or challenge arguments—then writing
and rewriting—or practice, practice, and more practice—will eventuate in better,
not worse, thinking.[20] That is so because writing, and thus critical thinking, is a
skill. People who do not write well can be taught to write better. In the process
they also learn more. So writing to think, because thinking is always about
something, is also writing to learn.

Newell's study of eleventh-grade students provides evidence that writing is
an effective method for learning and thinking. His work produced two major
findings. First, "students involved in essay (discursive) writing, especially those
who had limited knowledge of a topic, acquired more knowledge of key concepts than equivalent students who had either taken notes or responded to study
guide questions." Second, those students who wrote essays "engaged in a greater
number of overall cognitive (reasoning) operations (i.e., planning, generating,

organizing, goal setting, translating, and reviewing)" than did the note-takers or those who answered study-guide questions.[21]

According to Langer and Applebee, analytical writing, by which they mean the essay writing that most of us envision (or envisioned) as typical of high school writing assignments, leads students "to more complex manipulations of the material they are writing about. . . . [W]hen information is manipulated in more complex ways, it tends to be better understood and remembered" (1987, 136). Langer and Applebee conclude that if we want students to think more reflectively and to reason more deeply, then teachers should assign analytical writing; the more, the better.

Should such writing be assigned in any course? Will writing help students learn better in science and math? That was the impetus behind Writing across the Curriculum programs that began in the 1970s. In response to widespread concerns that post secondary students were deficient in writing and reasoning skills, educators began to use writing, regardless of the content or methods involved, as a way to learn a subject. Writing was considered a measure not only of what students had learned in a course, but also of whether, and how, they could organize that learning and apply it to novel situations. Educators also found once the programs were under way that writing stimulated students to learn more and to think better.[22]

Does writing work in math, the subject that seems most removed from writing and that has its own language? William Zinsser argues that writing works for any subject: "It is by writing about a subject we're trying to learn that we reason our way to what it means" (1988, 22). Writing is about making sense and discovering meaning, regardless of the subject.

Zinsser introduces his readers to Joan Countryman, head of the math department at Germantown Friends School in Philadelphia. For years she has had her students write about math. This writing has the wonderful effect of "free[ing] them of the idea that math is a collection of right answers owned by the teacher," while reinforcing the notion that "what makes mathematics really interesting is not the right answer but where it came from and where it leads" (149).

Countryman's experiences teaching math through writing, and writing through math, led her to an observation that has at some time popped into the minds of all math students: "I don't think we should even teach long division anymore; kids spend so much time learning to do it, and getting it wrong, that they never see the point of it—why would you *want* to do it. But with a calculator doing the drudgery, you can ask an interesting question, like 'How much fabric do I need to cover this chair?'" (151)

Countryman is not suggesting that teachers cease teaching mathematics— adding, subtracting, multiplying, dividing, and all that is based on such figuring. She is suggesting, however, that at some point, perhaps when dividing four or more numbers by three or more numbers, teachers call a halt to a process that a calculator can do instead. At that point, the student has learned the process of long division; to carry it out further, and the numbers farther, is pointless. It is pointless, because we should honor technological advances that do not replace the process but that provide a stopping point for us. Calculators and computers can free us to think about what makes a problem interesting and what makes math useful.

The question that she finds interesting, and for which math is useful, is "How much fabric do I need to cover this chair?" To many students this question is not interesting. Yet there are multitudes of questions mathematically based or related that students will find interesting. Some might want to write about the geometry of tennis; some might want to think, and therefore write, about how far someone could hit a pitched baseball. Answering such questions is not writing *about* math; it is writing, or doing, math—that is, learning math by writing about questions that are based on or that use math.

The point of this, she says, is to have her students see math "as a way of asking questions" (157), which is a way to think. "Writing," she concludes, "is what forced [students] to think through both math and its relationship to their lives" (161). If her students had done straightforward mathematics, "then they wouldn't have thought about what they were doing as thoroughly as they did when they wrote about how to do it."[23]

Of course, writing across the curriculum may work well with post secondary students, but is it appropriate for students in secondary and elementary schools? We should bear in mind at this juncture that I am not proposing writing across the curriculum per se as the core of the elementary- and secondary-school curriculum; I am proposing instead a program of language arts not limited solely to writing. But because the key to teaching critical thinking as the core across the curriculum is writing, then writing across the curriculum is an excellent place for our schools to start.

How Writing Teaches Critical Thinking

Each exercise of discursive writing is a minicourse in critical thinking. Every step requires decision making. Each step requires evaluation and logic, a linear progression from idea to idea. The second sentence should follow logically from the first. Does it? What is the connection? Should more be added? The composition of each sentence depends upon evaluating what one has said and upon considering what one now needs to say to proceed toward the conclusion or to the next point. What is the next point? What should it be? Can I get there from here? How can I get there? And so forth.

This process of thinking—of planning, questioning, evaluating, reviewing, deciding—is true for every phase of writing, for every sentence, paragraph, section, and chapter. The longer the manuscript, the greater the number and complexity of decisions. Nowhere is this process more evident than in the essay.

Howard and Barton argue that students must learn to write essays:

> From both writers' and readers' points of view, the essay is a framework for thinking in writing employing every strategy for reasoning, weighing of evidence, and persuasion required for virtually any subject or discipline. It is not too much to say that the essay format is the basic structure for making sense to others on paper. Whatever the specific format—the business report, book review, newspaper editorial, scientific or scholarly paper—the elements of the traditional essay recur again and again in different guises. (1986, 42-43)

The problem, of course, is that writing essays is difficult, because, as Bertrand Russell pointed out, thinking is difficult. It is so difficult, he observed, that most people would rather die than think. Unfortunately it seems that many do. To write and therefore to think well, students have much work to do:

> Students speak and write vaguely because they have no criteria for choosing words; they merely write what pops into their heads. . . . They do not recognize that words generate implications. . . . Not recognizing that what they say has implications, they do not recognize the responsibility to have evidence to support what their words imply. As a result, they routinely confuse believing with knowing, reasoning with rationalizing, evidence with conclusion, data with interpretation. (Paul, 1990a, 48-49)

In short, students do not grasp the logic of language. Practice alone does not quite make perfect; some appreciation for the logic of language permits, or eases, the mastery of it. So, it is to the logic of language as it pertains to writing that students, and we, must turn.

Many students, at all levels, think that good writers know before they write what they think on a particular subject. Writing, therefore, seems to such students to resemble dictation from mind through hand to paper or keyboard. Writing is simply a matter of recording what one thinks.

This view is not the fault of the students. "[F]or most of this century," observe Maimon et al., "teachers of writing ignored [the] vital connection between writing and thinking and focused instead on writing as the transcription of letters and punctuation marks" (1989, 161). Most elementary and secondary school English teachers today, it seems, maintain that focus, if they teach any writing at all. The basis for this focus is the idea that writing is to communicate and that that consists mostly of simply recording one's thoughts.

Yet this is rarely the case. Writing is an act of discovery or, more accurately, an act of construction—the construction of meaning. Meaning does not jump fully formed from one's mind like Athena from the head of Zeus. When someone writes, it is virtually assured, unless he is a tired academic, that he has never before written these words or seen these words in this exact combination. He is struggling first and foremost to discover what he thinks.

This is the purpose of critical thinking: to find or make meaning. It is also the principal purpose of writing. Before writing can be a method of communicating to others, it must first be a method of communicating to oneself or, as Hannah Arendt might say, communication among the parties to an internal dialogue. That is, writing is a means of discovering what one thinks about a topic and why one thinks that. Once meaning is constructed or discovered, then it can be communicated to others.[24]

The practice of writing helps us gain control of our language to the extent that there are not, in Ann Berthoff's phrase, "too many meanings at a time" (1990, 16). Such control, from piece to piece and within any piece, is not easy, for writing begins in chaos and moves through mystery. The skill is learning how to take advantage of, how to use and control, both (Horton, 1982, 156).

Writing originates in chaos, because the logical and coherent essay that one considers a finished product begins in a welter of notes, quotations, ideas, diagrams, data, observations, impressions, intuitions. "Mess [chaos]," observes Horton, "is material; material for thinking; for shaping into essays" (156). Added to this chaos is the chaos of what we do in sorting through the chaos: "When we write, we are simultaneously naming, inferring, referring, recognizing, remembering, marking time, wondering, wandering, envisaging, matching, discarding, checking, inventing: all at once, we are carrying out these acts of mind as we are writing something down" (Berthoff, 1990, 86).

The mystery is that from this chaos we ever write anything coherent at all. Indeed, the process by which we do so is mysterious: there are no sequential steps to writing. The steps or stages really overlap, just as our thinking does. Because thoughts come to us uncontrolled—come to us in mobs and flocks, come to us unexpectedly or at odd and awkward moments, come as flashes or images and as polished phrases—we must be ever vigilant. "While you are still gathering material, you begin to write sentences or even paragraphs." But a gap appears because you need more information or you need to read more. "Even in the last stages of writing, when you are polishing sentences, you might discover that finding just the right word changes the way you see your whole subject" (Horton, 1982, 157). The last sentence or the title might appear first; the first sentence might be worked on last.[25]

So how does writing structure or order thought? It does so by recapitulating what we humans do by nature all of the time. We compose. It is how we make sense of the world. "In looking and naming, looking again and renaming, [students] develop perspectives and contexts, discovering how each controls the other. They are composing; they are forming; they are abstracting" (Berthoff, 1990, 23). We look for patterns and for forms. "A composition," Berthoff tells us, "is a bundle of parts"; discovering the parts and developing ways of bundling them are interdependent operations (1978, 3). This is the basis of how we find models for interpreting the world, also known as ideologies. It is also how we write: putting things together to make sense of them.

> When we think, we compose: we put this with that; we line things up; we group and classify and categorize; we emphasize or pass over, start and stop and start up again, repeating ourselves, contradicting, hedging, declaring and questioning, lying and denying. . . . When we read, we re-compose, juxtaposing this character with that character, the theory with the supporting evidence, the argument with the alleged facts, etc. We compare premises with conclusions, ifs and thens, the beginning of the story with the ending, seeing what goes together to make up the whole, seeing how the composition is put together, enjoying it, learning from it. (10)

Composing is difficult because writers must do two things at once. They must consider what the whole is going to be and thereby determine what parts will fit, and they must use the parts to generate the whole. Ann Berthoff summarizes this process by saying that writers "construe as they construct" (46 and passim). In other words, writers figure out what they want to say by saying, or writing, it. The process is not linear; it is more dialectic: back and forth; start, stop, start again; form patterns, reconsider or oppose them, form other patterns. Berthoff's advice: keep everything tentative. Always be open to the possibility of a better way to look at or present an idea, but always realize that at some point a piece must be finished. Democracy is like this: participants must keep in mind that an issue may not be settled or ultimately resolved; they keep in mind that better alternatives may pop up and that issues can be reopened.

Writing, therefore, is a process of composing, of seeing patterns or relationships and ordering them. What we make out of the chaos of "images, half-truths, remembrances, syntactic fragments" is meaning; what we order are relationships among the parts to generate meaning. When we say to someone, "I see your point," we are telling him that what he has said is meaningful to us because we can translate his idea into, we see his idea in terms of, what we have already seen, what we already know. Whether in visual perception or mental insight, "[w]ithout remembered forms to see with, we would not see at all."[26]

Meanings are relationships. To see someone's point, to see what he means, is to understand or to make sense of that point "with respect to, in terms of, in relation to something else (44). We cannot make sense of something except in relation to something else, whether it is black ink on a white page or the symbol or concept that the black ink forms through words. Objects need a background in order to stand out; concepts need a context in order to convey meaning; just as the brain and retina compose an object of perception, so thinking, the active mind, composes ideas or concepts that we understand. Owen Barfield reminds us that "all meaning—even of the most primitive kind—is dependent on the possession of some measure of [the] power [to recognize resemblances and analogies]. Where it was wholly absent, the entire phenomenal cosmos must be extinguished. All sounds would fuse into one meaningless roar, all sights into one chaotic panorama, amid which no individual objects . . . would be distinguishable."[27]

Grammar

Having seen relationships, having constructed or discovered meaning, the writer must now order those relationships to make the meaning clear. The rules for ordering our meanings, or structuring our thoughts, constitute grammar. They enable us to lay out our reasoning about some topic. Without such rules we cannot make intelligible the patterns or relationships we see. One could fail to understand a sentence because the words are exotic and arcane; one can also fail to understand because the words do not fit together in a pattern or relationship that we can figure out.

How important, then, is grammar to our thinking? It doesn't appear to be very important to our talking, which itself is thinking, so how important can grammar be? But the point of talking is principally, and perhaps exclusively, communicating. When talking, we don't have to think about rules, logic, and such because the point is to get the message across. Whether we are doing so is indicated by the immediate reactions of our listeners. When listening, we are willing to make great allowances for speakers. We fill in words for them; we nod assent, which permits them to finish their thoughts in some sort of symbolic shorthand, if they finish those thoughts at all; or we frown, which tells them to pause or back up.[28] Generally, people can easily make themselves understood when speaking. Consider this example from Richard Mitchell:

> I have been reading . . . your magazine for sometime and I truly do enjoy reading it. The onliest thing is, is that it is hard to study out what it means. At least always. [You] make things out harder than they have to be sometime, and you could learn from us [students] as well. You take Philosophy, as anyone would call it a hard "subject" . . . because you would want to read about the material dialects and the rational. Still, I think you would very seriously do it but end up finally with book learning that is all right in its place. However, life must go on as they say. . . . You take doctors and lawyers and even, I hope you don't my saying so, some of your college professors, and you will find there is more than just one stuffed shirt between them. That is because all those "subjects" they study they make them so serious as though somebody's or other life depended on it. Life isn't all a rose colored glass, you know. (1981, 111-12)

Read aloud, this passage can be interpreted; listeners can generate some meaning out of it (whether it is the *intended* meaning is another matter). More amazing is to consider that this excerpt is not part of a transcription of a student talking, but is a portion of a college student's letter written to Richard Mitchell. Moreover, a reader of the original letter would note that the ellipses and my emendations make the writing clearer, not muddier. How, we might ask, could anyone write this way? While we make allowances for gaps, run-on thoughts, stops and starts when someone is speaking, we have higher expectations when someone is writing, because we recognize that writing, as endlessly revisable, ought to be a reflection of careful, sequential thought.

Grammar, we might conclude, is essential to *precise* thinking or to thinking we wish to get right. Proper grammar, as Orwell reminds us in "Politics and the English Language," keeps us from having foolish thoughts.[29] Does it? Richard Mitchell notes that entire worldviews can be altered by simple grammatical forms. "To understand the world, we make propositions about it, and those propositions are both formed and limited by the grammar of the language in which we propose" (1979, 12).

This seems exaggerated. Surely grammatical forms cannot be that important. My youngest son is perfectly capable of expressing some complex ideas, to say nothing of his wishes, and he has little knowledge of, or need at this time for, grammar. The issue, however, is not what my son can talk about, but what he can write about.

The issue is about discursive prose, because that is the mode of language of careful, continuous, and coherent thinking. Discursive prose is the concrete and permanent record of ordered thinking. The inability of students to spell or punctuate correctly can signify more than a trivial oversight or a weakness of technique. It can signify further inability: the inability or frequent failure to attend to details or to work with precision. Such inability, or failure, can have ramifications beyond grammar; for example, in examining brakes, tightening airplane bolts, designing gas tanks, completing income tax forms, or making political decisions.

The last point goes too far. Can we really identify a causal link between the failure to spell and punctuate correctly and disastrous oversights that can cost lives or put us in jail? The point is that such small details as spelling and punctuation may well betoken larger, deeper mistakes. "If a statistician or your computer at the bank subtracted 6 from 9 and got 2, you would not feel mildly irritated and amused. You'd ask what the hell is going on here, and you'd become suspicious, wondering what the hell *else* is going on here" (Mitchell, 1979, 70; emphasis in the original). Inattention to the details of writing may well point to a general habit of thoughtless inattention; it must point out at least the thoughtless inattention of the writer. That is, the writer was not paying attention. But why not? Why wasn't he paying attention? What was he paying attention to? These are the essential questions to ask not simply of our children, but of our children's teachers as well. How did Johnny and Joanie come to write, and come to think, like this?

The first concern is that they came to write this way because they read too little. Persons who have read millions of words, who have seen the same words again and again and have heard the rhythms of excellent prose, learn the sights and sounds of good writing—spelling, punctuation, syntax.[30]

There is no other way to judge how persons think except through their use of language. We judge how persons think by attending to their discourse, either reading it or listening to it. We wish to make sense of it, and that requires that the speaker/writer or the listener supply a chain of logical propositions. Such propositions require exactitude, which brings us back to the importance of attention to details. To read or listen carefully demands our attention. We look for clues and guides to meaning.

Imagine that you could not understand or use, in writing or speech, prepositional phrases. Try rereading the paragraph above after having eliminated all the prepositional phrases. It makes no sense. Nor could it be rewritten to make sense without prepositionalism. That is so because lost is not just a useful grammatical function. Lost, as Mitchell points out, is "the whole concept of the kind of relationship that is signaled by the prepositional phrase" (1979, 12). What is the relationship?

Grammar, to repeat, is nothing short of the rules governing the establishment of relationships. Punctuation is "the visual equivalent of spoken intonation"; it symbolizes "the pauses, stops, and stresses that contribute so much to our meaning" (Howard and Barton, 1986, 99). It contributes to our meaning by making clear the relationships of parts to wholes and of what parts go with which wholes. When a newspaper headline reads "Chile Bars Ads Showing Torture from Television," the headline writer did not mean to convey that television tortures viewers, though he and others might think it; he meant that the Chilean government had barred television ads that showed torture. Because the headline writer did not pay attention to the grammatical rule in English that modifying words and phrases should be placed as close as possible to the word(s) they modify, his meaning is either ambiguous—the generous interpretation—or off, because it is not what the article under the headline is about.

If we want to control our thoughts, then we must know the rules that govern their formation, articulation, and expression. The moral, political, and social world is a world of discourse, and discourse is controlled by grammar. Thus, in English modifying words are placed as close as possible to the words they modify because the relationship between those words is a close one. Proximity makes for clarity—of relationship and of expression. When words are at a distance from their modifiers, the result is not just a slip in grammar; it is a slip in the mind. Because the mind has not made the connection, has not established the relationship, the written English does not reflect it. It is a grammatical oversight, but not simply a rule that the writer has missed.

"A language is only incidentally in the business of naming things. Its important business is to explore the way in which things are, or perhaps might be, related to one another" (Mitchell, 1979, 32). When the Bible says that Adam began naming things, it is a way of saying that humans were becoming conscious of differences, of the need to differentiate among other worlds and to relate those differences to another. If all things in our world were related, there would be no need for the word *family*. Since we are not all related, there is need for a word to signify or identify distinction. Whenever something is named, it is also a statement that it is not something else.

What is the point of this talk about grammar? It is to bring back the importance of teaching grammar not as rules of usage but as ways of establishing and examining relationships in English. In this way writers can be sure of saying what they mean and of making that meaning clearer. Grammar is a way to condition the mind. It is not just, as most English teachers have said, to help us communicate or, as most students and some teachers have thought, a way simply to torture students. It is a way to structure our thinking. The structure of our languages, whatever the language, structures, as Wittgenstein said, a worldview: "The limits of my language are the limits of my world."

In English, for example, though the same is true for most languages, the most common statements take the form of a sentence that identifies an agent—one who acts—the agent's deed, and the object of his deed: "I want the strawberry shortcake." In short, we live in a world of agents and objects called nouns, to which we give attributes called adjectives, and which we put into action through verbs.[31]

Unfortunately, the mind likes to wander; focused attention requires effort or intense interest. "If we want to pursue extended logical thought, thought that can discover relationships and consequences and devise its own alternatives, we need a discipline imposed from the outside of the mind itself. Writing is that discipline" (Mitchell, 1979, 40). Writing is not natural. It is a learned practice that can develop into a habit. But clear writing is a sure sign of clear thinking. "It seems drastic, but we have to suspect that coherent, continuous thought is impossible for those who cannot construct coherent, continuous prose" (1979, 40).

Those of us who teach for a living may well have had an experience similar to Mitchell's:

> At one time I thought that I was the victim of a conspiracy. . . . I was certain that the Admissions Office had salted my classes with carefully selected students, students who had no native tongue. Many of my students seem unable to express themselves in any language whatsoever. They aren't utterly mute, of course. They can say something about the weather and give instructions about how to get to the post office. They are able to recite numerous slogans, especially from television commercials and the lyrics of popular songs and recent—very recent—political campaigns. They are able to read traffic signs and many billboards and even some newspapers, and they can claim certain emotions

with regard to various teams and even individual athletes, whose names they often know. They can spin more or less predictable reveries about the past or the future either in very simple concrete terms or in sentimental banalities, or both. But they cannot pursue a process; they cannot say why evidence leads to a conclusion; they cannot find examples for analogies. (1979, 156-57)

This situation, as Mitchell goes on to say, was not a conspiracy. As we know and have experienced, this kind of student is too often the frequent result of our educational system. This kind of student may even be the typical, or "average," student.

Can the solution to this problem, the problem of students who cannot think critically, be as simple as teaching them to write, or to read and write and speak and listen? I think that it can be. Writing is thinking on paper. To think we must form propositions and "devise connected chains of predications" (157). Those who lack fluency in language cannot do that, for they lack the means to think sequentially, deeply, at a high order; they cannot think critically. It appears that the simple matter of being logical is a function of language.

That is the point of practicing writing and of learning grammar: to guide the creation of logical meaning. Punctuation helps establish, emphasize, or deemphasize relationships among words and sentences. The structure of the writing, the order of the words, sentences, and paragraphs all convey relationships among the parts to generate a meaningful whole. This, of course, assumes that the writer is aware of the proper usage of words, punctuation, and syntax to create and convey meaning. Otherwise, the writer's meaning cannot be conveyed. The reader will say, "I don't get it. What's the point? I don't follow you." Any reader, including the writer herself, will search out order to find meaning. When the writer cannot control the relationships among words, sentences, and paragraphs, the reader will either give up or create meanings of his own. This is not a stage of interpreting the text; it is the stage of comprehending what the writer is saying, of being able to recapitulate the author's point.

Students must learn to control the relationships. Simply putting words to paper is not enough. They must practice forming and revising relationships. That requires repetition and a careful reader—the teacher. That requires dialogue between the student and a more experienced, a more practiced and skillful, writer/reader. Meanwhile, the student, as she writes and revises, is also practicing her inner dialogue, which with practice can stand in for the teacher. An audience of oneself, however, can never substitute for others when the guest is to know whether one has been understood. That requires an additional, and different, relationship: one between a writer and an audience outside herself.

One concern about learning and conforming to grammatical rules is that it will stifle creativity and one's own voice.[32] Grammar does establish guidelines for establishing relationships. Because grammar structures and orders our thinking, does it limit our thoughts? Do grammatical rules establish boundaries to what we can think? This seems implausible. How could we know that our thoughts were limited without someone expressing in language a thought that would push past or test our boundaries? That thought would be considered unintelligible, not because it was poorly formed grammatically, but because it outstripped the reader's or listener's experience. That thought could be a grammatically correct parable, or an articulate, but abstract idea about distributive justice. Yet the language did not limit the writer or speaker when he articulated it. It made sense to him; it had meaning for him. "Good writers," observes Barry Sanders, "continually test the possibilities of expression by pressing against whatever the rules will allow. In successful writers, that struggle produces sentences marked by innovation and invention" (1994, 182). So we readers must work a little harder, while the writer might need to explain his meaning to us in language closer to our own experience. This is part of the dialectic, the dialogue, of thinking.

That is so because meaning is not like Easter eggs, as Ann Berthoff puts it. Meanings are relationships that are shifting, unsettled, and dynamic. "Meaning is a current between the poles of intention and expression" (1981, 116). When a reader or listener "gets it," then the current is strong. When she doesn't, we tinker with our articulation, with our thought.

This is why dialogue is so important: as readers we want and need to translate the text into language or terms that we understand, but without distorting what has been written or said. So we go back and forth, asking questions and probing the text. In the process we stretch ourselves, our thinking. But we cannot break out of language, for any interrogation of language presupposes language; and any language presupposes grammar or rules for making sense and meaning in that language. "Rules of grammar," opines Sanders, "hold sentences together the way physical laws hold the natural world together and constitutional laws hold society together" (1994, 182).

So the formal properties of writing—parts of speech, grammar, syntax—guide how we think in English, or in whatever our language is. Students, and all citizens, need to learn how the rules of grammar are useful to creating and conveying relationships, and thus meaning, among propositions, qualifiers, modifiers, sentences, and phrases. These rules help us establish and convey what aspects of what we have to say are most important and less important. When we read and listen and write, we need to pay close attention to the grammar and syntax of what is said or written. That is how we sort out meanings. The rules of grammar are not arbitrary commandments that force uniformity and mental sterility on writers. Grammar is the codification of how we think, of how the mind works, in English (or in whatever language, including English, you wish this book had been written). Writers do not strive to put modifiers close to the words they modify simply because a grammatical rule says that is how it should be done. Writers strive to do this to construct a specific relationship and thus convey a specified meaning. The rule is a reminder that in English words are as close as possible to the words they modify. This is how we think in English, how we generate clear images and precise meaning.

As all teachers know, writing enables them to see how their students' minds work. Careful readers can see the thinking involved in getting to a conclusion; writing is a demonstration of a writer's reasoning. So the reader sees what the writer knows and how he came to know it. This is why it is useful in any discipline and in all disciplines. Every discipline has a literature, a body of good writing, that is also good thinking, that students and teachers can look to and learn from. What makes the writing good, regardless of the discipline, is that the thinking is provocative, trenchant, groundbreaking, subtle, but clear. The thought in it is logically arranged. Because writing is essentially an exercise in logic, if one learns to write well, one will also learn to think well. This is why, as Sandra Stotsky observes, many teachers and researchers today see "writing as possibly the foremost tool for promoting thinking and learning" (1991a, 193).

Having discussed the nature of critical thinking and the value of teaching it through writing, I turn now to consider how best to implement the teaching of critical thinking—that is, how best to teach it through language arts and through democratic decision making. For it is one thing to generate a theory of deliberative democratic education; it is quite another to implement such a theory. The practice of deliberative democratic education, its continual exercise, will transform thinking, to paraphrase Dewey, into effective power (1991 [1910], 391).

Notes

1 John Dewey, "What Psychology Can Do for the Teachers," in *John Dewey on Education,* ed. Reginald Archambault (New York: Random House, 1964).

2. What is so unsettling, to my mind, about the information superhighway is not just that contributions to our information networks are uncensored, or that the information explosion is now geometric and beyond control. More unsettling is the absence among many users of the ability to discriminate. The absence is all the more conspicuous now that every mental eructation can be recorded, stored, retrieved, and reconfigured into a version of human experience that the "author," and others, without any standard of discrimination that separates meaning from garbage, may interpret as significant human history.

3. The literature on the failure of secondary schools to teach critical thinking is now extensive. As excellent representative samples see John Goodlad, *A Place Called School* (New York: McGraw-Hill, 1983) and Theodore Sizer, *Horace's Compromise* (Boston: Houghton Mifflin, 1984) and *Horace's School* (Boston: Houghton Mifflin, 1992). For excellent discussions or descriptions of those exceptional schools that do teach critical thinking, see Deborah Meier, *The Power of Their Ideas* (Boston: Beacon Press, 1995); Rexford Brown, *Schools of Thought* (San Francisco: Jossey-Bass, 1991); Edward Fiske,

Smart Schools, Smart Kids (New York: Simon and Schuster, 1991); and Theodore Sizer, 1984 and 1992, cited above.

4. 1983, chapter 4. "Teaching to the test" is not solely an American phenomenon. In Japan many scholars and commentators say that schools teach the young to memorize but not to think. Memorization is seen as the key to success on the college entrance exams that largely determine the futures of Japanese students. The Japanese educational system, comments Alfons Deeken, a Japanese-speaking professor of philosophy at Sophia University in Tokyo, is in crisis. "Many Japanese students are absorbing even greater amounts of information, but they don't acquire the ability to make value judgments on basic human values." In Sheryl WuDunn's words, Japanese "students are able to absorb rules and vocabulary but often cannot use what they have learned in the real world." This makes critics anxious that many of the seemingly best and brightest of Japanese students are vulnerable to the mind-control tactics and techniques of such religious cults as Aum Shinrikyo. Quotations are from "Japanese Critics Assert Schools Led Best and Brightest into Sect," *New York Times,* 22 May 1995, 1, 4.

5. See, among others, Marva Collins (1990), Albert Shanker (1995), and Sizer, *Horace's Compromise,* 1984, and *Horace's School,* 1992.

6. 1988, 32, 38. All Siegel references, unless otherwise specified, are from this text.

7. 1990a, 374. All parenthetical references to Paul, unless otherwise noted, are from this text.

8. John Locke remarked that "there is nothing more ordinary than children's receiving into their minds propositions . . . from their parents, teachers, or those about them; which, fastened by degrees are at last (whether true or false) riveted there by long custom . . . beyond all possibility of being pulled out again. For men, when they are grown up . . . are apt to reverence them as sacred things and not to suffer them to be profaned, touched, or questioned." (*Essay Concerning Human Understanding,* book 4, chapter 20, "Of Wrong Assent or Error.") Students when grown, but also still growing up, should scrutinize such propositions.

9. McPeck, 1981a, 5. See also McPeck, 1990, chapters 1 and 2.

10. McPeck, 1981a, 6, 7. McPeck's reference to reflective skepticism raises an issue that goes to the heart of the definition of critical thinking. In my view, critical thinking is not just challenging or questioning, which McPeck implies by characterizing it in general as applying the appropriate skepticism. Such a view leads to dichotomous thinking, by suggesting that creative thinking is to be separated from critical thinking. Yet clearly there is a creative dimension to critical thought, just as there is a critical dimension to creative thought. "In fact," comments Francis Schrag, "*all* thinking, whether the task be the creation of a film or the writing of the review of that film, to take one example, has exploratory phases in which suggestions are generated and developed and evaluative phases in which ideas are checked and tested prior to execution" (Schrag, 1988, 28; emphasis in the original). Creative thought helps us generate ideas, even in expository work; creativity is required to weave themes and points together, to create analogies or make connections, and to choose our words and order them. That we speak of two kinds of

thought—creative and critical—indicates only where we place the emphasis and not that one kind is excluded from the other.

To keep clear that these two are both present in critical thinking I might have followed Dewey and used terms such as "active thinking" or "reflective thought." Yet I want to situate my own views within the context of the debate over critical thinking, and so I shall stay with that term, knowing that by the term I imply both critical and creative thinking.

11. Conversely, one who wishes to argue that reading and writing are not single skills, such as E. D. Hirsch, needs to explain why they are not. See Hirsch's article in the *American Educator,* summer 1985; quoted by McPeck, 1981a, 39. So, too, Neil Postman must explain why "no one is a 'good reader,' period" (1979, 164). A person, Postman comments, may be a good reader in history, but not in religion; or in biology, but not in politics. That may be so, but why is it so? It might be more difficult to read biology articles and texts without sufficient background in and familiarity with the concepts and the vocabulary of biology. A careful reader can, however, with attention and patience, identify the thesis of the article, find the main points, differentiate the evidence or findings from the conclusion and assumptions. Often the density of work does not depend on the complexity of the subject as much as it depends on the lack of clarity and organization of the writing. Poor writing can disguise as profound many thoughts that are actually muddled or mundane. This may be more difficult for laymen to spot than for experts in the field. That difficulty means that laymen have to work harder; it does not mean that they must be poor readers.

12. In *How We Think,* John Dewey argues strongly that reflective thinking is one general method: "[N]o matter how subjects vary in scope and detail, there is one and only one best way of mastering them, since there is a single 'general method' uniformly followed by the mind in effective attack upon any subject" (202). That method consists, says Dewey, of preparation, presentation, comparison, generalization, and application.

By preparation Dewey means relating a new topic to ideas and experiences already familiar to the student. Having "activated" the old knowledge, the new knowledge is then presented to the student. The new idea is then directly compared with other similar ideas so that the elements common to all of the ideas can be drawn together into a generalization. This generalization is then applied to new contexts, thus solidifying the idea in the student's mind as well as stimulating additional information.

13. *The Apple and the Spectroscope.* Quoted in Berthoff, 1981, 116.

14. 1991 [1910], 2, 3. Dewey defined reflective thought as the "active, persistent, and careful consideration of any belief or supposed form of knowledge in the light of the grounds [reasons] that support it, and the further conclusions to which it tends" (1991 [1910], 6).

15. The notion that writing is inextricably linked with thinking is found in the medieval *trivium,* the curriculum that combined logic, grammar, and rhetoric. Today we find these three separated, so that texts on logic pay little attention to writing whereas texts on writing make only passing references to reasoning. See Howard and Barton (1986, 13-14)

who also mention the important influences of modern-day semiotics for seeing language as an instrument of thought.

16. 1981, 29. Unlike writing, which is not lost, the knowledge gained in the age of orality "had to be constantly repeated or it would be lost: fixed, formulaic thought patterns were essential for wisdom and effective administration" (Walter Ong, *Orality and Literacy,* London: Methuen, 1982, 23-24; quoted in Sanders, 1994, 11).

17. *Litera scripta manet,* "The written word remains," as Horace said. Barry Sanders observes that *manet* is a pun on *manes,* "the remains of the dead." Thus, words remain inert or dead, without meaning, until revivified by the reader (1994, 120).

18. J. Gage, "Why Write?" in *The Teaching of Writing,* eds. D. Bartholomea and A. Petrosky (Chicago: National Society for the Study of Education, 1986), 24; quoted in William McGinley and Robert Tierney, "Traversing the Topical Landscape: Reading and Writing As Ways of Knowing," *Written Communication* 6, no. 3 (July 1989): 243-69.

19. See, for example, Langer and Applebee, 1987, on this point.

20. Discursive writing is any writing that intends to inform, explain, or persuade. It is synonymous with but sometimes lacks the formality of expository writing.

21. The quotations are taken from McGinley and Tierney, 1989, 254-55; the parenthetical phrases are in the original. See G. Newell, "Learning from Writing in Two Content Areas," *Research in the Teaching of English,* 18, 1984. See also K. A. Copeland, "Writing as a Means to Learn from Prose," *Research in the Teaching of English,* 1989, whose work with 120 sixth graders showed that both good and poor writers of compositions learned more information and could more readily apply that information to new situations than students who responded to multiple-choice questions, wrote only summaries, or synthesized major concepts without writing.

22. For more on the history and nature of Writing across the Curriculum programs, see McGinley and Tierney, 1989; T. Fulweiler and A. Young, eds., *Language Connections* (Urbana, Ill.: National Council of Teachers of English, 1982); J. Gage, 1986, Langer and Applebee, 1987; N. Martin, *Writing across the Curriculum* (London: Ward Lock, 1975); and J. S. Mayher, N. Lester, and G. M. Pradl, *Learning to Write, Writing to Learn,* Boynton/Cook, 1983.

23. For more on writing in mathematics, see *The Mathematical Experience* (Boston: Houghton Mifflin, 1981), and *Descartes' Dream: The World According to Mathematics,* (New York: Harcourt, Brace Jovanovich, 1986), both by Philip J. Davis and Reuben Hersh. For an example of a teacher who uses writing as a tool to teach critical thinking in math, but with poor, rural students, see "Mississippi Learning" by Alexis Jetter, *New York Times Magazine,* 21 February 1993, and "Algebra Project: Bob Moses Empowers Students," *New York Times Education Life,* 7 January 2001, Section 4A.

Claudia Henrion, a professor of mathematics at Middlebury College, concludes that "seeing mathematics as a language leads naturally to the assumption that everyone can learn to be math literate. . . . We would never say to a student: 'Sorry, you're not bright enough to learn English'" (quoted in Jetter, 51).

24. This is why teachers often find the true introduction to a student's paper in the student's conclusion. The student has only come to realize what she thinks about a sub-

ject when she has finished writing about it. Thus I sometimes advise students to rewrite their papers by starting with the conclusion, because now they know what they are going to write about.

25. Speaking of mystery, Howard and Barton observe that "ideas have a way of adding up to something only dimly perceived at the moment of their articulation" (1986, 31). Therefore, the authors recommend that students keep writing, even when the thoughts seem silly and unconnected. "Let your mind roam over the topic in any direction jabbing at, alluding to, and nailing down ideas as they occur to you" (31). When does one stop this process? When one senses that repetition has set in.

26. Rudolf Arnheim describes acts of perception as involving "active exploration, selection, grasping of essentials, simplification, abstraction, analysis and synthesis, completion, correction, comparison, problem-solving, as well as combining, separating, putting in context" in *Visual Thinking* (Berkeley: University of California Press, 1969), 13; quoted in Berthoff, 1990, 32. It is no wonder, therefore, that our word "theory" derives from the Greek, *theoria,* which itself derives from the base *thea* or "sight." To see with the mind's eye we must undertake the same steps or acts as those in perception or visual seeing. To see we not only look upon something, but we also match and order and look again.

27. *Poetic Diction*; quoted in Berthoff, 1978, 36-37. To escape chaos we see relationships, we make distinctions. When you understand someone, see a person's point, you are seeing relationships between what he/she is saying and what you already know. To be articulate means more than enunciating clearly. It derives from the Latin word for "joint" (*artus*) and refers to the relationships among parts. As Berthoff puts it, "without articulation, there can be statements but no composition" (1978, 134). "Analogy is the principal means of articulating relationships and thus of forming concepts" (1978, 136). An analogy is a rhetorical form in which one thing is described in terms of another. This is why analogies articulate relationships: we see things in terms of other things.

28. "Oral peoples," Barry Sanders points out, "have no need of dictionaries, just as they have no need for grammar, for orality holds to no standards of correct usage— neither in syntax nor in spelling" (1994, 69). What about dictionaries for looking up meanings?

29. [T]he slovenliness of our language makes it easier for us to have foolish thoughts" (1945, 77). Hannah Arendt observed of Adolf Eichmann that, because of his literal thoughtlessness, "when confronted with situations for which . . . routine procedures did not exist, he was helpless, and his cliché-ridden language produced . . . a kind of macabre comedy" (1977, 4). His language, and thus his thinking, also produced monstrous deeds about which Eichmann seemed insensate.

30. Writing aside, students often cannot comprehend, and therefore do not read, complex sentences. They lack "a repertory of sentence patterns and syntactical structures," as Ann Berthoff calls it (1981, 21), that can enable them to understand and use complexity. They lack this repertory because they have not been read to or have not read enough difficult material. They have not been challenged.

31. For an example of a different worldview, see Mitchell's discussion of the "Jiukiukwe," whose language structures their worldview through the passive voice, 1979, 20ff.

32. See, for example, Sheridan, 1992.

1) importance b writing for teaching habits : 1 thinking; but which habits? not necessarily deliberative habits, but potentially those.

2) writing in conjunction w/t practice of democratic decision making = critical thinking?

3) modest proposals for curricular reform

Chapter Six

Reform Schools: Implementing the Democratic Curriculum

Teaching Critical Thinking

Since we are always thinking about something when we are thinking, then, as McPeck points out (1990, 43), when we think critically, we need something to think critically about. So information or content is crucial to critical thinking. It is not the case, therefore, that an emphasis on the processes of critical thinking will downplay, let alone ignore, the importance of content.

Course content, naturally, will vary with the age of the students. So, too, will the sophistication of the writing and thinking. Though some fifth graders may be able to read for pleasure Dickens's *A Tale of Two Cities,* fifth graders do not write at an adult level. Bombarding young children with adult concepts and abstractions, such as would be the case if we tried to teach elementary school children critical thinking through informal logic, will have predictably unfavorable results.

Yet children's critical thinking can be improved when their own level of thinking is taken into account. That level is reflected in their writing. Writing practice and instruction will improve their thinking, as it improves their writing, if their thinking remains in the realm of their experience. Young children want to make sense of and find meaning in their experiences. To demand that they write, or try to write, is to demand that they make sense systematically.

To facilitate this process we could teach the youngest students to write in the same manner that they learn to talk. Talking for children is functional; they talk to make things happen. Babies cry when they are hungry and want to be fed. Children ask for milk when they are hungry and want a drink. Yet in school, as Roger Shuy points out, "[s]tudents write in response to the teacher's demand to write. They do not write to accomplish a personal goal, as they do with talking. Their writing, in short, is neither self-generated nor functional. . . . That is, student writers write on demand about topics they don't originate, to unknown audiences, for purposes not their own, while sitting at desks or tables in classrooms, under supervision, during specific hours of the day" (1987, 390).

Some of this context for writing we cannot and should not change. Children need supervision; they need schedules and classrooms, deadlines, assignments, and guidelines. Yet their writing can be more "natural." Teachers can relax the standards that demand from young students a level of formality not required of them in talking. Students can devise, plan, and execute their own topics and purposes; and students can produce interesting, high-quality work for no audience other than themselves, their peers, their families. In other words, teachers do not have to be the audience or the only audience; nor does all of the writing have to be evaluated.

 One way to proceed is to use what Shuy calls a "Dialogue Journal." Here a classroom of students writes daily in their journals to their teacher, and their teacher writes daily in those journals to the students. This dialogue method relaxes the formal standards of writing. The result is that the students use the format as a bridge between talking, which they already do, and writing, which they are learning (1987, 392). Also, because the students can use the journal to complain, promise, excuse, blame, criticize, ask questions, and evaluate, this format "opens the door to the development of rational argumentation."[1] Finally, the dialogue journal helps young writers adjust to the solitary nature of most writing, while also providing some of the conversational support of dialogue.

In the NIE study on dialogue journals, students wrote in their journals about anything that interested them; they wrote about the world they knew or wanted to know. They were also permitted, even encouraged, to complain. These criteria enabled the students "to feel socially and personally enfranchised," to present their points of view on topics important to them and to give voice to their own thoughts and feelings (1987, 393). The teacher used their complaints to teach them to think clearly, to offer reasons and evidence to support their grousing. Students came to see through their writing that complaints in forms such as "math is boring" were insufficient. The teacher used such situations to ask questions that would elicit reasons and information. These questions were not didactic; the teacher did not know the answers to her own questions. What the teacher thereby displayed to her students was her own curiosity and her involvement in the students' worlds.

Though Shuy does not discuss it, the language used by the teacher in her journal responses is also significant. The teacher can model for the students greater control or mastery of the language. This is not, of course, the purpose of her writing, but it can be an important by-product. Surely it will not be the focus of the students. Yet they get to see repeatedly, in direct response to their own writing and ideas, the responses of an adult who takes them seriously and takes seriously what they say.[2]

Anton Lawson, a professor of zoology, concludes in his own work on teaching science through writing that the difference between the educational experience of a doctoral student and that of a kindergarten student should be one of degree, not kind. Whatever the level of experience, all students should be constantly asking the questions, "How do you know?" "What is the evidence?" and "What are the alternatives?" Each student pursues answers to such questions, of course, in a manner appropriate to his or her age and realm of experience.[3]

An appropriate question to ask kindergarten students to investigate is "What caused the yellow spot in the grass at the front of the school?" or "Why did the aquarium water turn green?" On the other hand, high school students might investigate how multicellular organisms grow, or why some chemicals change colors when mixed. As Lawson points out, while the possible causal agents in the questions for kindergarten students are all observable, those for high school students are theoretical.[4]

Lawson makes no recommendations for what configurations students must assume to pursue their answers. Whatever the age or level, they could do so singly or in small groups; they could discuss the questions in groups or as a class; after discussion, they could write up their reasoning individually or jointly. Lawson's focus is on the nature, or appropriateness, of the questions.

This focus is congruent with the views of many who teach critical thinking through writing. Questioning, observes Ann Berthoff, "is the life of thought. Learning to see what you're looking at really means questioning" (1981, 75). The questions asked, at all levels, might be of the following kinds:

1. questions of origins: "Where did this view come from?"
2. questions of support: "What reasons or evidence do you have for thinking this?
3. questions of conflict: "What if the opposite were true? What is the opposite? What would you say to someone who objected by saying . . . ?
4. questions of implications and consequences: "What follows from believing this?" "What follows if this is true?" "What do we have to accept to believe this?"

We might even imagine a question-centered curriculum in which questions of the students' own choosing drive the course content.[5] This, too, is congruent with the views of many educators. Howard Gardner comments that "finding some topic or skill with which one feels 'connected' is the single most important educational event in a student's life" (1990, 104). David Hawkins concludes after years of observing schoolchildren: "[C]hildren can learn to read and write with commitment and quality just in proportion as they are engaged with matters of importance to them, and about which at some point, they wish to write and read" (1990, 6).

Asking and pursuing their own questions, where this is feasible, is to engage children in matters of importance to them. To focus on students' interests is to follow John Dewey's advice to touch students where they care. Students, he observed, work hardest and think best when they think about issues that concern or interest them.[6] Indeed, we might differentiate authentic learning from artificial learning by emphasizing the difference between a topic or issue that matters to the student, though not necessarily chosen by the student, and one that the teacher dictates. Even when the two topics coincide—a topic generated by the teacher that matters to the student—the student needs to be able to modify the topic, if he chooses, to make the learning authentic. The best way to pursue these topics, in addition to reading about and discussing them, is to write to learn, where further questioning will occur with every source and with the writer's every step. Here the thinking can be broad, systematic, and, because of the questioning, critical. [7]

As students mature, teachers should come to expect more depth in and structure to student thinking. Increased attention should then be paid to grammar and syntax. Junior high students, for example, could be asked to form and advance or challenge clear arguments. They could begin close textual analysis, paying attention both to what the author (and the students) say and to how the author (and the students) say it. Diagramming arguments might be one way to accomplish this.

A standard practice in English classes, now long out of fashion, was to diagram sentences. This practice enabled the student to see in graphic form the relationships among parts of a sentence. Just so, an argument can be diagrammed. The premises can be separated from the conclusions. In larger arguments, such as extended essays, the conclusion in one part might be a premise in the next, or in a later, argument. Diagramming the argument(s) helps to keep straight the premises and the conclusions, especially where there are several arguments in the work. Such a process can also be employed in reverse, so that one begins with an outline as a blueprint and then develops the detailed arguments from it.

Assessment

With so much emphasis on writing,[8] how should a student's work, performance, and progress be assessed? Not as they are currently. If our goal is to develop students who can think critically, then we undercut our purpose and shortchange our students by using and promoting standardized, "objective" tests. For the most part, these are multiple-choice tests, with one right answer for each question. Credit is given for every correct answer; none is given if the answer offered is wrong. No attention is paid to how the student arrived at her answer; no allowance is made for critical, or innovative, thinking that might produce a different but also a "correct" answer. At no time is the student asked to give reasons for her answers.

A curriculum with critical thinking at its core and with an emphasis on writing would probably make no appreciable difference on test scores, the decline of which many critics of public education use to argue that our schools are in crisis. Our critical thinking curriculum might even make the scores worse.[9] Yet it would not be the curriculum that would then be wanting, but the means of assessing its efficacy and results. If offered a choice, parents and teachers, professors and citizens, would undoubtedly prefer students who could use factual information as evidence rather than students who can only identify information correctly, students who could apply their grammatical and syntactical skills to explore a text or poem or problem rather than students who could only recite rules without demonstrating any understanding. The result of placing weight on test scores is that the test content and format come to dictate rather than reflect both the content of and the methods in the curriculum.

To test the level of thinking proficiency, tests must require writing. But to measure the performance and progress of our students at the national or state level, perhaps only minimal testing should be used. In place of tests we could evaluate students' portfolios of writing.

Assessment is important, since parents, teachers, citizens, and the students themselves want to know whether and what students are learning and accomplishing. To this end, every student should accumulate through her years of schooling a portfolio of work and of commentary by teachers, peers, and experts. The portfolio would serve, therefore, as systematic evidence of each student's performance and progress, strengths, and weaknesses. Parents, teachers, and students could retrieve and revisit the work. They could examine past performances and compare them with their present work. Those interested could track the overall development, or individual development, of different skills, from the motor skills of first graders to the increasing depth of thought and expression of ninth graders.

It is too much to expect college admissions officers or prospective employers or even parents and new teachers to wade through the wealth of each student's accumulated accomplishments, though each portfolio should have separate sections for each grade's work. Therefore, at the end of grades four, seven, and eleven, students could have all of their work in that grade sent for evaluation by experts. In addition, students could sit for set, national essay exams.

Neither of these methods of assessment would be sufficient in isolation. Portfolios can become political weapons used by school personnel. Before being sent off, portfolios might be culled and edited for the purpose of picking out a student's best work, which may not be truly representative of that student's overall work. Set exams could help offset this problem of selective editing. At the same time, students who might have had a particularly bad day when taking the essay exams would have their portfolio work that might more fairly, and clearly, reflect their capabilities. The problem is not resolved for those students who might claim to have had a bad day but didn't, and who then presented a highly edited portfolio. The solution, I think, would be to permit, or even require, students to take the exams again.

Who, then, would be the experts assessing the portfolios and grading the exams? For fourth graders the experts would consist of junior high teachers; for

seventh graders, high school teachers; and for eleventh graders, college professors. In each case, the teachers would evaluate the work of those who might
someday be their own students. Clearly, they would have a vested interest in
seeing that their future students were well prepared. There would be a good
chance that these particular students would not become the assessor's students,
but, then again, they could. In all cases the evaluations should be through blind
review. There would be nothing gained and much, potentially, to be lost by dis-
closing the identities of the students. In fact, those assessing should know neither the students' identities nor their schools, region, or perhaps even state.
Assessors could come from the same state as the students, but not the same
district or county. The assessor's identity, of course, would also remain unknown. Such steps would maintain the integrity of the process; discourage ven-
dettas against schools, teachers, students, parents, or the assessors; and prohibit
recruiting of specific students.

Assessors would essentially be operating from behind a Rawlsian "veil of
ignorance." The assessors would be ignorant about career plans, interests and
ambitions, likes and dislikes, race and gender, and socioeconomic status not of
themselves, as in Rawls, but of those students whom they were evaluating. No
assessor would know anything about a student except how well he or she can
write and therefore think.

Assessment would take place in the summer, when teachers and professors
have more time off. Assessors would also be compensated for their work, which,
contrary to many seasons past, would permit them to have remunerative and
fruitful summer work. While remuneration is some incentive for teachers and
professors, there is no way of avoiding the recognition that this work would be
time-consuming and very labor-intensive.

What about differing standards? Wouldn't the assessments be uneven because the standards are subjective? Teachers are in the business of evaluating
student performance. It rarely happens that excellent writers and thinkers are
considered poor students, though it can happen that teachers can be fooled by
those who have strong vocabularies and the skill to mimic complicated literary
constructions, but who also have little to say. Schools of education could use-
fully contribute by offering workshops in assessment to aid assessors. Although
it strikes me that it is not that difficult for teachers to recognize, as opposed to
produce, good thinking through writing, if standards did become an issue, assessors could discuss with one another the hard cases.[10] College admissions officers
evaluate hundreds, even thousands, of applicants by reading and discussing the
applicants' files. Perhaps three assessors could read each portfolio, through blind
review, and could then discuss those cases where there were discrepancies. Failing to arrive at consensus on such cases, they might give an overall grade or assessment, but with comments as to where and why divisions or discrepancies
proved to be irreconcilable. The same process could be adopted for those grading the essay exams.

What topics or content would such essay exams cover? In subjects such as American history, there should be a choice of essays so as to make the exam fair to those students whose interests lie in, or whose teachers may have focused more on, the founding of the nation and not, say, the Civil War. The mandatory, or set, section of the exam should involve the students in reading and in some fashion reacting to a text. In this way, no specific background information would necessarily be assumed. Questions could either relate directly to the text or could use the text as an entrée into more general topics to be chosen by the students and to which they might have given some thought. Perhaps there could be truly open-ended approaches where the students could generate their own topics. In all sections, including math and science questions, students would have to write to demonstrate critical thinking.

Clearly, schools, districts, counties, and states that committed themselves to teaching critical thinking could also commit the funds for some sort of assessment program. The issue is not money, but will. If we can mount and fund successful exploratory missions to distant planets, military missions to foreign countries, rescue and humanitarian missions at home and abroad, we can mount and fund an educational mission on behalf of our future citizens. Despite the frequent rhetoric, equal education for all is not a national priority. If it were, we would not permit, as a nation, the "savage inequalities" that plague our public school system.[11]

Teacher Training

The place to begin the implementation of an education in deliberation is with the teachers. Learning will not be strong unless the teaching is strong. But if the teaching of critical thinking is not yet strong, isn't it ironic that the assessors of that thinking will be teachers? Simply recognizing good and poor writing is not the same as assessing it. Assessment requires judgment and justification; it requires the exercise of, and it presupposes practice in, critical thinking. In order to be assessors, teachers themselves must be assessed.

There is no way around the fact that teachers, especially in this curriculum, must be able to think critically. Teachers are people who think for a living, regardless of what subjects they teach or the ages of their students. So the first, best advice to teachers and prospective teachers: if you don't want to think—to think about your subject, your students, their questions, your questions to them, how best to approach a topic, how to connect one topic with another, why you do what you do and how to do it better—then don't teach. "Thinking," by which Richard Mitchell means critical thinking, "is not unlike playing the violin; it isn't simply natural. Even if we can do it, we don't often do it" (1981, 194). But teachers need to think critically all the time. Therefore, the best place to begin educational reform is to make this revelation the centerpiece of teacher education.

The requirements of critical thinking, especially of writing (I shall discuss the other three components of language arts later in this chapter), that would be built into this curriculum demand that teachers be proficient both at assessing and at teaching writing. Training teachers in these skills is, of course, the purview of schools of education, where most, if not all, of the faculty are expected to demonstrate in their own work those very skills. Publication, presentation of papers, and research in general are thought to be such demonstration. By and large, despite the disparities evident among publishing scholars, this is an adequate demonstration that teachers of teachers can write. Whether they can teach teachers to teach writing is another matter.

Yet there are people on campus—those who work in writing centers, who teach composition, and who attend assiduously, whatever their fields, to writing, whether their own or their students'—who can be enlisted to help teach teachers.[12] Professors must overcome their parochialism, and their single-minded protection of departmental turf, and recognize that capable instruction in and help with writing comes from all over the campus. Likewise, schoolteachers must overcome their provincial notions that the English department is solely responsible for teaching composition. Teachers of English are responsible for students' writing and arguing about literature. Other teachers, using the same grammatical and syntactical guidelines, are responsible for students' writing and arguing about the contents of their own disciplines.

The best writing teacher, of course, is practice. Therefore, teachers in training should be required to write extensively and to review, discuss, and assess writing, their own as well as that of students, professors, and peers. This latter exercise we traditionally call a seminar, but the writing in addition to the course content should be discussed (or the writing itself should be a salient part of the course content).

Teacher training for beginning teachers should happen during a student's senior year in college. Prior to this the student should major in, or focus on, academic subjects taught as regular courses and not as teacher-education courses. This would give the beginning teacher a grounding in the academic subject, or its cognates, that he might teach. Student teachers should begin classroom work under the supervision of teachers in active service. To facilitate this practice schools of education might create lab schools or teaching schools analogous to science labs and teaching hospitals. Designated master teachers and other supervisors would work in the classroom with their student teachers and their elementary or secondary school pupils. These master teachers would also participate in teaching the pedagogy courses in colleges and universities.[13]

Having earned certification to teach, a beginning teacher should then hold a two-year probationary position to ascertain how he takes to teaching and how he performs. For those who do not take well to teaching or who do not do well, their training in teaching critical thinking through writing could still make them highly employable, as businesses would value the ability of those who can think—write and speak—well. The probationary period would be analogous to a physician's internship or residency. At the end of the two-year period, those who are promoted should receive a regular contract and a raise.

It would be expected that teachers throughout their careers would continue to write to learn. This is not to suggest that teachers must be superb writers, though they must be able to write clearly and precisely, for they will serve as models for their students. Their students, therefore, should see them struggling with and through language; they should see teachers sharing and discussing their work with their colleagues. This could take many forms: book groups, for example, where a teacher writes and shares a review of a book that will begin a discussion of that book. Or a group of teachers might meet to discuss current controversies—political, social, cultural, educational. Members of the group would be required to write periodic position papers arguing for or against a position. Teachers would need to keep their skills sharp and to reacquaint themselves often with the vulnerability that comes from committing one's thinking to paper.

The Greensboro Plan

Critical thinking programs are most often carried out successfully when they acknowledge the need to train, or retrain, teachers. In such programs the central lesson seems to be that teachers must be intimately involved in all stages of implementing the program. As an example, I want to look at the Reasoning and Writing Project undertaken in 1986 and continuing today, in the kindergarten through high school (K-12) curriculum in the Greensboro, North Carolina, school system. I use this example not because Greensboro has all of the elements that I think are necessary in a critical thinking program, and not because their project is a blueprint for any critical thinking curriculum. I do so because the way in which they involved their teachers in implementing their curriculum is an excellent guide or model for other school districts or individual schools.

Greensboro is a medium-sized city near the Appalachian Mountains. Their public school system enrolls approximately 21,000 students, with about one classroom teacher for every fifteen pupils.[14] The Reasoning and Writing Project began in 1986 when the school board approved a proposal to infuse thinking and writing into the K-12 curriculum. To implement the program the board approved the hiring of two educators, both classroom teachers, to serve as facilitators. The important point to note here is that these facilitators were teachers, not administrators. Greensboro recognized immediately that the success of the program depended on the involvement, leadership, training, and enthusiasm of the teachers.

To begin the project the two facilitators established two demonstration schools where a group of fourteen teachers volunteered to serve as "nucleus teachers." The initial goal of the group was to write the philosophy of the program. The facilitators recognized that if the program were truly to be teacher directed, then the teachers themselves would need to work out the teaching philosophy and strategies.

This initial theoretical stage, Janet Williamson says, is essential. "[I]t is necessary for at least a small group of people to become educated, in the strongest sense of the word, about critical thinking and to develop a consistent and sound theory or philosophy based on that knowledge."[15] Educating themselves involved reading, soliciting views from propinquitous experts, taking relevant college courses, and attending related conferences.

In short, the nucleus teachers underwent a process of discovery, where they clarified what they meant by critical thinking and evaluated the best means of teaching it. Their work, in other words, was similar to what I have described as discovery through writing. Note, also, that the nucleus teachers formed their own reflective-discussion group, where they could engage in extended dialogue about a subject of great importance to them. Such a setting was crucial to understanding what critical thinking is and to creating an atmosphere where participants could openly point out and work on contradictions in their own reasoning.

The role of the facilitators at this point was to hold workshops for the nucleus teachers; to present new information to them; and to help them introduce, address, and work through various issues and problems (2). Such workshops, in addition to developing the knowledge and skills of the nucleus teachers, prepared them to run workshops for the faculty in the demonstration schools or in other schools throughout the district. Workshop attendance provided those teachers who had only marginal interest in teaching critical thinking with external incentives such as credit toward certificate renewal. The purpose of these inservice workshops was twofold: (1) to model for teachers the skills necessary for critical writing and discussing and (2) to involve the teachers themselves in the kinds of writing and discussing that they would demand of their students (18).

From the workshops and discussions among the nucleus teachers came the central tenet of the Reasoning and Writing Project: lasting change in student learning and performance occurs when teachers work with students to create an atmosphere of open inquiry for all participants. Rather than foisting new lesson plans on the teachers, the nucleus teachers proposed helping the faculty rework their current lesson plans to incorporate critical thinking into them. This "allows the teacher to exercise professional judgment and provides opportunity for the teacher to gain insight into his or her own teaching" (18).

By 1991 the program was operating in Greensboro in all the middle schools, in two high schools, and in at least ten elementary schools. The facilitators and nucleus teachers offered in their first four years over thirty workshops for faculty and school administrators. While many schools in Greensboro have found that other instructional techniques, such as integrated subjects and cooperative learning, dovetail with the Reasoning and Writing Project, nevertheless, it is the project that guides the curriculum. Otherwise, comments Williamson, "cooperative learning can degenerate into cooperative worksheets" (4).

Teachers in the primary grades focused on language development. That meant immersing children in what Ernest Boyer calls "rich language" experiences: "In a school saturated with rich language, children, from their first entry, would be speaking, writing, talking about words, listening to stories, and building vocabulary" (1987, 5). I would add here that children should also be immersed in questions about the ideas, stories, characters, and events that they are talking and writing about and listening to. Such questions, and the answers they pursue individually and collectively, can be the basis of early critical thinking. Students need to play with words and to build their vocabularies as a means of expanding their abilities to conceptualize, articulate, and analyze ideas. One lesson that these primary grade teachers learned was the need to respect the children's language, to understand their language limitations, and to understand and appreciate the basic linguistic competence that students bring to school.[16]

What lessons can teachers, scholars, students, parents, and administrators learn from the Greensboro experience? There are at least five essential lessons: (1) involve teachers directly in creating the curriculum; (2) generate a clear and comprehensive philosophy of education focusing on reflective thinking; (3) rely on voluntary teachers; "there is no gain in 'forcing' teachers to teach in a way they do not favor" (4); (4) make reasoning and writing the principal mode of instruction; and (5) be sure that there are frequent workshops and opportunities to share experiences and information among teachers—that is, provide feedback, information, and encouragement so that teachers can participate in their own reflective discussions on their teaching and the curriculum. What stands out here is the need for teachers to be directly involved, along with the recognition that teachers themselves need training and experience in teaching critical thinking as well as in reflective teaching itself. There must be regular opportunities for teachers, to use a cliché, to practice what they preach.

Reading, Speaking, and Listening

If my proposal is for a language arts program across the curriculum, and not just for writing across the curriculum, then I have given short shrift to the other three modes in the uses of language. As Ann Berthoff comments, to study critical thinking one must "learn the uses of language in the four modes" (1981, 118): speaking, reading, listening, as well as writing. Therefore, all courses must involve students continually in the four modes of language use. Francis Bacon had something like this in mind when he remarked that "reading maketh a full man; conference a ready man; and writing an exact man."

Of course, all four modes must be developed, and they are developed in much the same way. Reading, speaking, and listening, like writing, all require asking questions: when reading, asking questions of the author; when listening, of the speaker; when speaking, of oneself. The basic questions in all four modes are, "What is the fundamental idea?" "How is it being defined?" "What evidence or reasons support or challenge it?" "What are its implications?"

Since this is an educational program, which assumes that students need guidance, the primary questioner is often the teacher. This is not unusual or unexpected. Teachers are themselves active learners, probably more active than their students. They must ask probing questions and questions of clarification; they must stimulate students to go deeper or further in their thinking; they must attend carefully to what students say; they must pay close attention to who is talking and who is not so as to encourage some to participate and to limit the participation of others. In all of this they model for their students what careful reading, attentive listening, and direct speaking or questioning is.

Richard Paul likens the teacher in this regard to that real-life grand inquisitor: Socrates. This teacher is one who seeks out clarification of positions as well as reasons behind those positions; who "actively considers alternative points of view . . . and tries to reconcile differences."[17] This teacher asks open-ended questions for which there is no expected, and no right, answer. This seems to be precisely Socrates' method. He asked questions to which he himself had no satisfactory answers.[18] This distinction is important for differentiating open-ended questions from the more typical information-oriented classroom questions. Consider the following illustration:

> John Dewey once asked a class he visited, "What would you find if you dug a hole in the earth?" Getting no response, he repeated the question: again he obtained nothing but silence. The teacher chided Dr. Dewey, "You're asking the wrong question." Turning to the class, she asked, "What is the state of the center of the earth?" The class replied in unison, "Igneous fusion."

The teacher's question is certainly not the one Dewey was asking, for his question presupposes nothing like digging a hole to the center of the earth. It might be a hole only one spade deep. What would students find then? The implication, it seems to me, is that Dewey had no preordained answer. He was simply curious. But the students did not know how to think about such a question; nor, apparently, did their teacher.

Socrates shows us something else about thinking. Thinking is often social. It is also dialectical in that interpersonal deliberation moves in dialogue, back and forth. This is so whether the dialogue is among you and others or among your many internalized "others." Hannah Arendt refers to this inner dialogue as the "duality of myself with myself that makes thinking a true activity, in which I am both the one who asks and the one who answers" (1977, 185).

We have already seen how students can be introduced to critical thinking and dialectical deliberation through the dialogue journal. Dialogue or discussion, the schoolhouse arena for speaking and listening is a complement to writing. Dialogue, too, is reasoning. In discussion with others, especially in the context of arguments, "a wide variety of things [is] happening. There are statements, questions, changes of tack, backing up of statements with reasons, giving explanations, fitting things together, changes of belief, withdrawal of assertions, evaluation of reasons, and the gradual development of commitments and theories (Girle, 1991, 51).

The significant difference is that discussions do not always freeze one's thought, or freeze the moment, the way writing does. The words are out; they are challenged; your challengers await a response. Yet a good discussion, supervised if not guided by a Socratic teacher, is not a free-for-all or a ganging up of listeners on a speaker or writer. A good discussion is structured, as writing is structured, to take students toward clarification of their ideas, to take them to a closer look at the reasons and evidence that support those ideas, and to take them into the explicit and out of the implicit. Speech and articulation of positions and ideas, like writing, must be practiced, especially if we are preparing students for participation in dialogic democracy.

"Good schooling," Mortimer Adler tells us,

> should involve a great deal of discussion, interchanges of questions and answers between students with one another. . . . Those engaged in educationally profitable discussion will be engaged in agreeing or disagreeing, arguing when they disagree, and giving reasons for disagreements. They will be making and defending generalizations or challenging generalizations made by others. They will be judging by weighing evidence pro and con, or by examining the validity of reasons for making one claim or another concerning what is true or false, more or less probable. They will be asking and answering questions about consistency or inconsistency of things asserted or denied about their presuppositions and their implications, and about the inferences involved therein. (1986, 28)

Thus Adler gives an apt summary of the kinds of ideal and thoughtful discussions that educators should pursue. Still, he leaves unsaid, or at best implicit, one fundamental idea: to read or listen critically, which means well, a student must grasp what is being said. She must enter sympathetically into the perspective of the writer or speaker, to identify without judgment the assumptions, reasons, conclusions, and consequences. To comprehend the thinking of another, the reader or listener first accepts without doubt what is written or said. This is not to suggest that she suspends interrogation. The initial interrogation, however, is to uncover meaning. The reader or listener tries to be as fair as possible to the speaker or the text; she searches for meaning without distorting what is said or written. Once comprehended, the meaning is then probed with skepticism.

McPeck, who, we may recall, equates critical thinking with such skepticism, remarks that "the most refreshing—indeed, the most liberating—thing about honest argument is that it requires taking the other person's reasons seriously, no matter how bizarre they might seem, and addressing them head-on. In argument, notice, people have to treat each other as equals. . . . This is precisely the kind of thinking and discussion that the schools should be trying to foster" (1990, 52). He is exactly right. But this kind of discussion and argument is not natural to persons, any more than good writing is. Students must practice this kind of discussion, this kind of speaking and listening. Because it is not natural, the requirements of good listening and speaking—namely, taking another's ideas and reasons seriously—must be built into the process, into the practice, to assure that it happens.

Classroom discussions are, of course, an excellent venue for practicing good listening and speaking. So, too, is the democratic assembly, which I shall discuss in the next section. But for young students let the classroom be their laboratory for critical thinking. Young students might read fairy tales or make up their own tales. They could lay out the plot and describe the main characters as a way to focus attention on comprehending the tale through attentive reading or listening. Then they might discuss aspects of the tale: did Goldilocks trespass against the bears? Is she the heroine of the tale? Does the giant have a right to be angry in *Jack and the Beanstalk?*

Of course, good discussions require good teachers. To conduct such discussions and engender critical thinking, these teachers should be persons "comfortable with and experienced in critical discussion, critical reflection, and critical inquiry; [they] must be willing to make questions and not assertions the heart of [their] contribution to student learning; [and they] must treat no idea as intrinsically good or bad" (Paul, 1990a, 128).

Our schools often have too few such discussions, because they have too few such teachers. Our current teacher preparation may militate against them. Not only do we perpetuate the educational expectations of a centuries-old model, but we also perpetuate a pedagogical method that dates from the Middle Ages, when books had to be copied by hand. Then the mode of instruction was for students to commit the texts to memory and to have that memorization tested by the teacher. Books were too rare to be borrowed and had to be chained to the library shelves or tables, a practice that can be seen today in the upper library of Merton College, Oxford. Teachers, therefore, lectured or read from the texts as the most efficacious means of transmitting knowledge. Students were then tested on the accuracy of what they retained.[19]

The invention of movable type, to say nothing of the advent of computers and photocopiers, should have obviated this approach. By and large, it didn't. Today, even in high schools and junior high schools, teachers rely on lecturing. Students from early on are taught to look to the teacher for answers. Often what passes for discussion, then, are exchanges between the teacher who asks the questions—the answers to which he undoubtedly already knows—and the students who strive with varying success and often waning attention to read the teacher's mind.

But how are teachers to run reflective discussions with thirty or more students in one classroom? All must be involved to the extent that they pay attention; all must be involved in stimulating tasks that do not leave some bored and others overwhelmed. Writing dialogue journals might enable the student and teacher to interact one-on-one, though many teachers will resist the increased workload, but running class discussions is another matter. To control the classroom and, simultaneously, to cover the curriculum, many teachers decide to lecture, offer question-and-answer sessions, and focus on worksheet learning as the way to teach skills.

Such fallback strategies show lack of imagination.[20] Collaborative learning in small groups provides plenty of discussion and eliminates some of the problems of how thirty students in one classroom can consistently interact. When the students meet in small groups, the teacher can spend more time with certain groups or students within the group. Students can even teach other students. Because they must explain the material, those who teach may learn more than those who are taught. But those who are taught can have one-on-one interaction and thereby have their specific questions addressed.

As students take more responsibility for their learning, the teacher's role shifts from one of supplying knowledge and information to one of facilitating the students' discovery, creation, and use of knowledge and information. This is not to say that teachers forsake their own responsibilities for teaching and evaluating students. Yet the tasks that constitute teaching and evaluating change in this context. Teachers need to evaluate what students as individuals and in groups need to know or ask or learn to move forward with a project; they need to plan how to move a project, or the learning, forward; and they need to evaluate when the learning context calls for an approach different from collaboration.

The classroom teacher also sets the tone. She must be committed to, and therefore she must stay with, the collaborative strategy. Otherwise, she may grow frustrated as the students struggle to take responsibility for their learning. Likewise, the teacher's commitment must be to the process of learning even more than to the product or to how much is learned.

Mathematician and science educator Jack Easley argues that most discussion of math and science content should be left to the pupils themselves and that teachers should serve fundamentally as moderators of class discussions. Students "should work in small but heterogeneous groups, trying to convince and understand one another. Through arguing, children discover their own views' strengths and weaknesses and also discover contrasts between their views and the views of others" (Paul, 1990a, 212). Among the many lessons that Easley has learned through experience are these three:

1.   groups to convince others through clear speaking and writing;
2.   Peer-group dialogue helps children recognize and deal with alternative schemes;

3. As children come to see that they have different ways of approaching and looking at problems, as well as of solving problems, they will revise and modify their understanding to allow them to convince and understand Primary school children should first strive in their heterogeneous others.[21]

It is clear from Easley's experiences, and from those of other educators discussed in this section, that reflective discussions are not debates. "Nobody," Ann Berthoff comments, "learns from debates. . . . The disputant is commonly too busy making a point to trouble to see what it is" (1990, 24), and the listener is too busy thinking of a response. In other words, the point is not understanding but victory. In a debate "people argue to score points, *defeat* the other person, make their point of view [sound] good. They experience 'argument' as *battle,* not as a mutual or cooperative search for a fuller understanding" (Paul, 1990a, 216; emphasis in the original). Unfortunately, models for this kind of "arguing" are pandemic, the two most prominent being our adversarial legal system and our government, more and more the terrain of lawyers.

While debate formats seem a popular activity around which to form classroom discussions, any temptation to use that format should be scrupulously avoided. Besides the pertinence of the battle analogy, debates often reduce complex issues to only two sides. Students need to be made aware, and reminded, that complex issues generate not two but multiple perspectives. Reducing complexity to polar extremes not only distorts or ignores the multiple perspectives and encourages simplistic thinking, but it also makes consensus and resolution virtually impossible. The two sides seem irreconcilable because they represent the polar extremes.

In reflective discussions, as in writing and in deliberative democratic procedures, multiple perspectives are not only tolerated but also embraced. They are sought out so that participants, or writers, can be confident that they have as comprehensive a view as they can get. Students need to be, and will strive to be, as fully informed as possible to avoid ill-formed or misinformed solutions or conclusions.

Of course, the ingredients that make up reflective discussions in our schools are also to be found, or built into, democratic dialogue: participants work together to address and attempt to resolve common problems or conflicting issues; participants propose ideas, probe the roots of and support for those ideas, test the ideas reflectively, gather and move between different points of view, determine whether contradictions can be transcended or embraced, test the strengths and weaknesses of ideas and positions, and consider the long-term effects or ramifications of these views should they win the day.

The topics in democratic dialogue, the methods of arriving at outcomes or decisions (a vote or a consensus), the time allotted for discussion, and the relationships of the participants (strangers or neighbors, friends or relatives) will all be different. Yet, while the contexts of reflective discussions change, the procedures for carrying on such discussions do not. Dialogue is "structured conversation." It is the means by which "a community publicly reasons its way toward truth and understanding" (Splitter, 1991, 101-2). This is true both for a classroom and for a democratic polity.

Democratic Standards

Teaching critical thinking speaks both to the requirements of democratic participation and to the needs of autonomous persons. Teaching critical thinking is another way of describing the teaching of deliberation—the weighing of evidence, reasons, and alternatives that occupies the center of democratic dialogue and autonomous choosing.

Yet if this proposal is for critical thinking as the core of a national curriculum, then it appears that I am ignoring or contradicting the pedagogical view that there is no single best way to learn. Instead, I'm arguing that not only is writing the best way for all students to learn and to explore thinking critically, but critical thinking itself is also what all students should learn. This ignores differences among students in temperament, inclination, or, as Howard Gardner phrases it, "frames of intelligence" (Gardner, 1983b).

Recognition of different learning styles and the like led educational reformers in the 1960s to shift emphasis in schools away from required courses and into electives. To suggest that all students should learn the same symbols, virtues, lessons, and learn them in the same way was to violate the heritage, values, and identities of some by imposing on all a common "culture" through a common curriculum. Doesn't critical thinking as the core across the curriculum, even in the guise of language arts, do precisely that? Doesn't it impose a particular, and perhaps peculiar, understanding of rationality? Doesn't it focus on reason over emotions, argument over articulation and acting out, analysis over accommodation, and independence over relationships?

In brief, I do not think that such accusations hold up. No one can complain that articulation is not essential to discussions, even if the complainant does not recognize that writing is also a form of articulation. No one can think that accommodation of multiple perspectives is left out of deliberation and reflective discussion. The same must be said of relationships, which are often key in learning to think critically. Relationships are fundamental to discussions and collective decision making, both in the classroom and in the polity. Finally, emotional positions can be articulated in writing and speaking; they, too, are part of the multiple perspectives. Yet they will also be examined for the reasons and arguments behind them.

In a multicultural society, however, it would seem almost impossible to achieve consensus on the content of education. Because there would be significant disagreement as to what and how schools should teach, multiculturalism points toward school choice. Through school choice, especially charter schools, parents and students may find a subject range and pedagogical approach that suits them.

But don't those who advocate school choice make *arguments* for it? Don't they need to do so if they are going to convince legislators and fellow citizens of the merits of choice? When placed in that context, isn't it likely that we can reach agreement that we all want our children, neighbors, coworkers, and fellow citizens to be thoughtful; that we prefer that they use persuasion instead of violence; that they can articulate and defend their ideas, values, and beliefs and can challenge those of others, and even their own, with counterarguments and countervailing reasons; and that they know how to learn on their own, especially when that leads to asking for help from others?

The best way to learn anything at all, the only way to learn anything on one's own, is to think and to question; that is, to think critically or reflectively. To be able to do that well one needs to know how to control and order one's thinking, how to understand and criticize a speech or a text. Teaching critical thinking provides the tools whereby all citizens can control not only language but also their own learning. This teaching provides the tools by which they can participate in local, regional, and national conversations wherein participants can articulate, promote, defend, and challenge values and positions.

This is not to overlook the social constructivist view that the rules of grammar, syntax, and rhetoric that shape thought are only the conventions of the communities to which "we thinking and willing persons of Western European-American literate culture belong" (Bruffee, 214). This is true; the culture of the United States is derived largely from Western Europe. It happens that this is a culture in which the predominant language is English. Those who wish to maximize their chances of success in this culture, those who wish to participate in its political and economic as well as most of its social and cultural institutions, need to learn English. This is true today, and it will be true tomorrow, though I recommend more than learning to read, to write, and to speak English. That is basic literacy. I recommend learning to control English, to think critically in it. That is why critical thinking must be the core across the curriculum.[22]

We live in a culture and a polity built upon, and that prizes, what Howard Gardner calls "linguistic intelligence" (Gardner, 1991). Because that is so, competence in the semantic, phonological, syntactic, and pragmatic operations and applications of language is important to all citizens and persons in society. In the world of everyday actions and interactions, this type of thinking predominates.

Yet the *content* of what students write and discuss and read has no limitations. Thus students can study maritime subjects, performing arts, even sports, on the condition that they meet the democratic standards of critical thinking and reflective discussion—extensive and intensive preparation and practice in writing, reading, speaking, and listening.[23]

In this way the core of critical thinking can accommodate the different frames of mind discussed by Gardner. Students turned off by conventional academic subjects or invigorated by other subjects could gravitate toward a curriculum based on another kind of intelligence; for example, a curriculum based on spatial-intelligence in which students focus on the observable, tangible, and tactile aspects of art, architecture, archaeology, or paleontology (Gardner, 1983b).

Regardless of their choice, students would still have to meet the democratic standards; the core of the curriculum would still be critical thinking. Otherwise, in what way would students establish that they focused on art, architecture, archaeology, or paleontology?

Adherence to these standards is not stultifying. Students with what Gardner calls "personal intelligences"—the intrapersonal intelligence to delve into and differentiate feelings or the interpersonal intelligence to attend to the feelings and behaviors of others—would thrive by studying psychology, psychobiography, and drama that portrayed characters' inner lives, about which students could write and discuss their own observations and insights. Even here the thinking in these different modes needs to be structured, developed, and expressed. Critical thinking is crucial to one's interpretation of a text, a person, an event, a display, just as the intelligence or mode is crucial to the selection of the text, person, event, display. The thinking involved might include making scale models, doing hands-on building or testing, undertaking library searches, interviewing experts or observers or veterans. But every project will require some aspect of critical thinking, of language arts. The final product may not be a paper or presentation, but no one can undertake a project or complete it without critical thinking.

When language arts are seen as the principal vehicle for developing and expressing critical thinking, then multiculturalists need not fear the inculcation of formulaic or lockstep thinking. Every writer and speaker has her own style of expressing thought. Rules of grammar and syntax do not elicit uniform articulation, but are used to permit the writer to control language to say precisely what she wants to say. English is a language rich and flexible enough to offer expression to virtually any point of view and articulation of every way of life.

On the other hand, maybe the absence of formula or doctrine is exactly what multiculturalists fear. They fear the absence of *their* doctrine. Do we transgress against groups or cultures, therefore, if they honor social solidarity more than autonomy and critical thought? In teaching students to think critically we are providing them with the skills to challenge the values and views with which they have been raised. Critical thinking threatens inherited ways of life. But in the face of such threats, parents and group leaders will have to argue for their values and views and against alien values and views. Thus they, too, will be urged to think critically. Can it be that their valued way of life is merely an indoctrinated way of life and that the core of their values lies exclusively in its unassailability?

Indoctrination is not education. Indoctrination is the forging of an emotional allegiance to beliefs and practices of a doctrine the assumptions of which remain beyond question. Is teaching critical thinking a form of indoctrinating students into relying on reason or rationality? The dilemma is that we cannot assess such a challenge unless we use reason. We cannot critically assess rationality unless we are already rational. If we wish to make it possible for students to question ends and assumptions, including the nature, place, and value of rationality, then we must teach them to be rational and to think critically. Yet the inculcation of reliance on reason is not the same as indoctrination. The point of indoctrination, remember, is to sidestep challenges to the doctrine, not to confront them. Reason or rationality, on the other hand, permits and even demands the scrutiny of the doctrine of reason itself.

Adherence to and enforcement of the democratic standards of critical thinking are, therefore, especially important in fundamentalist schools. The sacralizing predispositions of such schools may preclude participation in dialogues or in reading texts in which different and divergent views must be heard and wrestled with. It is important to bear in mind that without the core of critical thinking a fundamentalist school could construe the contents of courses in sectarian ways. Courses could be constructed such that the students never heard or read anything outside of the Bible or other sanctioned courses. Central to scholastic requirements is not accumulated credits or impressive transcripts, but an emphasis on and a commitment to critical thinking. Thus some alternative views must be presented, perhaps not in *every* course, but in enough courses to give the student knowledge of and experience in challenging views, defending views, and hearing and discussing views that diverge from her own.

All students—whether in public, private, parochial, or home schools—need critical thinking to meet the demands of citizenship in a liberal democracy moving toward and involving more deliberative arenas. The democratic standards, applicable to every student, assure that these demands can be met. All who can thereby be self-governing may not, however, choose to be self-ruling. They may not, that is, choose to be autonomous or to apply critical thinking in their day-to-day living. Living out such a choice may not be easy, since those steeped in critical thinking and now exercising their autonomy may find that their critical capacities cannot be turned on and off like faucets; the habits of thoughtfulness might be deep. But those habits themselves must be open to critical scrutiny.

The connection between critical thinking and autonomy, as well as democracy, ought to be clear. Persons need to be able to make reasoned judgments on and decisions about issues that affect their self-directed lives and their collective life. Amy Gutmann observes that autonomy reposes on an alliance of rhetoric and reason (Gutmann, 1993b, 140). Nowhere is this alliance better pursued, expressed, and developed than through writing, which is the use of rhetoric to form, advance, and challenge arguments. This is not to discount oratory, reading, and listening, which also employ and develop the same alliance. But writing is the keystone, the centerpiece, because it teaches one to structure thinking. The other modes of language use play off of writing.

Because rationality is necessary but insufficient for autonomy, students can learn how to reason, deeply and well, without being required to exercise self-reflectivity. Teaching deliberation therefore does not mandate that students be self-reflective. Autonomy is not necessarily implicated in the teaching of critical thinking. Teaching such thinking is therefore propaedeutic to, but is not an education in, autonomy.

Yet autonomy means thinking about one's own thinking, and writing is at least the expression of one's own thinking. Therefore, when any student, at any age, revises his writing, then he is thinking about his own thinking. Writing that includes revision demands that students think autonomously. This refutes the claim that one can be educated for autonomy but not in autonomy.

While it is true that autonomy includes metacognition or thinking about one's thinking, it is not true that all those who can and do think about their own thinking are autonomous. In revising his writing, a student is not necessarily turning reflectivity onto himself, onto his self. Attention is directed to the meaning he has created or discovered and how best to convey that meaning to, or clarify that meaning for, others. Attention is not necessarily, and is probably not, directed to how that meaning reflects his life.

There is enough explosive power in teaching critical thinking, in teaching students to write clearly, read carefully, listen attentively, and speak directly, to offset the need for public schools to require students to think self-reflectively. That students may well do so anyway, especially under pressure or with a fillip from peers, relatives, or various circumstances, is not a justification that they might just as well do so under pressure or with a fillip from their public school teachers. Where a student's thinking will take her is unpredictable and limitless. But what a public school teacher demands must have limits.

Reflective thinking, to say nothing of self-reflective thinking, can be dangerous, as John Dewey observed:

> If we once start thinking no one can guarantee where we shall come out, except that many objects, ends, and institutions are surely doomed. Every thinker puts some portion of an apparently stable world in peril and no one can wholly predict what will emerge in its place.[24]

Fundamentalist schools are therefore not the only institutions threatened by the menacing aspects of critical thinking. If one purpose of public schooling is to prepare citizens to participate in our democracy, and if that democracy consists of little but voting, then our schools can rest content with fostering, at most, basic literacy. All the more reason for avoiding critical thinking is that it can lead to questioning the assumptions of authorities, the rationale behind policies, and the foundations of institutions. Critical thinking can thereby be subversive of our own democratic system.

Education in deliberation, with its focus on critical thinking through the language arts, is a means of developing students' voices as they ask questions and make reasoned judgments. But to try to establish a critical thinking curriculum in the dilapidated heaps we call inner-city schools is a travesty. The lack of resources, the lack of support, and the horrors that literally surround many of these schools add another context for the term "chaos." If a critical thinking curriculum were a national priority, perhaps we could do something about the inequities within and among school districts that our democracy seems all too willing to countenance.[25]

A graduate of high school, of any high school in this country, says Mortimer Adler

> should be able to show an understanding of a moderately complicated essay; an ability to write clear and concise expository prose; to perform reasonably complicated mathematical operations, to sort out issues, to solve various types of problems, to think through an argument and evaluate it, to formulate a persuasive argument and deliver it orally, to listen critically to a speech and respond relevantly to it. (1983, 51)

Such a view comes close to what I have described as the skills of critical thinking: writing clearly, speaking directly, listening attentively, and reading carefully. Would any parent object? How does learning such skills undercut ethnic or cultural identity? Notice in Adler's statement that there is no mention of, and no need to mention, self-reflectivity. Public school is not the place to call one's self or way of life into question, though post secondary education is such a place. In the context of adult education, in all its manifestations, we assume maturity and with it the need to explore and exercise autonomy.

Yet what Adler describes and what I have described are not quite enough. Daniel Resnick observes that adolescents rarely "approach academic learning with the same intensity they direct to sports, other extracurricular activities, and out-of-school work" (1990, 28). Why is this so? It is so, according to Resnick, because school experiences and requirements offer little tangible reward. It is difficult to convince students that the reading, writing, speaking, listening, and calculating required of a critical-thinking curriculum will pay off in the long run. We preach the payoff, but do they experience it? This is why the schoolwork is required; children will not do it on their own. But schools can offer more immediate payoffs; they can offer real experiences as tangible rewards that also serve as educational preparation for these future citizens. Schools should be run democratically, where students of particular ages, in conjunction with teachers and staff, make decisions that affect some of the actual operations of the school. Indeed, to add a pedagogical justification to this idea, Robert Moses, echoing John

Dewey, found through his Algebra Project that students learn best when lessons begin with or focus on real-life problems rather than on abstractions ("Mississippi Learning"). How such a democratic school might actually use such problems is the principal topic of the concluding section of this chapter.

Democratic Schools

Although a search in any research library of the topic "democratic schools" will reveal a fair amount of material, it is disappointing how little of that material discusses democratic practices in schools. Instead, one finds literature dealing either with "schools for everyone," where the primary focus is on the important topic of equity in education, especially for the poor and minorities (about which I shall have more to say in the epilogue) or with the equally important topic of how to empower teachers to control their schools and classrooms.

A case in point in the latter category is the article by Landon E. Beyer (1988) with the promising title "Can Schools Further Democratic Practices?" The essence of Beyer's position is captured by the following: "If schools are to become sites for building participatory democracy, they must allow workers there the very sort of autonomy that is lacking in most public school systems" (267). Workers in this case are teachers who must be allowed "the opportunity to exercise self-governing capacities" (267). Granted, teachers need such opportunities; democratic schools, obviously, must acknowledge that. But what of the students, who in Beyer's view seem to be the products of schools and not workers themselves? Perhaps Beyer does not mean to overlook students; he simply wishes to suggest that at the outset, to build democratic schools, teacher empowerment must be the first step. With this I wholeheartedly concur, and later Beyer maintains that "[i]f participatory democracy is to work, people must have the opportunity to experience its efficacy firsthand" (268). Since students are people at the same participatory site, surely Beyer means to include them in these opportunities. But while teachers engage in democratic practices in which they reflect on their reasons for curricular and pedagogical choices, alter "the criteria for such choices so that ethical and political dimensions are considered along with more traditional, technical concerns," and contemplate "the short- and long-term consequences of actions for both students and teachers" (268), students have the opportunity only to discuss among themselves and with teachers "issues of form and content" (268). About the power to change form or content, about students' real decision making in the classroom or in the school at large, Beyer offers nothing.

Similarly, Carl Glickman in *Renewing America's Schools* argues that "there is only one primary goal for American public schools . . . to prepare students to become productive citizens in our democracy" (8). Our schools, in his estimation, should "produce caring, intelligent, and wise citizens who willingly engage in the work of democracy" (9). If democracy is at the center of the curriculum, he continues, then teachers, administrators, students, and parents will have a clear focus on what is to be done in schools. This focus will "show students how to connect learning with real issues of their surroundings. . . . [M]ore students [will] learn how to write cogent compositions, [will] learn basic skills, [will] use higher-order thinking, [will] learn aesthetic appreciation, [will] excel in academics, and [will] graduate" (9).

How can Glickman be so confident? He observes: "The reason why many of our students do not do better in schools is not that they are deficient, or that teachers are incompetent or uncaring; the reason is that these students do not see the relevance of such learning to altering and improving their immediate lives in their communities. For them, school is a bore" (9).

Unfortunately, the remainder of Glickman's book is useful only for pointing out two principal ironies. First, Glickman's view of democracy is firmly rooted in the representative model. Thus, while he acknowledges that there is direct democracy and that some schools have even used it, he prefers (and offers no argument for such a preference) a hybrid model in which a governing council sets the agendas, guidelines, and timetables, but in which final decisions are made by the "citizens" as a whole. Ironically, when the council takes an issue to the citizens—and the council does not always have to do so; it can make the decision on its own—it takes the issue in the form of a recommendation, which the citizens are then to vote up or down. There is no mention of discussion or deliberation among the citizens; there is only "a vote" (40-41). While it seems certain that the students will have reinforced for them through this method their duty to vote, it is less clear that students will see in this form of democratic governance, as well as in a similar representative form that awaits their maturation, the relevant connection, as Glickman promises, to their learning to write cogent compositions, to their learning basic skills, to their using higher-order thinking, or to their learning aesthetic appreciation. School may still pretty much seem to be a bore.

Second, Glickman can be content to offer such a model of school democracy, even while complaining that "[m]ost policies in public education are undemocratic" and "are not decided by those who will be affected" (23), because most of the issues or policies that he has in mind are teachers' issues and policies. Thus, in the face of his premise that "if a school is to foster educated citizenry for a democracy, then the school itself must be an example of a democracy" (37), Glickman states that the focus of decisions "should always be . . . how to enhance schoolwide teaching and learning" (37). There is little question that these issues are teachers' issues. Indeed, of the possible decision areas that Glickman lists (33) virtually all are teachers' issues. Thus ideally, he says, while all major groups in the school (administrators, students, staff, parents, faculty) should be represented on school governance committees,[26] "teachers should be in the majority" (35). This begins to smack of democratic centralism. Why only teachers' issues? Why should professional issues even be decided democratically? Why only representative councils, with teachers in the majority and no room for deliberation among the students and other groups? Glickman provides no answers.

Why is so little written about involving students in deliberative or participatory democracy? Why, as John Kornfeld asks, is so little of practical value written, despite the many calls for democracy in the classroom, to help teachers attain that goal (1993, 75)? The answer, he suggests, is that as "[a]nyone who has spent any time in an elementary classroom would agree . . . it is far easier to talk about the values of democracy than to instill them in students" (75).

One philosopher who understood the importance of student participation in democracy in schools and who understood how to instill its values was John Dewey. According to Dewey, we gain knowledge of anything through experience and reflection on that experience. This, of course, is the centerpiece of his educational philosophy. So if we want knowledge of democracy, then we must experience democracy.

Dewey thought, as Tocqueville did, that active democratic participation could draw people out of apathy and the hardened shells of narrow interests. Also, like Tocqueville, he thought that people could be convinced of this only through their own experience. That is, people had to participate before they would see the value of participation. How, then, are people convinced to participate initially? Dewey proposed that such participation should be in schools, where participation, if it involved issues of real concern for students, would lead students to see its value.

Real problems, Dewey argued, would be of real concern to students. So in addition to activities of writing and classroom discussion, students should engage in "active inquiry and careful deliberation in the significant and vital problems" that confront the community, however defined (1991 [1910], 55). One community, in Dewey's mind, about which students are often concerned is the school itself. "Pupils," he commented, "are taught to live in two separate worlds, one the world of out-of-school experience, the other the world of books and lessons" (1991 [1910], 200). Granted, both are worlds of experience, but the two are rarely brought together so that book lessons and classroom discussions connect with decision making on issues that affect the community. One logical, and practical, possibility is to make the operations of the school part of the curriculum. Let the students make, or help make, decisions that directly affect some of the day-to-day operations of the school. Make the school itself part of the curriculum.

Dewey thought of schools as "embryo communities" (1915, 174), "an institution in which the child is, for the time . . . to be a member of a community life in which he feels that he participates, and to which he contributes" (1972, 88). We need not become sidetracked in questioning just what Dewey means by, or what we should mean by, "community" to grasp the sense that he is after. Because students spend much of their day in school, we can think of it as a place where they live as well as learn. Indeed, students spend more time in school during the school year than anywhere else, except sleeping. Therefore, it is not surprising that Dewey wanted to give students experience in making decisions that affect their lives in schools. What is surprising is that so little democracy takes place in schools and that those who spend the most time in schools have the least opportunity to experience it.

What, then, in my terms is a democratic school? As I envision it, a democratic school is any school that has a democratic component such that students engage in the practice of deliberative decision making that controls some aspects of the functioning of the school or the classroom. In other words, a democratic school is one in which students participate in deliberative democratic structures and processes not simply to provide them with democratic experiences as propaedeutic to future democratic participation, but also to enable students to make actual collective decisions that affect some aspects of their lives in school.

Of course, not everything in school should be decided democratically. There are some areas in which decisions require expertise—a combination of experience and knowledge—that rules out students as decision makers. Chief among such areas is pedagogy. As Dewey pointed out (1937), if teachers are ever to develop expertise, let alone be considered experts, then they must be involved in making the decisions most intimate to their profession. Teachers, in conjunction with administrators and with only minimal interference from school boards, should make decisions about the curriculum and pedagogical philosophy of their school. To deprive them of such decision making not only undercuts or retards their exercise of autonomy, but also alienates them from what they do: teach. That they must defend their decisions before administrators and school boards is, of course, another matter.

Students must be left out of such decision making for the same reason that members of the school board must be: both groups lack the professional judgment, broadly defined, to make those decisions. Teachers are the experts on what students need to learn and how they need to learn it and on what *these* students need to learn and how *they* individually and collectively need to learn it. Because the teachers and administrators in a particular school have firsthand and often intimate knowledge of the range and nature of abilities and problems of their students, as well as the particular circumstances in which the learning takes place, then they should make pedagogical decisions, not the school officials who are further removed.

To make such decisions requires increased interaction among faculty, including more collaboration inside and outside the classroom. Could a faculty decide that in their school students will not focus on learning to think critically or to discuss democratically? Certainly they need not take the advice of an outsider, a political theorist who isn't even a public school teacher. That is a decision that they can legitimately make provided they follow the democratic procedures. But from the perspective of a liberal state that promotes and perhaps mandates democratic standards, such a faculty will present a problem. There are boundaries within which schools must operate. In a liberal state, any school that decides democratically to end its education in deliberation, however ironic that may be, must declare itself to be a private school or should seek to become a charter school.

Because many students are still children, the decisions that they are to make should be age appropriate. Not all democratic procedures or school issues are suitable for all ages. Differences in cognitive, social, and emotional development, especially at the elementary-school level, complicate open democracy. Dewey commented that "full education comes only when there is a responsible share on the part of each person, in proportion to capacity, in shaping the aims and policies of the social groups to which he belongs" (1948, 209). While all students may have the same capacity as potentiality, activating those capacities requires development.

It seems too much to expect children below sixth grade, for example, to engage in open deliberation with adults, which might be necessary in the democratic assembly (about which I shall say more in due course). There are solid developmental-psychological reasons for differentiating between the democratic procedures, as well as the topics for deliberation, used in high school and those used in elementary school. While the age-dependent characteristics and details of, for example, the moral stages of Kohlberg or the cognitive stages of Piaget may be in question, there is no general quarrel among developmentalists that all persons pass through three invariant states of increasing cognitive complexity— from preconventional to conventional to postconventional, or their equivalents. What most often characterizes these states, and accounts for movement from one state to the next, is the ability of persons to take up the perspectives of others.[27]

Young children have difficulty taking up such perspectives. On those grounds alone deliberative procedures that require the consideration of multiple perspectives would seem unsuitable for elementary school children. Additionally, young children are far more reliant on the teacher's involvement in presenting problem situations in which the children's knowledge and skills can be applied and developed. R. S. Peters offers an important consideration in this regard:

> The cardinal function of the teacher, in the early stages, is to get the pupil on the inside of the form of thought or awareness with which he is concerned. At a later stage, when the pupil has built into his mind both the concepts and the mode of exploration involved, the difference between teacher and taught is obviously only one of degree. For both are participating in the shared experience of exploring a common world. (1966, 53)

The distinction between those moving into "the inside" of reflective thinking and those already there may seem so vast as to be a difference of kind, not degree. But the difference is always one of degree. Elementary school students have yet to develop the skills and knowledge, or have yet to gain the experience, to participate in procedures that require perspectivism—the taking up and considering of multiple perspectives.

Thus, there is a hierarchy to democratic decision making, and the higher levels are built of and rest upon the lower. That is, the lower levels are prior to the higher; without them there could be no hierarchy. The lowest level, and the one central to every level, is the democratic discussion. It is democratic discussion that forms the basis of deliberative democracy and democratic decision making, whether those decisions are made in high schools, universities and colleges, workplaces, civic associations, religious groups, senior citizen centers, sports clubs, or the public arena.

Democratic discussion constitutes the entire deliberative, or democratic, procedure for the lower grades, say K-4. The next level up consists of democratic discussion plus the democratic classroom. This combination is suitable predominantly for middle schoolers, fifth grade through eighth grade. By high school, students would continue to use democratic discussion, but the democratic classroom, absent homerooms, would drop out to be supplanted by democratic wards or democratic assemblies. I shall look more specifically at each of these democratic arenas.[28]

Democratic Discussions. The basis of classroom discussion is dialogue. The term comes to us from the ancient Greeks, for whom it meant a "talking through" of an issue. Those who have read any of Plato's dialogues can appreciate how the Athenians considered dialogue the best way of talking through and reflecting a philosophical issue to arrive at the truth about it. Thus dialogue is a fitting term for democratic deliberation.

What would elementary school children deliberate about? Discussions would focus predominantly on issues related to the curriculum—on stories, fables, or biographies; on science experiments, math problems, and historical events; on the students' writing or current events. Discussions could even focus on the curriculum itself; how, the teacher might ask, should we study penguins, our next topic in science? How should we decide whose stories to read next week? How should we celebrate your classmates' birthdays?

In such discussions the teacher needs to model reflective thinking. He needs to seek out clarifications of positions or ideas, to ask for justifications for holding these positions or ideas. He needs to summarize what students have said and to lead students from those statements to additional questions or illustrations. By doing so, the teacher models both reflective questioning and good listening. He listens carefully to what others say; he mirrors in his summaries what students have said; he looks for reasons and does not settle for mere opinions. Such discussions permit the teacher to respond immediately to what students say and allow him to recognize when a student is having trouble attending to the discussion or articulating a position. Because the dialogue is at this level mostly between the teacher and students, although student-to-student dialogue is to be encouraged, there is strong teacher supervision and strong teacher feedback. Students in these discussions can see and hear and thereby learn what good reflective thinking is.

What is democratic about these discussions? First, everyone must be allowed to speak without being interrupted or harassed. Even in these elementary school discussions some of the rules for the democratic procedures that adults use must be evident and be in force. One such rule is that any student can be asked, in this case by the teacher, to summarize accurately what another student has said (or what the text says). This means that listening requires attending to the ideas of others. Although a student might have to translate those ideas into different words or ideas that make sense to her, she must learn that she cannot do so in a way that distorts or misrepresents the perspective of the other student.

In brief, anyone who wants to speak in turn can do so without fear of being interrupted and without concern that her ideas will go unheard or will be distorted. Speaking and being heard accord respect. Mutual respect is shown by the way that others hear our positions and thereby acknowledge us as persons and by the way in which we speak to or address others. The teacher must reinforce and enforce the rule of uninterrupted speaking and the rule of attentive listening. As students mature and move on to higher grades, the students themselves will usually enforce the rules.

One way to initiate elementary school children into democratic dialogue—dialogue, that is, with one another—is to use the "circle meeting." Students' chairs are arranged in a circle, so that the children face one another. A discussion leader, who does not always have to be the teacher, selects the first speaker. The next speaker is the student on the first speaker's immediate left (or right), and so on around the circle. Each person can speak for up to three minutes about a prearranged topic or, at other times, about anything related to that day in the classroom. No one may interrupt a speaker or comment while a student is speaking. The circle meeting involves all of the students, gives them equal time to voice their views, and elicits views from everyone. The point is to permit all students to voice perspectives knowing that no one will challenge them, that they can speak for three minutes or for ten seconds, and that there is no pressure to produce a right answer. "Children," Rosemary Chamberlin reminds us, "are not simply embryonic citizens, trainee democrats or even future individualists. They are people with current feelings and wants who feel oppressed or undervalued if their own views are silenced or ignored, or their own wants dismissed as unimportant or irrelevant" (1989, 124).

Democratic Classrooms. The purpose of democratic discussions at the elementary school level is to engage students in the practices of giving voice to viewpoints, of hearing the viewpoints of others, and of questioning not only the teacher but also themselves. In the democratic classroom, however, the expectations are higher for democratic discussion. Moreover, dialogue among students is expected; the teacher is less the focal point. While they are expected to be able to mirror or summarize other students' perspectives, students are expected to articulate but also to challenge positions and proposals. In short, they are expected to become the Socratic speakers and listeners that the teachers are in early elementary classrooms.

At this level real conversations take place, potentially with many more perspectives to keep in mind. That complexity engenders rapid intellectual growth. "The experience of veteran teachers and the evidence from recent research both argue that . . . intellectual activities are most effectively developed by a dialectical process, by testing and reacting, by *conversation.* What counts is the quality of that conversation" (Sizer, 1992, 89; emphasis in original). That quality depends upon the standards set, and chief among those standards is, comments Sizer, "the willingness of all in the conversation respectfully to challenge incomplete or shoddy thinking" to create "a culture that endorses constructive reflection."[29]

Thus an emphasis on respect continues as students learn to challenge respectfully. To do so students must first demonstrate that they have accurately heard the position and then offer criticisms of it—that is, reasons or evidence against it. The purpose of democratic discussion at this point, then, is not only to guarantee respectful challenges of different views, but also to structure constructive reflection and deliberation.

To assure that students take one another seriously—that is, to assure that they listen attentively to one another—Thomas Kasulis uses the "listening-point circle" in his classes. In the circle, "students may be called upon at any time to summarize what another student just said and to relate it to a previous point. Then the previous speaker explains whether the listener really got the point or not" (1991, A32). This technique not only pushes students to listen carefully, but also pushes them to speak with clarity. The immediate feedback from a listener, assuming that the listener was paying careful attention, leaves no doubt as to how well the original speaker has communicated her positions or arguments.

Democratic discussions at this level might well involve problems that the students want, or are asked, to solve. In a discussion of this sort, the teacher would lead the students through the elements in the democratic procedures that constitute deliberative decision making at the adult and young adult level. These procedures I shall discuss in detail in the section on democratic assemblies, but the point is to generate multiple perspectives as multiple contributions that might lead the group to an acceptable solution or conclusion. Multiple perspectives can create a healthy tension that requires participants, including the teacher, to rethink and even abandon a position. Such a point of tension delineates a "space of regulated confrontation."[30] Clearly, younger students would not be able, or be expected, to recognize or handle such tension.[31]

In the democratic classroom, while the discussion focuses heavily on student dialogue, it is the teacher who guides students through the procedures found at the next level. In the discussions, students share their views with others; these views are heard and often responded to by other students; these views are taken seriously in that they are discussed as potential contributions and they require argument (reasons and evidence) if they are rejected. There is much interaction and collaboration among students, especially as they endeavor to locate and deal with the points of tension or conflict.[32]

Beyond teacher involvement, also separating democratic classrooms from the democratic discussions of the earlier level, is the nature of the topics or issues. In addition to those related to the curriculum are issues related to the organization, administration, activities, and operations of the classroom itself. To govern behavior in the classroom, the students might write their own constitution. They could begin by asking themselves, through a democratic discussion, what rules they think are necessary for their classroom. Does everyone have to obey rules? Why do we obey rules? What do we do when students don't obey the rules?

Surely this topic is in keeping with Dewey's call to address students' interests and concerns. Students want rules to live by, but they want more than to know what those rules are; they want a say in what those rules will be. Rules made by those who will live under them have a greater chance of being honored. Why? As. J. R. Lucas says, "Even when a decision is not wholly agreeable, we may be more willing to accept it for having had some part in the discussions which preceded it. At the least, we understand the reasons that led to its being adopted. We may not agree with them or we may feel that other more cogent considerations have not been given the weight they deserve, but we have some appreciation of the force of the arguments which were finally adopted" (1976, 137). This, of course, is also the perspective of autonomy and deliberative democracy.[33]

The rules adopted by a classroom will rest on arguments. That is one of the points of democratic discussions. This is what the seventh-grade students at the Georgia O'Keeffe Middle School in Madison, Wisconsin, discovered. "[I]f there were to be rules, then those who would have to live by the rules needed to have a say" in the making of those rules (Brodhagen, 1995, 86). The students wanted to write their classroom constitution, and to do so "teachers and students alike had to stand up and explain, provide evidence, or otherwise convince the group why a particular idea or statement was necessary" (1995, 87). The result was that the students codified in their classroom constitution the rules of conduct, including punishments for infractions of the rules, as well as some of the topics in the curriculum.[34]

Without subjecting deep or extensive pedagogical issues to the judgments of callow youth, students can suggest issues for the class to discuss and can establish agendas for investigating those issues. Some of those issues could include topics within the assigned curriculum that students might like to study or to study in a different way. Teachers might hold democratic discussions not to make decisions but to elicit from the students issues for future agendas. Teachers might ask how the classroom could be improved and ask students to specify areas that need improvement.

At the school at Iceland Wharf in Copenhagen, Denmark, the teachers ask every class at the beginning of the year to plan the topics that it might like to study during the year (Bagge, et al., 1989). The crucial point here is that whatever the students can decide is acted upon. Thus, a constitution that governs class decorum must be followed; rules made democratically are rules to be enforced. The exercise of creating a constitution must not be seen as an academic exercise or game.[35]

Another difference that separates elementary school democratic discussions from those in democratic classrooms is that the older students will be asked to work in small groups as a way of scrutinizing the class itself. In other words, in democratic classrooms the classrooms themselves, the behavior and activities of the students, the atmosphere and life within the classroom, become issues for democratic discussion. Small groups allow participants more air time to articulate their perspectives and ideas and permit a sharper focus on the specific perspectives that arise. There is also less pressure to sound smart or to avoid sounding foolish. Small groups, as many studies of collaborative learning have shown, are usually relaxed and promote cooperation. Equally important, working in small groups prepares students for the small-group processes that are an integral part of the democratic procedures found in high school as well as in deliberative democratic procedures themselves.

Democratic Assemblies/Democratic Wards. Schools are not merely the site for preparing or the means of preparing students for the workplace, citizenship, and life. They are also sites of political concern where rules and conflicts need to be addressed and deliberated about, and where decisions on rules and conflicts need to be made collectively. Students at the high school level are ready for such decision making. Are they really? Do they have the maturity—that is, the experience and judgment—to think through the possible intricacies of an issue? Can they identify key assumptions? Can they draw inferences and follow implications? Can they hear viewpoints with which they disagree? Can they accept the contributions of those whom they detest? Will they listen; will they speak; will they participate fully?

Some of these questions are easily answered affirmatively if the education that has preceded high school has been an education in the skills of deliberation—the core across the curriculum. Yet some of those questions seem to speak of character more than of content: will students show a willingness to participate? The short answer is that character at this stage has nothing to do with it; students will be required to participate as part of the curriculum.

At the same time, many of the issues that the school is deciding will appeal to the students. Democratic assemblies might decide on physical education requirements; the time that school starts in the morning and ends in the afternoon; the lunch schedule; when the library should be open (on weekends?) and when, and whether, students should staff it; whether students should be responsible for policing the school premises; whether students should maintain the grounds and buildings; whether an official student responsibility should be community service such as coaching younger athletic or dramatic or debate teams; student responsibilities in the cafeteria, such as whether students should prepare the meals; the lunch menus; student dress codes; open-campus policies; whom to invite to speak at the school during the year and at graduation.

Drugs are endemic in our nation's high schools. Isn't it time to draw the students into helping resolve the problem on their own campuses? What about problems of racism? Sexism? Violence on campus? Imagine that someone has defaced a school wall with obscene graffiti. It is not a matter for the Discipline Committee, because no one has been caught or has confessed, and no rules exist covering such incidents. How might this matter be handled in a democratic school? Hold the example in mind as I describe the democratic procedures used to make collective decisions.

Democracy involves making group decisions, and therefore it makes sense to specify the methods or procedures by which democratic assemblies will decide. Whatever the procedures, they should build on the structures of democratic discussions and democratic classrooms. Those earlier structures served as the basis for learning and using deliberation, but in limited contexts. One set of decision-making procedures suitable, therefore, for a democratic school would consist of four stages: (1) pooling perspectives, (2) scrutiny of perspectives, (3) small-group conferences, and (4) voting. I shall take each one in turn.[36]

Pooling Perspectives. All students in the school are divided into wards or assemblies, which will involve fewer than the 100 persons Jefferson prescribed for his wards and that constitute the wards of deliberative democracy. The number should be in keeping with the homeroom concept: no more students than can be accommodated at one time in a typical homeroom—roughly thirty-five to forty students.

In the pooling stage all participants can have their say. For example, participants can make contributions to understanding or resolving the graffiti issue without fear of censure and without having their contributions subjected to critical scrutiny. To encourage such contributions, a school might propose having students initially meet within their wards in small-group conferences and then convene as an open ward or assembly to pool perspectives.

However a school decides to implement this stage, it is vital that every person recognizes that the pooling is open to any and all contributions. Moderators of the wards, those appointed to ensure that the process unfolds and moves along properly, have the power to ask participants, either before or after they have spoken, to summarize or to mirror the perspective of another. This is a way of checking that contributions are accurately heard.

The possibility that one might need to mirror another's perspective is important, for all perspectives, no matter how contentious, bizarre, offensive, or seemingly irrational, must be allowed to enter the pool of perspectives. For what students are doing at this stage is simply gathering perspectives as the database from which possible solutions, say, to the graffiti problem, will be drawn or on which possible resolutions will be based. While not all perspectives will be included in the final solution or decision, since they will be scrutinized critically at the next stage, all must be allowed into the conversation and must be understood. We might refer to this stage, following Ronald Beiner, as the stage of "hermeneutical judgment," which involves understanding rather than explanation or analysis. The participant opens "himself to the phenomena. [H]e seeks to penetrate into the actual experiential horizons of those involved in a situation, to gain hermeneutical appreciation of the agents' own understanding of the situation" (1983, 159-60).

The nondiscriminatory nature of this stage is vital to the process, for it is illegitimate at this point to rule out any perspective. There is no sure way to know whether, and how, a flamboyant or offensive idea might affect the thinking of others. Such an idea might spark a conceptual breakthrough that transcends or incorporates divergent views. To dismiss peremptorily certain views limits the possible solutions available to the ward, solutions that may not be readily visible unless all perspectives are pooled. At the same time, there is no sure way to discriminate between those views that should automatically be excluded and those that should automatically be admitted.

Scrutiny of Perspectives. Why "automatic" exclusion or admission of particular views? Surely there are ways to assess perspectives, to challenge those that are palpably misguided, misinformed, malformed, or irrational. Such challenges take place in the second stage, not the first. The second stage, the stage of scrutiny, is the time for critical analysis.

Contrary to modes of argumentation, especially in politics, that are traditionally adversarial—in which predetermined positions are staked out and the purpose of argument is to expose the vulnerability of others' positions and the superiority of one's own—the key concept in this stage is exploration. Positions must be defended by reference to reasons and evidence; those holding views that are challenged are expected to make the best case for them. At this stage students will clearly demonstrate their critical thinking skills. Yet positions are not scrutinized solely to uncover their weaknesses or contradictions and thereby dismiss them. Instead, they are also examined to ascertain whether anything in them is beneficial or "salvageable" before they are savaged. Positions are analyzed or broken down, and the constituent parts are examined for salutary, suitable, or substantial elements.

Small-Group Conferences. Ultimately, participants will judge for themselves, individually and collectively, the cogency and utility of any perspective. This third stage is perhaps the most deliberative of all the stages. The ward will divide within the room into small groups of six to eight participants. The purpose of the smaller groups is to increase the dialogue among participants. The groups discuss the various perspectives or proposals offered. They weigh the evidence and arguments for and against positions; they raise questions about those positions and work through their assumptions, implications, and inferences.

While this stage may not necessarily add to the scrutiny of the second stage, it allows for more dialogue and participation. Although many in the ward may have spoken during stages one and two, this stage holds out the possibility of drawing out, and from, even more participants. Research shows that the smaller the group, the more likely that participants will speak, will focus on the topic, will follow the discussion, and will show initiative, cooperation, and an interest in influencing others and in offering solutions.[37]

The purpose of the conferences is not discussion for the sake of discussion, but to come to some conclusion or decision as to what should be done about the issue at hand. Each conference group tries to draw or to create from the pool of perspectives a position or decision that seems to accommodate or incorporate as many salutary perspectives as possible. The ideal would be to find a perspective that either embraced all worthy points of view in the pool or transcended the contradictions among perspectives. Although contradictions cannot be resolved or reconciled, they can be transcended by finding or creating a view above or beyond the constituent perspectives.

Such conclusions or decisions are attempted, or accomplished, by exploring and examining perspectives to discover or generate a collective common position or interest. The position or interest is common not because it is made up of or out of all available perspectives in the pool, but because it is made from all and is contributed to by all, even those perspectives ultimately rejected. From all the stones available, we build a bridge, but it is not a bridge built of all available stones.

Voting. Once the small groups have finished deliberating, the ward reconvenes and takes reports from the conferences on the results of their deliberations. The conclusions or recommendations of the groups would then be scrutinized, with the expectation that the groups will defend, again with reasons and evidence, the results of their deliberations and will argue in a similar fashion against the conclusions and recommendations of other groups.

Having completed this stage of scrutiny and deliberation, or having run out of time,[38] the ward votes through private ballot, show of hands, or some other mechanism decided by the ward, on the surviving recommendations. Votes are counted, and a final decision, made by the entire group, will be reached on a recommendation.

While this recommendation is the ward's decision, it may not definitively resolve the issue. First, the result of each ward is then presented to the Democratic Assembly consisting of representatives from all the wards. Here the representatives undergo the same democratic procedures, including small-group discussions, to come to a recommendation on the issue. Once a recommendation is made in the assembly, the representatives return to their wards to discuss, and defend, that recommendation. The wards then ratify or defeat the recommendation. Ratification by a majority of the wards passes the recommendation. Failure to secure approval by the majority requires the Democratic Assembly to meet again, with a special focus on the criticisms of their original recommendation, and to render a new, or to reinforce the original, recommendation. A recommendation cannot be passed into law without support of two-thirds of the wards. In the graffiti example, the wards and assembly might pass a schoolwide rule: anyone caught defacing school property must spend her/his free time over five consecutive Saturdays working on specific jobs related to maintenance of the grounds and the building(s).[39]

When to call a halt to the democratic process is itself a recommendation to be made by the wards through the democratic procedures, as is the ratification process itself. Some schools, for example, might want to extend the ratification process; some might want less or more than a two-thirds majority. Indeed, the democratic procedures themselves should be discussed and decided by the schools themselves. Some schools might want teachers to serve as moderators in the students' wards and then to form their own wards to deliberate later on a particular issue. Some schools might want teachers to be part of the student wards, with moderators picked by lot to serve for a specified time. In some schools teachers' wards could be the equivalent of the Senate to the students' House. Differences between what the teachers and the students want could be hammered out in a joint committee and then presented to the wards as a joint resolution. The principal of the school might serve as the executive and hold veto power, which the House and Senate can override. Perhaps this makes the school board, then, the Supreme Court.

Deliberative Democracy

However schools decide to carry out the democratic procedures, they must be sure that those procedures take advantage of the skills of deliberation and that, as far as possible, the procedures mirror the deliberative procedures that students may enter when they are citizens. The procedures outlined above are ones that could serve as democratic procedures in deliberative democracy. There might well be modifications, such as less small-group work and fewer, if any, attempts to ratify recommendations made "up the line."

Benjamin Barber's multichoice ballot is a good example of how wards or neighborhood assemblies would feasibly deliberate, especially with regard to initiatives. Rather than simply voting a proposition up or down, participants in wards would be given a range of choices. The range might include such categories as "yes in principle—strongly for the proposal; yes in principle—but not a first priority; no in principle—strongly against the proposal; no with respect to this formulation—but not against the proposal in principle . . . and no for the time being " (1984, 286).

Something very much like the school procedures needs to be in effect to meet the requirements of democratic deliberation and thus of autonomy. The purpose of deliberation in both schools and society is clear: it should result in good policy decisions, which does not mean that all decisions will necessarily turn out to establish good policies; experience may prove some of them to be weak, even deplorable, in practice. But all decisions should be the result of good—that is, sound—critical thinking.

In school as well as in society participants are encouraged to articulate their perspectives, to defend and issue challenges, and to listen to and consider perspectives that they otherwise might not imagine or entertain. While such participation might foster an attitude of open-mindedness, the participant need not bring that attitude to the democratic procedures, though she must exercise that behavior while in those procedures. If she does not, if she does not listen and therefore cannot reproduce accurately the perspective of another, then she shall be censured. One must listen carefully to what is said not necessarily because one has an attitude of caring, though one may, but to understand another's perspective and arguments for it. A listener does not have to value the perspective that she hears, but she must strive to understand it, since she can be held accountable for what she hears. Indeed, one might care deeply about a speaker, but not listen well; one may not care at all for a speaker, but listen attentively. The latter is not the goal of either an education in deliberation or of democratic procedures, but it is an acceptable result.

While we all want participants who speak sincerely and who will not misrepresent their interests or positions, it seems that such characteristics can be downplayed in dialogic or deliberative democracy. The focus must be on articulating, hearing, probing, challenging, and defending positions through arguments and questions. Because positions will be scrutinized, there is little to be gained by misrepresenting oneself or one's position. It must be the strength of the argument that is the focus and that can win the day. The rules of the procedures establish the norms of conduct and behavior. As Michael Oakeshott put it, the "conditions formulated in rules [are] indifferent to the merits of any interest or the truth or error of any belief" (1975, 172).

Ralph Waldo Emerson said that "our [democratic] institutions . . . are all educational, for responsibility educates fast. The town meeting is, after the high school, a higher school."[40] Real issues for which students take responsibility will educate fast. So, too, as Emerson says, will politics. The democratic procedures used in both settings seek to structure an environment that uses a certain set of behaviors all related to deliberation, behaviors in which there are rules that underscore requisite behaviors as well as the sanctions imposed for failure to comply. This is in itself a lesson in responsibility.

Schools, however, are not the same as political communities, as Mary Ann Raywid (1976) reminds us. They are different in at least three ways. First, political society is concerned with such overarching social issues as defense, health care, welfare, and the like. Schools seek only to educate students. Second, whereas political participation is voluntary, schooling is compulsory (until students are sixteen). Last, citizens propose and choose ends and purposes for their communities; children are too young and inexperienced to do so. Thus such proposals and choices must fall to adults, especially in schools where adults act in loco parentis.

What Raywid overlooks, even assuming that all that she said is true, is how political issues are decided and political choices are made. Pupils need education and practice in know-how—that is, how to propose, how to question, how to decide, how to judge, and how to choose. When students are young and inexperienced, provide them with age- and experience-appropriate issues and choices. As much as possible, let the students undergo, or undertake, the same democratic processes, or their age-appropriate approximations, as citizens do. This, of course, is what will occur in an education in deliberation in democratic schools.

Yet in the proposal for an education in deliberation, I have made participation a requirement. Isn't it ironic that in an education whose foundation is critical thinking and deliberation, I have made participation compulsory? The argument for compulsion is that students must practice the skills of deliberation to develop and to control those skills. Without question, such practice and familiarity with the democratic procedures will help to make participants knowledgeable about, as well as confident and comfortable in, the procedures. Yet some might turn against participation, might be turned off by their experiences or by mandatory practices, the way some students are turned off by mandatory community services or by too many basketball practices.

Yet practice, required practice, is essential if skills are to be developed. It is one thing to know that free throws are shot from the foul line. But to have the skill of shooting free throws, one actually has to shoot them, again and again and again, if one is going to be good at it; that is, if it is a skill that one owns. To own the skills of deliberation and judgment, one actually has "to *use* the ideas, has [to] be in the *habit* of using them, and *use* is always far more complicated than simple recall or propositions or rules or even analysis" (Sizer, 1992, 26; emphases in the original).

Requiring practice through compulsory participation may turn off some students to democratic participation. I am not insisting that students value participation; I am insisting that they must be practiced in it. They must be able to do it, and they should be able to do it well. But they do not have to be the kind of persons who love deliberation, who can do it but must also want to do it. That is for them to decide. Students should come to see for themselves, through their experience and judgment, the value in deliberative democracy. They should not be socialized or indoctrinated into valuing participation as part of what it means to be a good citizen.

If education in deliberation cultivates students' judgment, then why not let them decide on some occasions whether to participate in the democratic wards and assemblies? If it is the democratic school's mission to develop in each student the skills of deliberation, then let them decide. The compromise position here, and it is a good one, is to permit students to decide when they will participate with the proviso that they must participate each year in some designated number of wards or assemblies. In this way, all can be assured of ample practice in the skills of democratic deliberation, while the students have the freedom to exercise their judgment as to which issues they will help resolve or decide. They can be steered, therefore, as Aristotle said, "by the rudders of pleasure and pain" *(Ethics,* 1172a21).

Giving students the choice of when to participate seems to eliminate any difference between student participation and citizen participation. Of course, what a student cannot do that a citizen (an adult) can do is decide whether to participate at all. Students must participate on at least some required number of issues, but no school official is going to ask them to explain their choices. The same is true for an adult; no one is necessarily going to ask for an explanation of why he does or does not participate. Indeed, for both students and citizens, autonomy may not ever be a factor in democratic deliberation. School officials cannot ask students to reflect on how an issue or decision affects their lives; conceivably, a citizen may himself never be asked and may never think about that.

Then how is democracy the public exercise of autonomy? For those who are self-reflective, who decide when to participate on the basis of the importance of the issue to living out their conception of the good life, democracy is the public exercise or expression of deliberations already performed in private (though not necessarily alone). The public exercise then has three benefits related to autonomy. One, the participant must give an account of his decision; that is, he must present and defend his positions to a wider, and different, audience, to persons with different perspectives and experiences. Deliberating in this setting solidifies or modifies his perspective as he takes responsibility for it. Second, he is now deciding with others on a policy matter that will affect his life, or his conception of the good life, or perhaps even his identify. Third, the policy matter clearly involves self-reflectivity where the self is now not just one's self but is the collectivity itself.

Yet by the same logic aren't democratic deliberations in schools also exercises in autonomy? Imagine, for example, that the issue before the democratic assembly, and the democratic wards, is when to begin the school day. Many want to begin the school day one hour earlier. Since some of the students live and work on farms, this arrangement might interfere with their morning work schedules. Allowances might have to be made to accommodate these students; such considerations or accommodations would be part of the deliberations. Yet might a student think to herself: "Gee, I have to start work at five in the morning. I can't finish my chores and get to school an hour earlier. Why do I have to do these chores anyway? I can never do anything in the mornings with my friends. Farm life is stupid. What's the value of being stuck all the way out here?"

It is plausible that this student's thinking could take such a turn, even though it is not required. But that is the point. The *school* cannot require her to call into question the nature of the life she leads. The thinking goes that far only because she has generated it herself; she is responsible for that. If she decided to write a report, stimulated by discussions with her boyfriend on Marx's notion of "the idiocy of rural life," should the school say no, because it might call into question her way of life? On the contrary, she should be encouraged to pursue her own lines of questioning; but they are her own lines of questioning. Perhaps as one source of evidence she will talk to her parents about farm life and thereby gain a different perspective.[41] Thus, some students will use self-reflective thought in the democratic procedures; some may make self-reflective judgments about when to participate; some in the procedures may even issue challenges that call into question the way of life of some students. All of that is acceptable. It is not acceptable, however, for any staff member in the public schools to insist on any such thinking.

In a different vein, would the democratic procedures in any setting address the problem of permanent minorities, an issue that may involve questions about personal identity? Imagine a school in which a white majority constantly overrules by outvoting the preferences of an African American minority. The minority is outvoted on the music for the prom, on the kind of food they want served in the cafeteria, on the dress code. Would collaboration overcome the problem of this permanent minority?

Surely the process should make all students immediately aware of the problem, though increased awareness and sensitivity are no guarantee of redress. The hope would be that all students would come to see the problem in a wider context by asking themselves, "What kind of community are we creating and living in when some of our members/some of us never get what they/we want?"

There are direct remedies for such a situation. On some decisions the faculty "Senate" might offer a counterproposal; the Head might veto a particular decision in order to move the students to focus on the positions of the African Americans. The school might experiment with a system of cumulative voting whereby each participant has multiple votes, all of which can be placed behind one preference, thus increasing the chances of victory if a bloc, say the African American students, voted for one preference.[42]

The point is to convey to all the possibility on the issue of "asymmetrical intensity," where an indifferent majority might overrule a passionate minority. In that case, participants might proceed "with utmost caution," if not reconsider the proposal. Here is a perfect place for the multichoice ballot that I mentioned in chapter 3.[43]

Such mechanisms may lessen the win/lose atmosphere that characterizes and plagues adversarial deliberation. Still, these mechanisms sidestep the central issue: even within democratic deliberations some groups continue to be at a disadvantage. The best solution, therefore, could be to introduce this dilemma of permanent minorities as an issue for democratic deliberation. Then the school would deliberate directly on how to resolve the dilemma; then the whole school, that community, would be responsible for grappling with what to do on this issue. In this way, the conflict would be brought out into the open.

Conflict such as this, commented Dewey, "is the gadfly of thought. It shocks us out of sheep-like passivity, and sets us at noting and contriving" (1988b, 125). Conflict can "bring to clearer recognition the different interests that are involved and that have to be harmonized in any enduring solution" (1988b, 115).

Democratic, or deliberative, procedures could well accomplish Dewey's desires. They could "bring these conflicts out into the open where their special claims can be seen and appraised, where they can be discussed and judged in the light of more inclusive interests than are represented by either of them separately" (1981, vol. 11, 56).

The authors of *The Challenge of Connecting Learning* made the following observation: "In the final analysis, the real challenge of college, for students and faculty members alike, is empowering individuals to know that the world is far more complex than it first appears, and that they must make interpretive arguments and decision-judgments that entail real consequences for which they must take responsibility and from which they may not flee by disclaiming expertise" (16, 17). From the perspective that informs *Democracy's Midwife,* this is the challenge not of college but of democratic secondary schools. One beneficial byproduct of an education for autonomy would be the obviation of post secondary education for all students but those wishing to enter certain professions or to pursue, perhaps only for a time, the life of a scholar—professional or amateur. With costs of a college education accelerating and with the collapse of the fiction that the work of most jobs *requires* a college degree, students would be relieved of the burden of thinking that "real" education begins with college.

Instead, we could immerse elementary and secondary school students in democratic practices where they will learn to make moral judgments and political decisions by applying the rules of critical thinking and the skills of deliberation. Democratic decision making in democratic high schools puts into play the procedures of critical thinking on real-life school issues. Such issues present in high relief conflicting perspectives, as well as conflicting rules. Such issues also teach how to participate responsibly, since they not only demand certain conduct or behavior, but also involve real consequences for real persons.

Younger students can certainly learn these skills and participate in these practices. They do not have to be postponed until college. Yet the vast majority of schools do not focus on, or often teach, these skills or engage in these practices. Since the routines and schedules of our schools continue to mirror the routines and schedules of nineteenth-century factories, we should not be surprised to find that schools produce few critical thinkers. But presumably societies make schooling to a certain age compulsory for reasons other than keeping their children off the streets or out of the job market. They do so to achieve certain results. If one of those results is to prepare students for active citizenship, then schools need to work toward achieving that result. If our society wants active citizenship, then schools need to work toward achieving that result. If our society wants active citizenship to mirror autonomous decision making, a process requiring at a minimum reflective thought and critical judgment, then schools need to prepare students for participation in something resembling deliberative democracy.

Frank Bryan, a political scientist who investigated "the degree to which the New England town meeting is an institution that promotes citizenship" (1995, 36), concluded that although town meetings hold no promise for mass democracy, they do teach participants lessons essential to the survival of the republic. "[C]itizens," Bryan wrote elsewhere, "cannot be factory-built or found in electronic villages. They must be raised at home." Home, or a setting like it, is necessary because "rearing takes place in real politics: places where community and politics meet, where individuals learn the habit of democracy face to face, where decision-making takes place in the context of communal interdependence."[44]

Schools can be places of "real politics," where community and politics meet and in which individuals can practice democracy face to face. Bryan captures as well what can happen to a community when members are without such practice and experience in real politics:

> Two years ago I spent a year in rural Mississippi. The thing that struck me most about the politics there was the absolute incapacity of the people to do face-to-face democracy. I refuse to attribute this to sinister motives and I found the people in rural Mississippi to be fundamentally a good lot. I think they want to be democrats, but they don't know how. Too many years of denial of fundamental human rights to African Americans, perhaps. But I sat one evening for two hours on hard bleacher seats in a little high school gym where a racially mixed group of 100 tried to organize a booster club for the local basketball teams. I saw not one iota of racism. I saw total ineptitude in talk democracy.

This must be in part due to the absence of institutionalized forums of open decision-making in history and in modern culture. (1995, 40)

Of course, the deliberative decision-making procedures in democratic schools are designed to provide students with practice and experience in "talk democracy." It is part of the standards of democratic education that students practice the skills of deliberation, which are themselves the cornerstone of that education. But open decision making is not simply about practice or rehearsal; it is also about real decision making, decision making in "real politics."

Parents, teachers, administrators, and students who are not interested in deliberative democracy or who think it a utopian dream (or dystopian nightmare) will not press for such skills, practices, or performances. Presumably, such persons will not be interested in autonomy, even in its private uses. But liberals will not be among such persons, nor will staunch democrats, even those who oppose participatory democracy but insist that our representative system requires thoughtful, independent, critical thinkers who can make informed judgments. Democratic schools are the launching pads as well as the proving grounds for those judgments.

What, then, do liberals say to religious parents who insist that any education in critical thinking, and therefore for autonomy, will undermine their religious convictions and thus their way of life? We can only say that here the clash between the religious freedom of the parents and the duty of the liberal state to prepare all future citizens for democratic participation must be decided in favor of the liberal state. There will certainly be deliberations, however, among the parties on this issue. Parents, or their lawyers, who want to argue effectively against the democratic curriculum must do more than simply assert that what is taught is incompatible with their faith. They must make arguments for their claims and against those of the state. They will want, won't they, their children to be able to do so as well. Students, their children, it must be remembered, will learn in an education in deliberation to make arguments *for* their views as well as against others' views. Parents who object to that kind of education seem to object to anything but indoctrination.

Is this to suggest that democratic dialogue and deliberative decision making are to be part of our national educational standards? It is indeed. Democratic discussions, democratic classrooms, and democratic wards/assemblies will, of course, be essential components of public education. There may be some parents, teachers, and community leaders who wish to avoid such essentials in their sectarian or private schools. That is their right. Their children or students need not participate in, or have, democratic assemblies or democratic classrooms. However much these students may be at a disadvantage by the absence of such arrangements, it is their right to opt out completely from those components of democratic education.

They may not, on the other hand, opt out from learning the skills of deliberation, of critical thinking, which is, to repeat, the cornerstone of democratic education. Nor can they avoid practicing those skills in democratic discussions where different voices and perspectives, different attitudes and experiences, may be heard and evaluated. Therefore, all students, as preparation for democratic citizenship, must learn and must demonstrate in discussions the skills of critical thinking and deliberative decision making, whether in the classrooms of a private school or, if homeschooled, in their homes.

Should the interests of the state—here, a liberal democratic state—therefore override the interests of a family or community? If the state can mandate national democratic standards that all students, regardless of their school setting, must meet, then the state's interests supersede those of the parents. If the converse holds, then the interests of the family supersede those of the state.

The individual states in the United States mandate various educational requirements that all schools, and all students, must fulfill, irrespective of that school setting (public, private, home), if those schools and programs are going to be accredited. Because the purpose of democratic education is to prepare all future citizens for active democratic participation, the state has an obligation to ensure that every citizen meets the requirements of such participation, regardless of what any individual state, family, or leader wants. Thus the liberal democratic state establishes national standards for democratic education.

It is one thing to live a life in which revelation or intuition is championed and reason is minimized; it is quite another life when reason(ing) is not developed. It is one thing to forsake and reject reason; it is quite another not to know from the outset what reason is or how to do it. To reject reason one must first understand what it is and how to use it. Simply to avoid reason requires nothing more than indoctrination. On this point, Jefferson was clear and correct: if we as a people do not inform our discretion, then we as a people cannot be safe in our freedom or our democracy.

Notes

1. 1987, 392. Shuy goes on to say that by using dialogue journals Staton, the principal investigator in the NIE study on which Shuy is reporting, "was able to demonstrate the actual development of reasoning ability throughout the school year" (392).

2. Vygotsky recognized the need in learning for collaboration between teacher and student. The teacher could aid the student in formulating and working out problems or situations that the student cannot quite manage on her own. See L. S. Vygotsky, *Thought and Language* (Cambridge, Mass.: MIT Press, 1962).

3. 1993, 170, 177. Lawson goes on to list what he thinks are age-appropriate thinking skills to be taught at different grades. The list is based on a survey of hypothesis-testing strategies among students K-12 and on Piaget's model of cognitive development.

4. This is also in keeping with Piaget's stages of preoperational, concrete operational, and formal operational thinking.

5. Ann Berthoff says, "whatever you really learn, you teach yourself. If you only learn what you are told, then you are only keeping in mind, for a longer or shorter interval, what was put there by somebody else. What you really learn is what you discover—and you learn to discover by questioning" (1978, 9) and, we might add, by writing.

6. See Dewey, 1916, 107-8ff and 153ff.

7. McGinley and Tierney point out through their studies of students' self-directed reading and writing projects that students marshall and use a broader range of their reading and writing powers when they explore a topic on their own. This broader range consists of wide and varying perspectives often missed when students closely follow the teacher's assignments.

8. What kinds of writing should students do? Almost any kind, comments Berthoff, a philosopher of rhetoric and composition with over forty years of experience teaching reading and writing: "short papers, long papers, throw-away papers, one sentence written ten different ways—ten different intentions written in one-sentence patterns; papers written out of class, papers in class, papers to be forgotten, papers to be revised and edited" (1981, 40). In short, any kind of discursive paper that begins with chaos and ends with meaning.

9. See Banesh Hoffman, *The Tyranny of Testing* (Westport, Conn.: Greenwood Press, 1962).

10. Every semester after the first exam in my introductory political theory course, I distribute to the class three essays from that exam. All three are on the same question, each written by a different student. I ask the class to assign a grade to each paper. With about 90 percent accuracy the students assign an A to the essay that we—my graduate assistants and I—also gave an A, a C to the one that we gave a C, and a D—or worse, they are harsh critics—to the one that we gave a D. Sometimes a florid essay without substance will receive several B's or even a few A's, but students in discussion can easily point out its flaws.

11. See Jonathan Kozol, 1991, and my epilogue.

12. Every school, and not just every college, should have a writing center staffed by experts (professionals and volunteers) and by teachers who can offer assistance with writing problems and the technical aspects of writing.

13. A side benefit of this arrangement is that it helps to overcome the snobbery of any teachers at the post secondary level who look down on schoolteachers. At the same time, promoting teachers to a level at which they could teach both in their schools and in departments or schools of education serves as well to elevate the status and esteem of teachers in their own eyes and in the eyes of the community. Along with the professoriate, these teachers, as well as those in a transition level between pure school teaching and this dual post, might grade the national essay exams. Finally, this method ensures that those who train teachers are not the most remote from practice, but are, instead, the least remote.

14. Janet L. Williamson, *The Greensboro Plan* (Santa Rosa, Calif.: Foundation for Critical Thinking, 1991), 1.

15. Williamson, *The Greensboro Plan*. Again, keep in mind that this presupposes no prior teacher training in critical thinking.

16. Williamson, *The Greensboro Plan*, 9. Perl and Wilson's four-year study of writing teachers at work shows, according to Farr and Daniels, that "the effective writing teachers viewed their students as bringing considerable linguistic skill to the task of learning to write. These teachers saw students as linguistically competent and described their own task as one of helping the student along to the next stage in a continuous process of language development. The less effective teachers, on the other hand, were more likely to view their students' language as being underdeveloped or deficient; they tended not to give their students as much credit for being able to use language effectively on their own terms." Marcia Farr and Harvey Daniels, *Language Diversity and Writing Instruction* (Urbana, Ill.: ERIC Clearinghouse on Urban Education, 1986), 47-48, quoted in Williamson, *The Greensboro Plan*, 10.

17. 1990a, 250ff, and chapter 19.

18. Of course, Socrates is also famous for pointing out why the answers of his interlocutors will not do. Instead of providing definitive answers, he brings his interlocutors to an awareness of their own ignorance, as he points out the inadequacy of their thinking and the depths of his and their perplexity.

Such a method and its results are to be contrasted with the kinds of responses of the people of Ephesus. They "are just like the things they say in their books—always on the move. As for abiding by what is said, or sticking to a question, or quietly answering and asking questions in turn, there is less than nothing of that in their capacity. . . . If you ask any one of them a question, he will pull out some little enigmatic phrase from his quiver and shoot it off at you; and if you try to make him give an account of what he has said, you will only get hit by another, full of strange turns of language. You will never reach any conclusion with any of them, ever" (*Theaetetus*, 180b-c, 309).

19. Another reason for lecturing was that before the seventh century writing was nothing but an uninterrupted string of letters. There was no punctuation (and rules of punctuation) and no spacing. The only way to make sense of this string was to divide it into separate words. The only way to do that was to read each line slowly and aloud, separating the words as best one could. Monks dictated these "words" to scribes. "Illiterate monks," comments Barry Sanders, "made better copies because meaning did not get in the way of accuracy" (1994, 134).

20. This is not to suggest that educators, students, parents, and citizens should accept overcrowding. No curriculum, no matter how innovative or progressive, can be effective in overcrowded schools and classrooms. Without question, great educational results can be achieved when the student-teacher ratio is lowered. In New York City, in the mid-1970s, Deborah Meier, a frustrated public school teacher, started the Smaller Schools of Smaller Classes reform movement. According to her model, each class should have no more than twenty students; no school should have more than twenty teachers. (See "A City School Experiment That Actually Works" by Sara Mosle, *New York Times Maga-*

zine, 28 May 1995.) Moreover, all of the teachers should be in the classroom and not, as is the current practice, in "out of classroom" positions such as curriculum coordinator, staff developer, or resource instructor (Mosle, 49). In the schools developed by Meier "[K]ids took notes, wrote stories, kept journals, composed essays—except now their work received more attention" (49). For more on class and school size, see Meier, 1995; "The Tennessee Study of Class Size in the Early School Grades" by Frederick Moeller, available from the American Academy of Arts and Sciences in Cambridge, Massachusetts; as well as the series of articles entitled "Multiple Choice" that ran in the *New York Times* during the week preceding Mosle's article. See especially within that series "New Schools Seeking Small Miracles," 22 May 1995.

21. These and other points of Easley's are summarized in Paul, 1990a, 212-13; for references to Easley's work, see Paul, 1990a, 223.

22. Critical thinking is what Barry Sanders describes as full literacy (1994, chapter 7). "Without the critical, reflective thinking that [full] literacy fosters, [persons] are unable to filter anything out, moving through life as victims, prey to every image that rolls off the TV screen or out of the movie theater—images, in large part, of violence and sadism" (137).

It should not be thought that I am here excluding the study of other languages and cultures. Indeed, as Richard Dagger points out (personal communication), studying other languages may even help us to know, to use, and to appreciate our own.

23. Critical thinking is the core across the curriculum, but it is not the entire curriculum. Students need content to think about, and that content can vary. Still, there should also be national standards that broadly specify content. My specifications here are not startling, unless they are startlingly conventional. As a minimum, high school graduates should have had the equivalent of four years of literature, three years of math, one year of computer, two years of history, two of laboratory science, and three years of a foreign language. This distribution gives each student knowledge and experience in the primary modes of knowing. I have in mind the empirical-analytical method of the sciences and the rational-interpretive method of the humanities. The social sciences, depending on the specific field and the topic within that field, are a mixture of these two modes. I say "the equivalent" because there are better methods for structuring content than those used in discrete departments and disciplines. For more on this see Meier, 1995, and Sizer, 1984 and 1992.

24. *Experience and Nature* (Chicago, Ill.: Open Court, 1926), 222; quoted in Siegel, 1988, 77.

25. I shall address the issue of inequity in more detail in the epilogue.

26. Glickman says that only older students should realistically expect to "have actual representation in school governance" (37).

27. See George Herbert Mead for the importance of internalizing the perspective of the group. *Mind, Self, and Society* (Chicago: University of Chicago Press, 1933).

28. I acknowledge that these divisions are largely arbitrary; some middle school children, for example, might be ready for democratic assemblies. I am simply trying to outline one possible deliberative hierarchy by taking into account at what ages students

are probably ready to move out of preconventional or conventional thinking and move toward conventional and postconventional thinking.

29. 1992, 89. As evidence of recent research Sizer cites Fred M. Newmann's report, "Linking Restructuring to Authentic Student Achievement," *Phi Delta Kappan* (February 1991), 458-63. Sizer himself is no novice in this area. Previously the dean of the Harvard Graduate School of Education and headmaster of Phillips Academy (Andover), Sizer is currently professor of education at Brown University and chairman of the Coalition of Essential Schools, a high school and university partnership that works to redesign the American high school to foster greater student learning and achievement. Currently there are over 1,000 high schools in the United States either implementing new practices on the basis of the coalition's principles or planning for or at least exploring the possibilities of changes in accordance with those principles. See Sizer, 1984 and 1992.

30. The phrase is from Pierre Bourdieu. See P. Bourdieu and J. Coleman, eds., *Social Theory for a Changing Society* (Boulder, Colo.: Westview Press, 1991), 384; quoted in Gutierrez, Rymes, and Larson, 1995, 467.

31. Richard Pratte (1988) suggests that young children, to prepare for dilemmas and conflict resolution, should role-play problem situations before actually encountering them. "Young children can use dolls, puppets, or masks; older students can be given role cards that define . . . their roles in the situation" (23). Such role-playing is a way for children to attempt to step into the perspectives of others without feeling as if their own identities are in jeopardy.

32. "The act of sharing ideas, of having to put one's own views clearly to others, of finding defensible compromises and conclusions, is in itself educative" (Sizer, 1992, 89). The literature on collaborative learning is vast and growing. For a summary, see Edward B. Fiske, *Smart Schools, Smart Kids* (New York: Simon and Schuster, 1991), 81-86.

33. See also Gutmann and Thompson, 1996.

34. To write a class constitution, the class could first study the making of the constitution by the Founding Fathers. They could then break into small groups to work on different sections of the document. Upon completion of a section, the group responsible for it would present it to and defend it before the entire class. There would be democratic discussion on each section, as students argued for and against proposed amendments and changes, as well as for and against ratification of that section.

35. For an excellent, though somewhat dated, discussion of democratic practices in the classroom, see Rosalind Zapf, 1959.

36. I have elsewhere discussed such procedures in the context of promoting compound individuality, the liberal self beyond individualism. I referred to the procedures in that context as the "generative procedures," where the principal concern was to generate a compound common good from diverse and competing perspectives. Because of that concern, and because of that context, many of the details of the generative procedures are different from what I am describing here as democratic procedures for democratic schools. Nevertheless, the basic structure remains the same. See Crittenden, 1992.

37. In addition to the literature on collaborative learning, see also B. M. Bass and R. T. M. Norton, "Group Size and Leaderless Discussions," *Journal of Applied Psychology*

35 (1951), and A. P. Hare, *Handbook of Small Group Research* (1976); both cited in Mansbridge, 1980, 371-72. Mansbridge states that small-group research shows that participatory groups attain consensus not only by bringing common interests to the group, but also by producing changes in interest when in the group process (282). This is in accordance with Tocqueville's views on how interests change through participation. Mansbridge summarizes: "Dividing a large meeting into small groups facilitates perceiving a conflict from another's point of view" (1982, 135). See also the *Harvard Assessment Seminars,* First Report, 1990; Second Report, 1992, both available from Harvard University Graduate School of Education and the Kennedy School of Government.

38. It is certainly possible, and feasible, to have a time limit on democratic decision making on any one issue, though that time limit may be counted by the number of meetings (over days or weeks) as well as by the number of hours. A necessary "expert" testimony might or might not be counted as part of the time limit.

39. See Apple and Beane, 1995, 2. School newspapers may take on new significance in democratic schools. Articles could provide information on the forthcoming agenda, or could offer point-counterpoint arguments on the issues. After legislation, the newspapers could describe and explain what happened and could offer editorials decrying or supporting the democratic outcome.

40. "The Fortune of the Republic," in *Complete Works,* Volume 6, (Cambridge, Mass.: Riverside Press, 1904), 527.

41. As I have said before, and I think it bears repeating, college is the venue par excellence for an education in autonomy. That, of course, is not all that college is. Yet both a student's collegiate academic work and the democratic procedures used in the college should involve, even elicit, self-reflection. Post secondary education, the workplace, the armed services are for young adults environments in which they should hold in mind questions about identity (Who am I?), purpose (Why am I here? Why am I doing this?), and destiny (Where do I want to go? What do I need or want to do?).

42. See Lani Guinier (1994) for discussion of such a case and of cumulative voting as a possible remedy.

43. Barber, 1984, 287. There are other possibilities as well. One is "the principle of proportionality" (see Peter Jones in Miller and Seidentop, 1983); another is "consociational democracy" (see David Miller in Graeme Duncan). Thanks to Richard Dagger for reminding me of these.

44. Frank Bryan and John McClaughry, *The Vermont Papers: Recreating Democracy on a Human Scale* (Chelsea, Vt.: Chelsea Green, 1989), 3. Bryan's conclusions rest on data collected from 1,215 (and counting) town meetings held between 1970 and 1994. For more statistical information, see Bryan, 1995, 44, n. 9.

1) a curriculum for colleges not primary schools? How to establish building blocks?

2) analogy answer idealued version of democratic politics?

3) most formely meetings/ assemblees want a cant follow most of these procedures

Epilogue

Youth, as the saying goes, may constitute only 20 percent of the population, but it constitutes 100 percent of the future. So our children are our future, and if we want to see America's future, then, as the wise man said, go to the schools and look around (Mitchell, 1981, 188). The sights, as we know, are not always prepossessing, for while our children are our greatest treasure, many are also our greatest victims. Inner-city youths often live surrounded by degradation of all sorts: human, physical, emotional, environmental. We place many of our children in buildings we call schools, though some of these buildings are so dilapidated that they are dangerous, collapsing wrecks; we ask these children to become literate and knowledgeable, though we do not provide enough books or paper or beakers or computers; and we ask them to learn from teachers who themselves are often scared, bored, burnt out, angry, and undereducated

When the test scores of these children reflect insufficient learning, when the dropout rate soars, when employers complain that high schools are graduating illiterates, then we may blame the children. If we push past the children, we may blame their families for their neglect and indifference and hostility. If we push past their families, we may blame society for the decline of morals and virtues. If we have the courage to ask how society got this way, we shall inevitably return at some point to the failures of our schools to educate our youth. The great question is, then, educate how?

That question pertains to all of our schools, not just to impoverished schools. In most of our schools, rich and poor, our students can think, but our public schools do not teach them to think critically. Wedded as they are to multiple-choice tests, our schools do teach thinking, but not systematic, precise thinking, which I have been calling critical thinking. Does this mean that our citizens, products of these schools, cannot participate effectively in democracy? If they could think critically, would they want to participate in our system?

The failure of our schools to teach critical thinking does not appear to jeopardize our representative democracy, because our democracy does not rest or depend upon the informed judgments and critical thinking of most of our citizens. Indeed, the kind of education that our public schools do provide is adequate, maybe even superb, for our democracy: future citizens learn enough to support, and participate in, the system but not enough to challenge it. And our representative system is perfect for this type of education: full citizen participation is not crucial to the perpetuation of the system.

In this book I have attempted to address what Sheldon Wolin describes as "the desperate problem of democracy"—to develop a fairer system for airing and resolving, where possible, conflicts and contestations.[1] My principal argument is not that democracy means that all political power must be exercised by the people. Rather, the principal argument is how the people exercise political power (as well as, but secondarily, when they can do so). That exercise must be deliberative, and it must be so for at least two reasons.

One reason is, as Aristotle said, that deliberative political decisions will reflect a collective wisdom not found in any single individual's ruminations, no matter how perspicacious the individual thinker. A second reason is that deliberative exercise is the expression or use of our capacities to make critical, reflective judgments. Those capacities are ones that a liberal society most often encourages of its citizens when the decisions taken are restricted to the private sphere. This sphere, also known as the civil society as opposed to the state, is the realm of autonomous choice.

Liberals want to be able to exercise their individual right of suffrage, but they also want to be protected from intrusions by the state into those areas of their lives that they consider private, beyond the reach of government or democratic majorities. Yet at times politics intrudes into the private or autonomous sphere of liberals. That occurs especially where issues of identity or issues central to definitions of self or of the good life become political—that is, when issues matter to groups, associations, neighborhoods, regimes, states, or the nation. As personal identities grow more intricate and open, especially in a multicultural society, and as conceptions of the good life collide, then issues that were once viewed as private and personal more and more become political.

This shift toward the political heralds, it seems, a shift in liberalism away from neutrality and toward autonomy, as persons want and need to seek political solutions to problems that deeply affect living out their good lives. The boundary between public and private becomes permeable, as autonomy becomes a focus in both spheres. Thus the process for making self-reflective choices in private is extended into public decision making; persons who are self-ruling in private want to be self-governing in public. If autonomy is the hallmark of both public and private decision making, then education should prepare future citizens and adults for such autonomy.

If our schools did educate for autonomy, they would also educate for a different kind of citizen. That citizen might challenge the representative system, for she might well want, and demand, to project her autonomy into the political sphere where decisions are made that affect her life but that are currently beyond her power or influence. Of course, she can join with other citizens and "vote the rascals out," the standard retort of those who champion representative democracy. But the public, or political, power to deliberate with others before deciding for oneself how to vote on an issue is largely denied all citizens but those elected to represent our views. To control, to author, to direct one's own life cannot be done by proxy; autonomy cannot be represented. To be fully self-ruling one must also be, and many will want to be, self-governing.

Thus my thesis is straightforward: many, perhaps most, persons who are self-ruling, or autonomous, will also want to be self-governing, or directly and deliberatively democratic. They will want, in other words, to make the decisions that affect their lives; they will not want representatives doing it for them. Therefore, if we are serious about autonomy and an education that prepares our future citizens to make autonomous political choices, then we must also be serious about the possibilities for, and plausibility of, more deliberative—what I also call dialogic—democratic arenas.

Preparation for political participation is not the only outcome of an education for autonomy. It is also a way to prepare persons for choosing the good life—planning, designing, evaluating, and pursuing the life that they think is good. In the liberal view, education for autonomy thus prepares students to be good citizens and good persons. Persons who are serious about autonomy, and this would include many liberal theorists, ought to want an education that will prepare persons for autonomy.[2]

Deliberative democracy rests on the presupposition that human beings are capable of self-reflective choice and have the capacity to act on such choices. Because all humans have these capacities, all are worthy of respect owed to people who can be self-ruled. People ought to be free to develop and exercise these capacities, though for children and young adults freedom is not enough. They also need to be guided toward the development and instructed in the use of those capacities so as to improve the possibility that those capacities will be actualized. This is the purpose of an education in deliberation, and in a liberal democratic society it ought to be guaranteed to all her future citizens.

But it isn't. "We talk of the importance of 'public' schools in a democracy," writes Theodore Sizer, "yet we know that our 'public' schools today are profoundly segregated by class—the wealthy suburbs and the inner city. The contrast between the Lake Forests and the Chicagos, the Scarsdales and the Harlems, is blatant. We all know this, but we mention it as rarely as possible" (1995, 83).

In this age of multiculturalism and value pluralism we Americans seem sensitive about exclusion on the basis of personal characteristics, but we seem almost inured to exclusion by lack of resources. This sort of exclusion is pandemic, with inequalities, as Sheldon Wolin says, increasing "at a cancerous rate" (1996, 106). We should not be surprised, therefore, to find the inequalities of the larger society reflected in our schools. Nor should we be surprised to see there as well the reflection of the increasing disparity between rich and poor.[3] Indeed, the inner cities of America, schools included, put the third world in our own advanced industrial midst. If we are two nations, as Andrew Hacker says, one rich and predominantly white, the other black and mostly poor, then we are also two educational nations, separate and unequal. A Harvard University study found that schools became more segregated in the 1990s. Despite the growing diversity among our population and support for integration as reflected in public opinion surveys, the 1990s show a marked increase in segregation, thus reversing a trend toward integration seen in a period between the 1960s and the 1980s. Gary Orfield, the study's principal author, found that schools with predominantly black and Hispanic students "had more transient student bodies, fewer teachers qualified in their subject areas, parents lacking political power, more frequent health problems, and lower test scores."[4]

Without equalized funding to our public schools we can readily imagine a two-tier democratic education in which the resource-rich schools teach their students to deliberate effectively, while the second-tier schools struggle simply to get students to, and keep them in, classes. Such a system reinforces the elitist aspects of deliberative democracy.[5]

One person who has not shied away from the topic of inequities or the outrage that the topic engenders is Jonathan Kozol. His book *Savage Inequalities* is a wholesale indictment of our system of school funding, as well as of our callous indifference to the palpable suffering of those subjected to these grotesque educational inequities. Consider:

- Camden, New Jersey, with the highest poverty rate for children in the United States, spends $4,000 per pupil. The state average is $5,000 per pupil. Princeton, New Jersey, spends on average about $8,000 per pupil. At Pyne Point Junior High School in Camden there are no computers, the science labs have no lab equipment, there are no goalposts on the football fields and no sports equipment. In Princeton, New Jersey, "the high school students work in comfortable computer areas equipped with some 200 IBMs, as well as with a hookup to Dow Jones to study stock transactions" (1991, 137-40, 158).

- At the high school in East Orange, New Jersey, there are no athletic fields; the track team has to practice in the school's hallways. At the high school in Montclair, New Jersey, there are "two recreation fields, four gyms, a dance room, a wrestling room, a weight room with a universal gym, tennis courts, a track, and indoor areas for fencing" (157). One of these schools is upper-middle class and predominantly white; the other is 99.9 percent black. I cannot imagine that I need to mention which is which.

- In Detroit, with a school population that is 89 percent black, the city school system "is so poorly funded that three classes have to share a single set of books in elementary schools" (198). At MacKenzie High School courses in word processing are taught without word processors. Students simply learn the keyboard in case they ever get to use a typewriter or computer. While Detroit spent $3,600 per pupil in 1988, Grosse Pointe, a Detroit suburb, spent $5,700 per pupil; another suburb, Birmingham, spent the most in the state: $6,400 per pupil.

- In Texas, where the state supreme court has ruled unconstitutional the current inequitable system of state educational funding, per pupil spending ranges from $2,000 in the poorest districts to $19,000 in the wealthiest (223).

- Public School 261 in District 10 in the North Bronx section of New York City is a converted roller-skating rink. The school has a capacity of 900 but actually serves 1,300. "Two first grade classes share a single room without a window, divided only by a blackboard. Four kindergartens and a sixth grade class of Spanish-speaking children have been packed into a single room in which, again, there is no window. A second grade bilingual class of 37 children has its own room but again there is no window" (85-86).

By contrast, Public School 24 in Riverdale "has a spacious library that holds almost 8,000 books. The windows are decorated with attractive, brightly colored curtains and look out on flowering trees. . . . In a large and sunny first grade classroom that I enter next, I see 23 children, all of whom are white or Asian. In another first grade, there are 22 white children and 2 others who are Japanese. There is a computer in each class. Every classroom also has a modern fitted sink."[6]

- East St. Louis, which is 98 percent black, is lined with chemical and metal plants. But rather than being sources of employment, these plants, which look to hire workers with educations better than the residents of the city can get, are sources of illness. "East St. Louis . . . has some of the sickest children in America. Of 66 cities in Illinois, East St. Louis ranks first in fetal death, first in premature birth, and third in infant death" (20). According to health care authorities, local plants are responsible for much of the mayhem: sewage running in the streets, foul air, high lead levels in the soil (20).

High unemployment in East St. Louis lessens the value of property. With low property values, the tax base is small. The result is a squalid educational system: sewage floods into and forces the closing of two schools; high school teachers meet five classes per day and have between 150 and 175 students; the school system uses more than 70 permanent substitute teachers, paying them each $10,000 per year (23-24); the science labs at East St. Louis High are 30 to 50 years out of date (27).

The governor announces that no additional money will be poured into East St. Louis, because the residents there must help themselves. Meanwhile in the same speech, he announces that a nearby wealthy community will receive a grant to improve that community's sewer system.

These deplorable inequities will not shock anyone who has looked even fleetingly at issues of race, class, and public education in the United States.[7] So what do we do about them? The first remedy must be to increase funding to, as well as change the funding mechanism for, public schools. While this sounds like the usual liberal nostrum of throwing money at a social problem, there can be little debate about the value of greater resources for our inner-city schools, provided that the money arrives, figuratively, on teachers' desks.

That, clearly, has been a problem in the past. As Albert Shanker, past president of the American Federation of Teachers, told a group of teachers, professors, community and business leaders, and heads of philanthropic institutions convened at the American Academy of Arts and Sciences to discuss the current state, and failure, of public education, the central school administration in New York City cannot account for most of the nearly $250,000 that is supposed to be spent in each classroom. "Schools don't buy many new textbooks. There aren't many new computers. Where does the money go? We don't know."[8]

To eliminate this type of bureaucratic black hole, each school should receive from their state a lump-sum budget, based upon dollar allocation per student. Each school would therefore be responsible for determining where the money was spent and for reporting that spending. Not only do individual schools know best where the money has gone, but they also know best where the money should go.

Without question poor schools need massive transfusions of capital. Those cynics who think otherwise should heed the words of many teachers and administrators spread throughout Kozol's book. When challenged on the difference money will make, these teachers and administrators say in unison that anyone from Princeton or Scarsdale or Beverly Hills is welcome at any time to switch places with an inner-city teacher or administrator or student to ascertain whether money would make a difference.

The authors of *A Nation at Risk,* something of a cynosure for school reform from the mid-eighties onward, state simply that "all, regardless of race or class or economic status, are entitled to a fair chance and to the tools for developing their individual powers of mind and spirit to the utmost" (1983, 8). Such rhetoric is still heard today. Little seems to have changed, except the situation may even be worse. Today we have the sorry spectacle of state legislatures in Texas, New Jersey, California, and my own state of Arizona either ignoring, dragging their feet on, or actively thwarting state supreme court mandates to make school funding equitable among and within school districts.

"If an unfriendly foreign power," the authors of the report also said, "had attempted to impose on America the mediocre educational performance that exists today, we might well have viewed it as an act of war" (1983, 5). Who does not believe that our mediocre educational performance is in large measure due to the horrific disparities in educational funding?

Too often citizens, parents, and even teachers and administrators, as well as students themselves, are quick to ascribe the mediocre scholastic performance of minority students to failures of character, family, or background. Yet several recent studies have found that the school environment itself can make a real difference in whether students succeed. An enriched and demanding curriculum, high expectations for all students, parental involvement in the school and in their children's education contribute positively to the achievement of students, including minority students. Underlying these elements in student achievement is the presupposition that the schools will be safe and will have adequate resources.[9]

To achieve equity among all schools, perhaps what we need is an act of war; perhaps that is the only way that our nation will marshall sufficient funds to redress our current resource imbalance. Without such equity we drive inner-city students below mediocrity into despair, where lives of crime and violence appear to be logical career choices.[10]

The act of war, of course, is not against a foreign power, but against ourselves. But who is the enemy? Parents trying to provide the best for their children? Administrators fighting for more control and more money? Teachers looking for greater autonomy in and resources for their classrooms? Teachers' unions? Bureaucracies? As a polity, we certainly have not deliberated on these issues. Nevertheless, we need to act now; we need the funds now. Let us take the funds from the national defense. If that seems too risky, though it is difficult to deny that educating our future citizens is in the national interest and part of our national defense (after all, there is precedent in the National Defense Education Act in the 1960s), then let us establish a federal tax, perhaps a sales tax on gasoline, to be available for every state that needs to revamp some schools. Funds from this tax should be earmarked for exclusive use in school financing to bring underfunded schools to a level equal to the best schools in each state. Included in this revamping would be help in transforming the schools into democratically operated schools educating their pupils in deliberation.

Such a federal tax would shift the burden away from property taxes, which are themselves the source of most of the inequitable funding, and onto the nation. This is a national problem, a national emergency, and a national issue perfect for a national referendum.

With increased funds for schools each state can send to its schools a budget sufficient to address five issues: safety, readiness, class size, resources, and teacher salaries.

Safety. The recent incidents of children shooting children in their schools have reinforced the idea that schools can be dangerous places, even killing fields. Can we make our schools safe havens? We can make sure that much of the violence of the streets remains out of the hallways and classrooms, though this does little to make the neighborhoods themselves safe. School issues are never far from social and economic conditions that surround them, but this is a start. At the very least we can assure that floors and ceilings are safe from collapse; that paint is lead free; that asbestos is removed; and that buildings are properly insulated, heated, and cooled.

> In poll after poll, parents, teachers, and the public rate violent and disruptive behavior as their number one concern with our schools. Yet students who bring weapons to school often are allowed to remain in that school or are simply transferred to another school. Few are suspended for any substantial period or expelled or placed in separate educational facilities. Does it make sense to sacrifice public education by refusing to take action on the 2 or 3 percent of students who are violent or chronically disruptive and who may ultimately force 97 or 98 percent of our children out of public schools? (Shanker, 1995, 48-49)

We should put such students in separate facilities, but let us take those students and facilities to the limit. Make these facilities highly supervised but academically demanding environments. Instead of incarcerating these students in facilities that are more like jails (or are jails), place them away from their families, neighborhoods, and friends in educationally intense boarding schools. Test thereby Mortimer Adler's claim that an education for the best (for British and American boarding-school students) is an education for the rest.[11] In such facilities students can get individualized attention. If they fail here or run away, keep at it until they are of legal age to leave.

Why do this? Because, as Lauren Resnick reminds us, the students with the greatest need for personal and expert instruction are the least likely to get it (1995, 61). For those students at the end of the line, a separation from their home and social environments may permit them to let down their persona and learn. Choate-Rosemary Hall may be a better model for the chronically disruptive than Spofford.[12]

Readiness. Among the goals of America 2000—the Bush/Clinton mission, along with the state governors, to lead the world in education by the year 2000—was the guarantee that every child in America would come to school ready to learn. That meant that all disadvantaged and disabled children would eat high-quality meals and would have access to high-quality preschool programs. All parents would have access to training and support to help them teach their preschoolers at home. All pregnant mothers would have sufficient health coverage to ensure that the chances of low-birthweight babies were minimized.

Without question these are laudable goals. It has been estimated, however, that simply supplying all children with quality meals and preschool programs will cost over $30 billion.[13] Still, we well understand the costs if we fail to provide such programs. Undernourished children who have received little or no medical care throughout their lives come to school at a decided disadvantage. They are not prepared to concentrate, to attend to their lessons, to learn from their teachers or their peers. Schools then spend inordinate amounts of their precious resources trying to take care of these children's many needs. Their teachers also must address those needs and simultaneously teach their classes.

The Committee for Economic Development, a policy group of 250 business leaders, concluded that to address the problems of our poorest and most vulnerable children, we as a nation must fully fund Head Start, a nutritional and educational preschool program, as well as WIC, a federal nutritional program for pregnant women and children under five. The committee was well aware that funding such programs was expensive. Yet the committee maintained that in the long run such funding would save money, since prenatal care, preschool programs, and nutritional supplements help keep children in school, off the streets, out of crime, off of welfare, and out of prison.[14]

Class Size. Results of the Tennessee class-size project indicate that small classes, especially in the early grades (K-3), powerfully improve student academic performance. "Thus, year after year, the students who were originally in smaller classes continued to perform better than the students from regular-sized classes with or without a teacher's aide" (Mosteller, 1995, 125).

The findings of the Tennessee study hold regardless of the setting—suburban, inner city, urban, or rural—the socioeconomic background of the students, or the ethnicity of the children. When Tennessee reduced the class size of K-3 classes in the 17 school districts with the lowest per capita income, the scores of the children in those districts jumped from below average in mathematics to above average. Not only scores but also state rankings (out of 139 school districts) increased, from an average for the 17 districts of 99th in reading and 85th in math in 1989-90, to an average of 78th in reading and 56th in math in 1992-93 (Mosteller, 1995, 122-23).

Additionally, the Tennessee study shows that the effects of early experiences with smaller classes carry over when the children return to regular-sized classes (Mosteller, 1995, 121). "In summary, the evidence is strong that smaller class size [13 to 17 children per class] at the beginning of the school experience does improve the performance of children on cognitive tests. Observations . . . confirm that the effect continues into later grades when children are returned to regular-sized classes. In addition, the implementation of the program for the economically poorest districts seems to be improving the performance of children in these districts by noticeable amounts" (123).

School size is also important in increasing the academic performance of students. Small rural schools in the Midwest consistently have the highest scores on the SAT (Scholastic Assessment Test), and schools with fewer than 300 students do the best. One key factor in this phenomenon appears to be the intimacy of the environment. Principals and teachers can know well the needs, strengths, and weaknesses of the students.[15] Deborah Meier (1995) argues that for best results schools should follow the 20/20 approach: no more than 20 teachers in a school; no more than 20 students per teacher.[16]

Resources and Teacher Salaries. Resources can make a difference. In Kentucky the state supreme court ruled that the entire educational system, because of the disparities in school funding, was unconstitutional. That ruling resulted in Kentucky's passing the Education Reform Act of 1990, which has produced, as the *New York Times* reported, "almost everything critics of American education call for: higher standards, more money, fairer allocation of resources, new curriculums, more creative teaching, better counseling, [and] improved technology."[17] The gap in spending between rich and poor districts has narrowed, and one benefit, in addition to the increased resources for poorer schools, is the improved academic performances of the state as a whole (1996, 6).

One area rarely discussed within school reform is increased teacher salaries. Teachers don't deserve increased pay, the shibboleth says, because they work only nine months per year. Yet such a view fails to consider how hard teachers work during those nine months. More to the point is the inability of teaching to draw our nation's top students and most talented college graduates. Teacher salaries do not successfully match up against starting salaries in many businesses or other professions.[18] Coupled with this is the relatively undemanding nature of the school work in, and thus the poor reputations of, schools and departments of education. "Teachers," as a result, "are drawn from the least well-prepared and least able segment of the college population."[19]

Of course, better salaries are not the only incentive necessary to draw better students into teaching. Schools and school districts must also treat teachers as professionals. As I have suggested, teachers need to be responsible for planning, implementing, and changing the curriculum. In coordination with parents and administration, teachers (among whom would be the principal teacher, which is what principals were originally) should manage their school's pedagogical orientation, as well as the hiring and firing of all teachers. Parents, their remonstrances to the contrary, are not the best judges of what children ought to be doing in the classroom. They may know well what they want for their own children, but they generally do not know what children at various ages, with differing motivations and learning problems, need in classroom settings.

Political equality means, at a minimum, that all persons are treated equally before the law, that all citizens share the same rights and liberties, and that no one can be excluded from the public business either by personal barriers (race, gender, ethnicity, and so on) or by lack of resources. Since part of the public business is to educate all of our children, all of our future citizens, we need to do so equally so as to assure that no child fails to develop the skills to participate simply because he lacks health care or nutrition or because her school lacks pencils, paper, books, fields, labs, and windows. Democracy requires political equality, and deliberative democracy, even more so than representative democracy, requires educational equality. This equality, in turn, requires equitable funding of schools. To achieve that equality does not at present require equal funding. It requires equitable funding. That is, poor schools and poor school districts will require greater funding than other schools and districts to reach equality. Once they have caught up, then funding can be equalized.[20] In this sense, perhaps we need a form of the Rawlsian difference principle so that any educational inequality must redound to the benefit of the least well-off schools.

It is a familiar story that when the Soviets launched Sputnik in 1957, American politicians suddenly awakened to the need for increased schooling in math and science for our youth. Little mentioned is the accompanying rise, evident predominantly in the 1960s, of educational expectations in general for all of our youth. As a nation, we held out the promise of a high school education, or higher, to all of our children, and we did so knowing that as late as the 1940s, the average American went to school for only nine years. To be brutally honest, this was a perversity deluxe, a perversity that continues today: while we promise and expect educational achievement, we deny to those most in need of it the very resources by which they can attain it. Imagine if John F. Kennedy had promised in the early 1960s that we would put a man on the moon, but would do so without dramatically increasing the funds to the National Aeronautical and Space Administration.

Until we as a society undertake the prodigious mission of minimizing the differences in life chances among our young—that is, until we establish approximate (as opposed to exact) equality of conditions—then there is little hope that equality of opportunity will be a meaningful liberal value or that democracy can constitute a just society. Nor, indeed, can we expect all students to meet national standards. Such standards cannot succeed as a benchmark of an educated citizenry until all of our public schools have equitable resources. To hold students to national standards but to deny them the educational resources to meet those standards is to encircle those students in failure and to consign them to a future of disillusionment and despair.

Conclusion

In many ways this book may seem quixotic, a charge familiar to political theorists. It is an exercise in political theory in the literal sense that it offers a vision (*theoria*) of how decisions important to the polity, or parts of the polity, might be made collectively. The cornerstone of decision making, for private persons and democratic citizens, is deliberation. Autonomous persons make private decisions by weighing evidence and considering alternatives on their own. Citizens make decisions in the same way, but do so in public and collectively. Both require deliberation.

The book also offers a vision of what kind of school system we need to develop deliberative democrats. This two-part vision—of movements toward deliberative democracy and of an education in deliberation—is a regulative ideal. As such, it offers justification for proceeding toward deliberative democracy more than the various institutions that would constitute such a democracy. It also offers the educational means for proceeding. Thus this work is not idealistic in the sense that I present a form of politics and an education that can never realistically exist. I only concede that the work seems idealistic, even unrealistic, from the present-day perspective where direct, deliberative democratic forums and an education in deliberation are so remote that they seem totally removed. Both are, however, future goals and future possibilities. From the liberal perspective, of which this book purports to offer one liberal vision, the value of education lies in its effect on preparing future citizens for participation in deliberative democratic politics and culture, as well as preparing persons to gain understanding, or better understanding, of the kinds of lives they wish to live and choices they need to make.

How does it happen that when a participant in a democratic dialogue is addressing others that she is also, as Emerson said, addressing part of herself? It happens through what Tocqueville called "self-interest rightly understood." She sees that at least for some others her own interests are no different from theirs. Even when interests are different, it is possible to find commonality within or among them or resolution of them. This is the purpose of reasoned public discussion. Each citizen is drawn into a conversation where from the panoply of reasonable interests the common good is recognized or made. Here self-interest is pursued, but through the alembic of civic concerns, multiple voices, and myriad interests.

We have lost the alembic. No conversational dynamic exists whereby the diverse interests of our multicultural society can be brought together, compared, argued for or against, and resolved or suspended or transcended. Too often groups, isolated and focused on their own exclusive rights and interests, have no forum for hearing the views of others. Persons seem locked into self-interest with no way of making it rightly understood. The forums and dialogue that are available are highly adversarial and purely disputatious. Perhaps our litigious society is really a sign that we so long for dialogue that we will settle for courtroom soliloquies, testimony, and examinations in place of discussion.

It is not, therefore, disagreement that must disappear, as if some common good existed or could exist to which all citizens could and would readily assent. It is the nature of the disagreements and the manner in which we disagree that are vexatious. As private persons, as citizens, and as students we need to learn to converse or discuss, which means to talk *with* others rather than *at* them. We need to have the opportunity to discuss in settings where we can affect, and effect, those decisions that shape our identities and lives. Both the ability and the opportunity involve reflective thinking, the development of which is the goal of public education.

Who we are and what we want are concerns, self-reflective concerns, that can extend self-rule into collective self-government. Here the self is not "I" but "we." This is not a matter of transformation, but of recognition: what I want or need can sometimes be accomplished and understood only in the political context of what *we* want or need. This is the basis of self-interest rightly understood, as self-governing collectively is a fundamental aspect of autonomous self-rule.

In Tocqueville's day the efficacy of some plans to exhort or energize the citizenry to participate made sense, for in local politics citizens could deliberate on important local issues and could make political decisions that directly affected their lives. Thus could the soft despotism of centralized democracy be eschewed. Today, however, participation in our system seems unlikely to make such a difference. Our democracy, as Tocqueville said of soft despotism, "seldom enjoins but often inhibits action; it does not destroy anything, but prevents much being born; it is not at all tyrannical, but it hinders, restrains, enervates, stifles, and stultifies" (1966, 692).

Good thinking, which I have been calling critical thinking, can be a threat to representative democracy. It can lead citizens to scrutinize campaign statements, slogans, and promises that were never intended to be scrutinized. It can lead thoughtful citizens to realize that many decisions in our large industrial nation can be and ought to be made by the citizens themselves. That realization threatens politicians and other elites, because it draws away some of their power. That power, however, belongs to citizens; it is democratic power. Such power begins with and emanates from the realization that citizens can democratically direct much, or important parts, of our collective life. That realization is nurtured in and through an education in deliberation, where an emphasis is placed on learning to be thoughtful, on learning to think critically, to act democratically, and to control our lives.

Tocqueville was well aware of the importance of autonomy, of mastery over ourselves, in directing our private and public lives. "However important," he observed, "this brief and occasional exercise of free will [of choosing political representatives] will not prevent [citizens] from gradually losing the faculty of thinking, feeling, and acting for themselves." Tocqueville continued: "It is really difficult to imagine how people who have entirely given up managing their own affairs could make a wise choice of those who are to do that for them. One should never expect a liberal, energetic, and wise government to originate in the votes of a people of servants" (694).

Scholarship, it has been pointed out, should be written for the future, and so this book is. The question that I ask, or that I started with, is not what kind of education our children need to become deliberative persons and good citizens. It is, rather, what education is required to be deliberative persons and good citizens in a democracy *better* than our own. Answering that question is the best way, and perhaps the only way, that our polity can improve.

An education in deliberation could be the greatest legacy that we can bestow on our children, our greatest treasure. Through such an education our children can learn to think and act for themselves; they can be prepared to manage, through thoughtful reflection and deliberative judgment, their own public and private affairs. With an education in deliberation as its midwife, democracy for the next generation might then be born anew.

Notes

1. The entire quotation from Wolin reads: "In the age of vast concentrations of corporate and governmental power, the desperate problem of democracy is not to develop better ways of cooperation but to develop a fairer system of contestation over time" (1996, 115).

2. This, again, is an area of agreement among Brighouse (1998 and 2000), Callan (1997 and 2000), and Macedo (2000).

3. See, among others, Andrew Hacker, 1992.

4. See "Schools More Separate: Consequences of a Decade of Resegregation," by Harvard University's Civil Rights Project, as reported in "U. S. Schools Turn More Segregated," *New York Times,* 20 July 2001, A12.

5. See Sanders, 1997.

6. Pages 94-95. For a corroborative discussion of two other New York schools see "Separate but Unequal," *New York Times,* 14 January 1999.

7. "[T]he biggest difference between schools . . . is not their publicness or privateness but the social and economic status of the students who attend them. . . . The rich, after all, have had both good public schools and good private schools. The good public ones looked [and functioned] a lot like the good private ones. The bad ones have looked alike, too" (Deborah Meier, 1995, 97-98).

8. Shanker is quoted in "Report on a Convocation," *Daedalus* 124, no. 4 (1995): 31.

9. See Sonia Nieto, 1994. Nieto cites studies by Lee, Winfield, and Wilson, "Academic Behaviors among High-Achieving African-American Students," *Education and Urban Society* 24, no. 1, 1991. See also Lucas, Henze, and Donato, "Promoting the Success of Latino Language Minority Students," *Harvard Educational Review* 60, 1990; and Moll, "Bilingual Classroom Studies and Community Analysis," *Educational Researcher* 21, no. 2, 1992.

10. "If you look at the period from 1947 to 1973 all five quintiles of the population had their living standards double. From 1973 to 1992 they stagnated; only the top 20 percent gained, its income rising by about 25 percent. The bottom 60 percent actually fell." Paul R. Dimond, special assistant to the president for economic policy; quoted by

G. Holton and D. Goroff in "Where Is American Education Going?" *Daedalus* 124, no. 4 (1995): 25.

The Federal Bureau of Prisons has increased its budget from $330 million in 1980 to $2.6 billion in 1995, an increase of almost 700 percent (statistics from Michael Massing, "Crime and Drugs: The New Myths," *New York Review of Books,* 1 February 1996, 18). To some, prison might look promising, for it can provide three meals, a bed, a roof, and even a library, though it provides no escape, ironically, from violence and crime.

11. See Mortimer Adler, *The Paideia Proposal* (New York: Macmillan, 1982).

12. Choate-Rosemary Hall is the elite coeducational boarding school in Wallingford, Connecticut; Spofford is the juvenile detention center in the South Bronx, arguably the worst section of New York City.

13. Harold Hodgkinson, "Reform versus Reality," *Phi Delta Kappan* 73, no. 1 (1991): 10.

14. See the CED report *The Unfinished Agenda: A New Vision for Child Development and Education,* 1995. See also *New York Times,* "Study Suggests Head Start Helps Beyond School," 20 March 1993.

15. Of the states whose students performed best in 1994 not one of them ranked in the top 10 on school spending. Those states were Iowa, Kansas, Minnesota, Montana, Nebraska, South Dakota, Utah, Wisconsin, and Wyoming. In fact, Utah ranked last in school spending among the 50 states. The spending in these states may well reach a level that we would agree is equitable, but what is the size of their minority and inner-city populations? While homogeneity of towns and schools used to be considered a key element in the success of the rural schools in these states, that position has now been challenged. See *New York Times,* "Study Says Small Schools Are Key to Learning," 21 September 1994, B12.

16. Darling-Hammond (1997) concludes from her own research that shrinking the size of schools and classes can be done with creative staffing, planning, and scheduling, and may not require substantially more funding to the schools. See also Darling-Hammond, "Beyond Bureaucracy: Restructuring Schools for 'High Performance,'" in *Rewards and Reform,* edited by Jennifer O'Day and Susan Fuhrman (San Francisco: Jossey-Bass, 1996).

17. "Revamped Kentucky Schools Are a Study in Pros and Cons," *New York Times,* 25 March 1996, 1. The "Cons" side consists of those who oppose the change in Kentucky in ungraded primary schools and who question the state's own assessment test, which relies on written portfolios. There is also some real concern as to whether the reported gains in achievement and on test scores are inflated.

18. Comparing the starting, mid-career, and end-of-career salaries of teachers with comparable professions (accountants, lawyers, and the like), even with the nine-month work year taken into account, will produce some shocking disparities.

19. Howard Gardner, 1990, 95. In support of this declaration Gardner cites *A Nation Prepared: The Report on the Task Force on Teaching as a Profession* (Washington, D.C.: Carnegie Forum on Education and the Economy, 1986). See also Gary Sykes, "Contradictions, Ironies, and Promises Unfulfilled," *Phi Delta Kappan* 65, no. 2 (1983).

20. See Kozol, *Savage Inequalities,* 1991. This is not to suggest that wealthy school districts cannot raise additional funds for school projects and property. There is nothing wrong with that. Instead, my point is that the funding for any school must be sufficient to provide the students with the resources they need to meet the democratic academic standards, whether those resources are teachers, property, school supplies, safety features, or nutrition.

1) why deliberative democracy at all? Because it produces better / more just results? Because it is procedurally fairer? Because it is 'good' for individual development? If one accepts these premises, the argument is quite good.

2) Attempt to ally strong democrats with liberal democrats through associating an education in deliberation with an education for autonomy.

3) The needs of American schools are so dire.... reform such of as these unlikely to resonate except among those schools (privileged, suburban) which least need them. This does not mean that the recommendations should not be made.... epilogue helps all dose of realism...

Bibliography

Adler, Mortimer. "Why 'Critical Thinking' Programs Won't Work." *Education Week* 6 (17 September 1986): 28.
——. *Paideia Problems and Possibilities*. New York: Macmillan, 1983.
American Federation of Teachers, the Educational Excellence Network, and Freedom House. *Education for Democracy*. Washington, D.C.: American Federation of Teachers, 1987.
Apple, Michael W., and James A. Beane, eds. *Democratic Schools*. Alexandria, Va.: Association for Supervision and Curriculum Development, 1995.
Appleby, Joyce. *Capitalism and a New Social Order*. New York: New York University Press, 1984.
Arendt, Hannah. *The Life of the Mind: Thinking*. New York: Harcourt Brace Jovanovich, 1977.
——. *The Human Condition*. Chicago: University of Chicago Press, 1958.
Aristotle. *The Politics*. Edited by Stephen Everson. Cambridge: Cambridge University Press, 1988.
——. *Nichomachean Ethics*. Translated by Martin Ostwald. Indianapolis: Liberal Arts Press, 1962.
Arkes, Hadley. "Can Emotion Supply the Place of Reason?" In *Reconsidering the Democratic Public,* edited by George E. Marcus and Russell L. Hanson, 287-306. University Park: Pennsylvania State University Press, 1993.
Association of American Colleges. *Liberal Learning and the Arts and Sciences Major: Volume 1, The Challenge of Connecting Learning*. Washington, D.C.: Association of American Colleges, 1990.
——. *Liberal Learning and the Arts and Sciences Major: Volume 2, Reports from the Fields*. Washington, D.C.: Association of American Colleges, 1991.
Bagge, Carl, et al. "Participation and Partnerships." In *Toward Democratic Schooling,* edited by Knud Jensen and Stephen Walker, 9-22. Milton Keynes, U.K.: Open University Press, 1989.
Baier, Annett. "How Can Individualists Share Responsibility?" *Political Theory* 21, no. 2 (May 1993): 228-48.
Bailey, Stephen K. "Political and Social Purposes of Education." In *In Education for Responsible Citizenship,* The Report of the National Task Force on Citizenship Education, 27-46. New York: McGraw-Hill, 1977.
Barber, Benjamin. *An Aristocracy of Everyone*. New York: Ballantine Books, 1992.

——. "Liberal Democracy and the Costs of Consent." In *Liberalism and the Moral Life,* edited by Nancy L. Rosenblum, 54-68. Cambridge, Mass.: Harvard University Press, 1989.

——. *Strong Democracy.* Berkeley: University of California Press, 1984.

Battistoni, Richard M. *Public Schooling and the Education of Democratic Citizens.* Jackson: University Press of Mississippi, 1985.

Baynes, Kenneth. "Liberal Neutrality, Pluralism, and Deliberative Politics." *Praxis International* 12, no. 1 (1992): 50-69.

Beard, Charles A. *An Economic Interpretation of the Constitution of the United States.* New York: Macmillan, 1936.

Beiner, Ronald. *What's the Matter with Liberalism.* Berkeley: University of California Press, 1992.

——. *Political Judgment.* London: Methuen, 1983.

Bellah, Robert, et al. *The Good Society.* New York: Alfred A. Knopf, 1991.

Benhabib, Seyla. "Judgment and the Moral Foundations of Politics in Arendt's Thought." *Political Theory* 16, no. 1 (1988): 29-52.

Benn, Stanley. *A Theory of Freedom.* Cambridge: Cambridge University Press, 1988.

——. "Freedom, Autonomy, and the Concept of a Person." In *Proceedings of the Aristotelian Society* 76 (1975-76): 109-30.

Benne, Kenneth D., George E. Axtelle, B. Othanel Smith, and R. Bruce Raup. *The Discipline of Practical Judgment in a Democratic Society.* Chicago: University of Chicago Press, 1943.

Berlin, Isaiah. *The Crooked Timber of Humanity.* Edited by Henry Hardy. New York: Alfred A. Knopf, 1991.

——. *Four Essays on Liberty.* Oxford, U.K.: Oxford University Press, 1969.

Berthoff, Ann E. *The Sense of Learning.* Portsmouth, N.H.: Boynton/Cook, 1990.

——. *The Making of Meaning.* Montclair, N.J.: Boynton/Cook, 1981.

——. *Forming/Thinking/Writing.* Rochelle Park, N.Y.: Hayden Book Co., 1978.

Beyer, Landon E. "Can Schools Further Democratic Practices?" *Theory into Practice* 27, no. 4 (1988): 262-69.

Bobbio, Norberto. *The Future of Democracy.* Minneapolis: University of Minnesota Press, 1987.

Bohman, James, and William Rehg, eds. *Deliberative Democracy.* Cambridge, Mass.: MIT Press, 1997.

Bowler, Shaun, and Todd Donovon. *Demanding Choices.* Ann Arbor: University of Michigan Press, 1998.

Boyer, Ernest L. "Early Schooling and the Nation's Future." *Educational Leadership* 44, no. 6 (1987): 4-6.

Boyte, Harry. "Commentary of Manfred Stanley's 'The American University as a Civic Institution.'" *Civic Arts Review* 2, no. 2 (1989): 10-12.

Brann, Eva. *Paradoxes of Education in a Republic.* Chicago: University of Chicago Press, 1979.

Bricker, David C. *Classroom Life as Civic Education.* New York: Teachers College Press, 1989.

Brighouse, Harry. "Civic Education and Liberal Legitimacy." In *Ethics* 108, no. 4 (1998): 719-745.

——. *School Choice and Social Justice.* New York: Oxford University Press, 2000.

Brodhagen, Barbara L. "The Situation Made Us Special." In *Democratic Schools,* edited by Michael W. Apple and James A. Beane, 83-100. Alexandria, Va.: Association for Supervision and Curriculum Development, 1995.

Brookfield, Stephen D. *Developing Critical Thinkers.* San Francisco: Jossey-Bass, 1988.

Brown, Harold. *Rationality.* New York: Routledge, 1988.

Bruffee, Kenneth A. "Thinking and Writing as Social Acts." In *Thinking, Reasoning, and Writing,* edited by Elaine E. Maimon, Barbara F. Nodine, and Finbarr W. O'Connor, 213-22. New York: Longman, 1989.

Bryan, Frank M. "Direct Democracy and Civic Competence." *Good Society* 5, no. 3 (1995).

Budge, Ian. "Direct Democracy: Setting Appropriate Terms of Debate." In *Prospects for Democracy,* edited by David Held, 136-55. Cambridge, U.K.: Polity Press, 1993.

Burnheim, John. *Is Democracy Possible?* Cambridge, U.K.: Polity Press, 1985.

Burtt, Shelley. "Religious Parents, Secular Schools: A Liberal Defense of an Illiberal Education." *Review of Politics* 56, no. 1 (1994): 51-70.

Butts, R. Freeman. *The Civic Mission in Educational Reform.* Stanford, Calif.: Hoover Institution Press, 1989.

——. "Historical Perspective on Civic Education in the United States." In *Education for Responsible Citizenship,* The Report of the National Task Force on Citizenship Education, 47-68. New York: McGraw-Hill, 1977.

Callan, Eamonn. "Liberal Legitimacy, Justice, and Civic Education." *Ethics* 111, no. 1 (October 2000): 141-55.

——. *Creating Citizens.* Oxford, U.K.: Oxford University Press, 1997.

Chamberlin, Rosemary. *Free Children and Democratic Schools.* Philadelphia: Falmer Press, 1989.

Cleary, Robert E. *Political Education in the American Democracy.* Scranton, Penn.: International Textbook Co., 1971.

Collins, Marva, and Civia Tamarkin. *Marva Collins' Way.* New York: G. P. Putnam's Sons, 1990.

Cone, Joan Kernan. "Appearing Acts: Creating Readers in a High School English Class." *Harvard Educational Review* 64, no. 4 (1994): 450-73.

Conover, Pamela Johnston, Stephen T. Leonard, and Donald D. Searing. "Duty Is a Four-Letter Word: Democratic Citizenship in the Liberal Polity." In *Reconsidering the Democratic Public,* edited by George E. Marcus and Russell L. Hanson, 147-72. University Park: Pennsylvania State University Press, 1993.

Conrad, Dan, and Diane Hedin. "Citizenship Education through Participation." In *Education for Responsible Citizenship,* The Report of the National Task Force on Citizenship Education, 133-56. New York: McGraw-Hill, 1977.

Constant, Benjamin. *Political Writings.* Translated by Biancamaria Fontana. New York: Cambridge University Press, 1988.

Crittenden, Jack. "The Social Nature of Autonomy." *Review of Politics* 55, no. 1 (winter 1993): 35-66.

——. *Beyond Individualism.* New York: Oxford University Press, 1992.

Cronin, Thomas. *Direct Democracy.* Cambridge, Mass.: Harvard University Press, 1989.

Cunningham, Luvern L. "Citizen Participation: Lessons for Citizenship Education." In *Education for Responsible Citizenship,* The Report of the National Task Force on Citizenship Education, 157-64. New York: McGraw-Hill, 1997.

Dagger, Richard. *Civic Virtues.* Oxford, U.K.: Oxford University Press, 1997.

——. "Education, Autonomy, and Civic Virtue." *Civic Arts Review* 3, no. 4 (1990): 11-16.

——. "Metropolis, Memory, and Citizenship." *American Journal of Political Science* 25, no. 4 (1981): 715-37.

Dahrendorf, Ralf. "Citizenship and Beyond: The Social Dynamics of an Idea." *Social Research* 41, no. 4 (1974): 673-701.

Darling-Hammond, Linda. *The Right to Learn.* San Francisco: Jossey-Bass, 1997.

Darwall, Stephen L. "Equal Representation." In NOMOS 25: *Liberal Democracy,* edited by J. Roland Pennock and John W. Chapman, 51-68. New York: New York University Press, 1983.

DeSario, Jack, and Stuart Langton, eds. *Citizen Participation in Public Decision Making.* New York: Greenwood Press, 1987.

DeToqueville, Alexis. *Democracy in America.* New York: Harper and Row, 1966.

Dewey, John. *How We Think.* [1910.] Reprint. Buffalo, N.Y.: Prometheus Books, 1991.

——. *The Later Works,* Vol. 14 (1939-41). Carbondale: Southern Illinois University Press, 1988a.

——. *The Later Works,* Vol. 13 (1938-39). Carbondale: Southern Illinois University Press, 1988b.

——. *Collected Works,* Vol. 2 (1935-37). Carbondale: Southern Illinois University Press, 1981.

——. *Reconstruction in Philosophy.* Boston: Beacon Press, 1948.

——. "Democracy and Educational Administration." *School and Society* 45 (3 April 1937): 457-62.

——. *Democracy and Education.* New York: Macmillan, 1916.

Dewey, John, and Evelyn Dewey. *Schools of To-morrow.* New York: E. P. Dutton, 1915.

Deyhle, Donna. "Navajo Youth and Anglo Racism: Cultural Integrity and Racism." *Harvard Educational Review* 65, no. 3 (1995): 403-44.

Diamond, Martin. *The Democratic Republic.* Chicago: Rand McNally, 1966.

Dietz, Mary. "Context Is All: Feminism and Theories of Citizenship." In *Dimensions of Radical Democracy,* edited by Chantal Mouffe. New York: Verso, 1992.

Dietze, Gottfried. *American Democracy.* Baltimore: Johns Hopkins University Press, 1993.

Douglass, R. Bruce, Gerald M. Mara, and Henry S. Richardson, eds. *Liberalism and the Good.* New York: Routledge, 1990.

Dunn, John, ed. *Democracy.* Oxford, U.K.: Oxford University Press, 1992.

Dworkin, Gerald. *The Theory and Practice of Autonomy.* New York: Cambridge University Press, 1988.

Elster, Jon. *Deliberative Democracy.* Cambridge, U.K.: Cambridge University Press, 1998.

——. *Sour Grapes.* New York: Cambridge University Press, 1985.

Engle, Shirley H., and Anna S. Ochoa. *Education for Democratic Citizenship.* New York: Teachers College Press, 1988.

Farr, James. "Framing Democratic Discussion." In *Reconsidering the Democratic Public,* edited by George E. Marcus and Russell L. Hanson, 379-92. University Park: Pennsylvania State University Press, 1993.

Farrar, Cynthia. "Ancient Greek Political Theory as a Response to Democracy." In *Democracy,* edited by J. Dunn, 17-40. Oxford, U.K.: Oxford University Press, 1992.

Fenton, Edwin. "The Implications of Lawrence Kohlberg's Research for Civil Education." In *Education for Responsible Citizenship,* The Report of the National Task Force on Citizenship Education. New York: McGraw-Hill, 1977.

Ferguson, Thomas, and Joel Rogers. *Right Turn.* New York: Wang and Hill, 1986.

Finley, M. I. *Politics in the Ancient World.* Cambridge, U.K.: Cambridge University Press, 1983.

Fishkin, James. *Democracy and Deliberation.* New Haven, Conn.: Yale University Press, 1991.

——. *The Dialogue of Justice.* New Haven, Conn.: Yale University Press, 1992.

Flathman, Richard. "Liberal versus Civic, Republican, Democratic, and Other Vocational Educations: Liberalism and Institutionalized Education." *Political Theory* 24, no. 1 (1996): 4-32.

Flower, Linda. *Problem-Solving Strategies in Writing.* 2d ed. San Diego: Harcourt Brace Jovanovich, 1985.

——. "Taking Thought: The Role of Conscious Processing in the Making of Meaning." In *Thinking, Reasoning, and Writing,* edited by Elaine E. Maimon, Barbara F. Nodine, and Finbarr W. O'Connor, 185-212. New York: Longman, 1989.

Frankfurt, H. G. "Freedom of the Will, and the Concept of a Person." *Journal of Philosophy* 68, no. 4 (January 1971): 5-20.

Fraser, Nancy. "Rethinking the Public Sphere." *Social Text* no. 25/26 (1990): 56-80.

Gadamer, Hans Georg. "What Is Practice?" In *The Conditions of Social Reason in the Age of Science,* 69-87. Cambridge, Mass.: MIT Press, 1981.

Gallie, W. B. "Essentially Contested Concepts." *Proceedings of the Aristotelian Society* 56 (1955-56): 167-98.

Galston, William. "Two Concepts of Liberalism." *Ethics* 105, no. 3 (April 1995): 516-34.

———. *Liberal Purposes.* New York: Cambridge University Press, 1991.

———. "Civic Education in the Liberal State." In *Liberalism and the Moral Life,* edited by Nancy L. Rosenblum, 89-102. Cambridge, Mass.: Harvard University Press, 1989.

Gardner, Howard. *The Unschooled Mind.* New York: Basic Books, 1983a.

———. "The Difficulties of School: Probable Causes, Possible Cures. *Daedalus* 119, no. 2 (1990): 85-114.

———. *Frames of Mind.* New York: Basic Books, 1983b.

Gatto, John Taylor. *Dumbing Us Down.* Philadelphia: New Society, 1992.

Girle, Roderic A. "Dialogue and the Teaching of Reasoning." *Educational Philosophy and Theory* 23, no. 1 (1991): 45-55.

Glendon, Mary Ann. *Rights Talk: The Impoverishment of Political Discourse.* New York: Free Press, 1991.

Glickman, Carl D. *Renewing America's Schools.* San Francisco: Jossey-Bass, 1993.

Goodlad, John. *A Place Called School.* New York: McGraw-Hill, 1983.

Goodsell, Anne, et al. *Collaborative Learning.* University Park, Penn.: National Center on Postsecondary Teaching, Learning, and Assessment (NCTLA), 1992.

Gould, Carol. "Feminism and Democratic Community Revisited." In *NOMOS* 35: *Democratic Community,* edited by John Chapman and Ian Shapiro, 396-413. New York: New York University Press, 1993.

———. *Rethinking Democracy.* Cambridge: Cambridge University Press, 1988.

Graham, Keith. *The Battle of Democracy.* Brighton, U.K.: Wheatsheaf Books, 1986.

Graham, Patricia Alberg. "Literacy: A Goal for Secondary Schools." *Daedalus* 110, no. 3 (1981): 119-34.

Graubard, Stephen R. Pp. v-xxx in preface to the issue "American Education—Still Separate, Still Unequal." *Daedalus* 124, no. 4 (1995).

Gray, John. *Post-Liberalism.* New York: Routledge, 1993.

———. *Mill on Liberty: A Defense.* London: Routledge & Kegan Paul, 1983a.

———. "Political Power, Social Theory, and Essential Contestability." In *The Nature of Political Theory,* edited by D. Miller and L. Siedentop, 75-102. Oxford, U.K.: Oxford University Press, 1983b.

Greider, William. *Who Will Tell the People.* New York: Simon & Schuster, 1992.

Guinier, Lani. *The Tyranny of the Majority.* New York: Free Press, 1994.

Gutierrez, K., B. Rymes, and J. Larson. "Script, Counterscript, and Underlife in the Classroom: James Brown vs. Board of Education." *Harvard Educational Review* 65, no. 3 (1995): 445-71.

Gutmann, Amy. "Civic Education and Social Diversity." *Ethics* 105, no. 3 (April 1995): 557-79.

———. *Multiculturalism.* Princeton, N.J.: Princeton University Press, 1994.

——. "The Challenge of Multiculturalism in Political Ethics." *Philosophy and Public Affairs* 22, no. 3 (1993a): 171-206.

——. "The Disharmony of Democracy." In *NOMOS* 35: *Democratic Community*, edited by John Chapman and Ian Shapiro, 126-160. New York: New York University Press, 1993b.

——. "Undemocratic Education." In *Liberalism and the Moral Life*, edited by Nancy L. Rosenblum, 71-88. Cambridge, Mass.: Harvard University Press, 1989b.

——. *Democratic Education*. Princeton, N.J.: Princeton University Press, 1987.

Gutmann, Amy, and Dennis Thompson. *Democracy and Disagreement*. Cambridge, Mass.: Harvard University Press, 1996.

——. "Moral Conflict and Political Consensus." In *Liberalism and the Good*, edited by R. Bruce Douglass, Gerald M. Mara, and Henry S. Richardson, 12-47. New York: Routledge, 1990.

Habermas, Jurgen. "Citizenship and National Identity." *Praxis International* 12, no. 1 (1992): 1-19.

——. *The Structural Transformation of the Public Sphere*. Cambridge, Mass.: MIT Press, 1991.

——. *Moral Consciousness and Communicative Action*. Cambridge, Mass.: MIT Press, 1990.

——. "Moral Development and Ego Identity." In *Telos* 24 (1975): 41-55.

Hacker, Andrew. *Two Nations*. New York: Scribner's, 1992.

Hahn, Harlan, and Sheldon Kamieniecki. *Referendum Voting*. Westport, Conn.: Greenwood Press, 1987.

Hanson, Russell L. "Democracy." In *Political Innovation and Conceptual Change*, edited by Terence Ball, James Farr, and Russell L. Hanson, 68-89. New York: Cambridge University Press, 1989.

——. *The Democratic Imagination in America*. Princeton, N.J.: Princeton University Press, 1985.

Harding, Neil. "The Marxist-Leninist Detour." In *Democracy*, edited by J. Dunn, 155-88. Oxford, U.K.: Oxford University Press, 1992.

Hawkins, David. "The Roots of Literacy." *Daedalus* 119, no. 2 (1990): 1-14.

Held, David. *Models of Democracy*. Cambridge, U.K.: Polity Press, 1987.

——, ed. *Prospects for Democracy*. Cambridge, U.K.: Polity Press, 1993.

Held, David, and Christopher Pollitt, eds. *New Forms of Democracy*. Beverly Hills, Calif.: Sage Publications, 1986.

Heslep, Robert D. *Education in Democracy*. Ames: Iowa State University Press, 1989.

Hirsch, E. D. "Cultural Literacy and the Schools." *American Educator* 9, no. 2 (1985): 8-15.

Hirst, Paul. "Associational Democracy." In *Prospects for Democracy: North, South, East, West*, edited by David Held, 112-35. Cambridge, U.K.: Polity Press, 1993.

Hochschild, Jennifer L. "Disjunction and Ambivalence in Citizens' Political Outlooks." In *Reconsidering the Democratic Public,* edited by George E. Marcus and Russell L. Hanson, 187-210. University Park: Pennsylvania State University Press, 1993.

Hoffman, Banesh. *The Tyranny of Testing.* Westport, Conn.: Greenwood Press, 1962.

Hollis, Martin. "Friends, Romans, and Consumers." *Ethics* 102, no. 1 (October 1991): 27-41.

Holmes, Mark. *Educational Policy for the Pluralist Democracy.* Bristol, Penn.: Falmer Press, 1992.

Hornblower, Simon. "Creation and Development of Democratic Institutions in Ancient Greece." Pp. 1-16 in *Democracy,* edited by J. Dunn. Oxford, U.K.: Oxford University Press, 1992.

Horton, Susan R. *Thinking through Writing.* Baltimore: Johns Hopkins University Press, 1982.

Hostetler, John A., ed. *Amish Roots.* Baltimore: Johns Hopkins University Press, 1989.

Howard, V. A., and J. H. Barton. *Thinking on Paper.* New York: William Morrow, 1986.

Hurka, Thomas. "Why Value Autonomy?" *Social Theory and Practice* 13, no. 3 (1987): 361-82.

Ignatieff, Michael. "The Myth of Citizenship." *Queen's Quarterly* 94, no. 4 (1987): 966-85.

Jacobson, Gary C., and Samuel Kernell. *Strategy and Choice in Congressional Elections.* New Haven, Conn.: Yale University Press, 1981.

Jacoby, Russell. *Dogmatic Wisdom.* New York: Doubleday, 1994.

Janowitz, Morris. *The Reconstruction of Patriotism.* Chicago: University of Chicago Press, 1983.

Jefferson, Thomas. *The Writings of Thomas Jefferson.* Edited by Albert Ellery Bergh. 20 vols. Washington, D.C.: Thomas Jefferson Memorial Association, 1905.

Jensen, Knud, and Stephen Walker. *Towards Democratic Schooling.* Milton Keynes, U.K.: Open University Press, 1989.

Jones, Peter. "Political Equality and Majority Rule." In *The Nature of Political Theory,* edited by David Miller and Larry Siedentop, 155-82. Oxford, U.K.: Oxford University Press, 1983.

Kahn, Kim Fridkin, and Patrick Kenney. *The Spectacle of U.S. Senate Campaigns.* Princeton, N.J.: Princeton University Press, 1999.

Kateb, George. *The Inner Ocean.* Ithaca, N.Y.: Cornell University Press, 1992.

Kelly, George Armstrong. "Who Needs a Theory of Citizenship?" *Daedalus* 108, no. 4 (1979): 21-35.

Kemmis, Daniel. *Community and the Politics of Place.* Norman: University of Oklahoma Press, 1990.

Kinder, Donald R., and Don Herzog. "Democratic Discussion." In *Reconsidering the Democratic Public,* edited by George E. Marcus and Russell L. Hanson, 347-48. University Park: Pennsylvania State University Press, 1993.

King, Patricia M., and Karen Strohm Kitchener. *Developing Reflective Judgment.* San Francisco: Jossey-Bass Publishers, 1994.

Kingdon, John W. "Politicians, Self-Interest, and Ideas." In *Reconsidering the Democratic Public,* edited by George E. Marcus and Russell L. Hanson, 73-90. University Park: Pennsylvania State University Press, 1993.

Kornfeld, H. John. "Teaching for Democracy in the Social Studies Classroom." *Theory and Research in Social Education* 21, no. 1 (1993): 75-83.

Kozol, Jonathan. *Savage Inequalities.* New York: Crown, 1991.

Krauthammer, Charles. "In Praise of Low Voter Turnout." *Time,* 21 May 1990: 88.

Kraybill, Donald B., ed. *The Amish and the State.* Baltimore: Johns Hopkins University Press, 1993.

——. *The Riddle of Amish Culture.* Baltimore: Johns Hopkins University Press, 1989.

Kukathas, Chandran, ed. *Multicultural Citizens.* New South Wales, Australia: The Centre for Independent Studies, 1993.

Kuklinski, James H., Ellen Riggle, Victor Ottati, Norbert Schwarz, and Robert S. Wyer. "Thinking about Political Tolerance, More or Less, with More or Less Information." In *Reconsidering the Democratic Public,* edited by George E. Marcus and Russell L. Hanson, 225-48. University Park: Pennsylvania State University Press, 1993.

Kymlicka, Will. *Multicultural Citizenship.* Oxford, U.K.: Oxford University Press, 1995a.

——, ed. *The Rights of Minority Cultures.* New York: Oxford University Press, 1995b.

——. *Liberalism, Community, and Culture.* Oxford, U.K.: Oxford University Press, 1989.

Kymlicka, Will, and Wayne Norman. "Return of the Citizen." *Ethics* 104, no. 2 (1994): 352-81.

Langer, Judith A., and Arthur N. Applebee. *How Writing Shapes Thinking.* Urbana, Ill.: National Council of Teachers of English, 1987.

Lasch, Christopher. "Democracy and the 'Crisis of Confidence.'" *democracy* 1, no. 1 (January 1981): 25-40.

Lawson, Anton E. "At What Levels of Education Is the Teaching of Thinking Effective?" *Theory into Practice* 32, no. 3 (summer 1993): 170-78.

Leca, Jean. "Questions on Citizenship." In *Dimensions of Radical Democracy,* edited by Chantal Mouffe. New York: Verso, 1992.

Locke, John. *Essay Concerning Human Understanding.* London: Dent, 1965.

Lucas, J. R. *Democracy and Participation.* Harmondsworth, U.K.: Penguin Books, 1976.

Lukes, S. J. *Individualism.* Oxford, U.K.: Basil Blackwell, 1973.

Macedo, Stephen. *Diversity and Distrust.* Cambridge, Mass.: Harvard University Press, 2000.

——. "Liberal Civic Education and Religious Fundamentalism." *Ethics* 105, no. 3 (1995a): 468-96.

——. "Liberal Civic Education and Its Limits." *Canadian Journal of Education* 20, no. 3 (1995b): 304-14.

——. *Liberal Virtues.* London: Oxford University Press, 1990.

MacPherson, C. B. *The Real World of Democracy.* New York: Oxford University Press, 1972.

Madison, James, Alexander Hamilton, and John Jay. *The Federalist Papers.* 1788. Edited by Isaac Kramnick. New York: Penguin Books, 1987.

Maier, Charles S. "Democracy since the French Revolution." In *Democracy,* edited by J. Dunn, 125-54. Oxford, U.K.: Oxford University Press, 1992.

Maimon, Elaine, Barbara F. Nodine, and Finbarr W. O'Connor, eds. *Thinking, Reasoning, and Writing.* New York: Longman, 1989.

Manin, Bernard. "On Legitimacy and Political Deliberation." *Political Theory* 15, no. 3 (1987): 338-68.

Mansbridge, Jane. "Self-Interest and Political Transformation." In *Reconsidering the Democratic Public,* edited by George E. Marcus and Russell L. Hanson. University Park: Pennsylvania State University Press, 1993a.

——. "Feminism and Democratic Community." In *NOMOS* 35: *Democratic Community,* 339-95. New York: New York University Press, 1993b.

——. "Feminism and Democracy." *The American Prospect* 1, no. 1 (1990): 126-39.

——. "Fears of Conflict in Face-to-Face Democracies." In *Workplace Democracy and Social Change,* edited by F. Lindenfeld and J. Rothschild-Whitt, 125-38. Boston: Porter Sargent, 1982.

——. *Beyond Adversary Democracy.* New York: Basic Books, 1980.

Manville, Philip Brook. *The Origins of Citizenship in Ancient Athens.* Princeton, N.J.: Princeton University Press, 1990.

Marcil-Lacoste, Louise. "The Paradoxes of Pluralism." In *Dimensions of Radical Democracy: Pluralism, Citizenship, and Community,* edited by Chantal Mouffe. New York: Verso, 1992.

Marcus, George E., and Russell L. Hanson. *Reconsidering the Democratic Public.* University Park: Pennsylvania State University Press, 1993.

Mason, Andrew. "Personal Autonomy and Identification with a Community." In *Liberalism, Citizenship, and Autonomy,* edited by David Milligan and William Watts Miller, 3-18. Aldershot, U.K.: Avebury, 1992.

Mathews, David. *Politics for People.* Urbana: University of Illinois Press, 1994.

McClure, Kirstie. "On the Subject of Rights: Pluralism, Plurality, and Political Identity." In *Dimensions of Radical Democracy: Pluralism, Citizenship, and Community,* edited by Chantal Mouffe. New York: Verso, 1992.

McDonald, Forrest. *The Formation of the American Republic, 1776-1790.* Baltimore: Pelican Books, 1968.

——. *Novus Ordo Seclorum.* Lawrence: University Press of Kansas, 1985.

McGinley, William, and Robert J. Tierney. "Traversing the Topical Landscape: Reading and Writing as Ways of Knowing." In *Written Communication* 6, no. 3 (1989): 243-69.

McLean, Iain. *Democracy and New Technology.* Cambridge, U.K.: Polity Press, 1989.

McPeck, John E. *Critical Thinking and Education.* New York: St. Martin's Press, 1981a.

——. "Critical Thinking without Logic." *Philosophy of Education.* Normal, Ill.: Philosophy of Education Society, 1981b, 219-27.

——. *Teaching Critical Thinking.* New York: Routledge, 1990.

Mehlinger, Howard D. "The Crisis in Civic Education." In *Education for Responsible Citizenship,* The Report of the National Task Force on Citizenship Education, 69-82. New York: McGraw-Hill, 1977.

Meier, Deborah. *The Power of Their Ideas.* Boston: Beacon Press, 1995.

Mendus, Susan. *Toleration and the Limits of Liberalism.* Atlantic Heights, N.J.: Humanities Press International, 1989.

——. "Strangers and Brothers: Liberalism, Socialism, and the Concept of Autonomy." In *Liberalism, Citizenship, and Autonomy,* edited by David Milligan and William Watts Miller, 3-13. Aldershot, U.K.: Avebury, 1992.

Meyers, Diana. *Self, Society, and Personal Choice.* New York: Columbia University Press, 1989.

Mill, John Stuart. *Utilitarianism, On Liberty and Considerations on Representative Government.* 1910. Reprint, London: Everyman's Library, 1972.

Miller, David. "Deliberative Democracy and Social Choice." *Political Studies* 40, no. 3 (1993): 54-67.

——. "The Competitive Model of Democracy." In *Democratic Theory and Practice,* edited by Graeme Duncan, 133-55. New York: Cambridge University Press, 1983.

Milligan, David, and William Watts Miller, eds. *Liberalism, Citizenship, and Autonomy.* Aldershot, U.K.: Avebury, 1992.

Mitchell, Richard. *The Graves of Academe.* Boston: Little, Brown, 1981.

——. *Less Than Words Can Say.* Boston: Little, Brown, 1979.

Moon, J. Donald. "Theory, Citizenship, and Democracy." In *Reconsidering the Democratic Public,* edited by George E. Marcus and Russell L. Hanson, 211-24. University Park: Pennsylvania State University Press, 1993.

Morgan, Edmund. *Inventing the People.* New York: W. W. Norton, 1988.

Mosteller, Frederick. "The Tennessee Study of Class Size in the Early School Grades." Pp. 106-20 in *The Future of Children* 5, no. 2, edited by Richard E. Behrman. Los Altos, Calif.: The David and Lucile Packard Foundation, 1995.

Mouffe, Chantal, ed. Dimensions of Radical Democracy. New York: Verso, 1992.

Mozert v. Hawkins County Board of Education, 827 F.2nd 1062 (6th Cir. 1987).

Murray, Donald M. *Write to Learn.* New York: Holt, Rinehart & Winston, 1987.

National Commission on Excellence in Education. *A Nation at Risk.* Washington, D.C.: U. S. Government Printing Office, April 1983.

Nauta, Lolle. "Changing Conceptions of Citizenship." *Praxis International* 12, no. 1 (1992): 20-34.

Newmann, Fred M. "Alternative Approaches to Citizenship Education." In *Education for Responsible Citizenship*, The Report of the National Task Force on Citizenship Education, 175-88. New York: McGraw-Hill, 1977.

Nieto, Sonia. "Lessons from Students on Creating a Chance to Dream." *Harvard Educational Review* 64, no. 4 (1994): 392-426.

Nietzsche, Frederick. *The Portable Nietzsche*. Edited by Walter Kaufmann. New York: Penguin Books, 1976.

Nisbet, Robert. "Citizenship: Two Traditions." *Social Research* 41, no. 4 (1974): 612-37.

Norman, Richard. "Citizenship, Politics, and Autonomy." In *Liberalism, Citizenship, and Autonomy*, edited by David Milligan and William Watts Miller, 35-52. Aldershot, U.K.: Avebury, 1992.

Norris, Stephen, and Robert Ennis. *Evaluating Critical Thinking*. Pacific Grove, Calif.: Midwest, 1989.

Nostrand, V. A. D. "Writing and the Generation of Knowledge." *Social Education* 43, no. 3 (1979): 178-80.

Nussbaum, Martha. "Aristotelian Social Democracy." In *Liberalism and the Good*, edited by R. Bruce Douglass, Gerald M. Mara, and Henry S. Richardson, 203-52. New York: Routledge, 1990.

Oakeshott, Michael. *On Human Conduct*. Oxford, U.K.: Oxford University Press, 1975.

O'Day, Jennifer, and Susan Fuhrman. *Rewards and Reform*. San Francisco: Jossey-Bass, 1996.

Oldfield, Adrian. *Citizenship and Community*. New York: Routledge, 1990.

O'Neill, Onora. "Autonomy, Coherence, and Independence." In *Liberalism, Citizenship, and Autonomy*, edited by David Milligan and William Watts Miller, 203-25. Aldershot, U.K.: Avebury, 1992.

Orwell, George. "Politics and the English Language." In *Shooting an Elephant*, 84-101. New York: Harcourt, Brace & World, 1945.

Oxford Dictionary of English Etymology. Oxford, U.K.: Oxford University Press, 1966.

Page, Benjamin I., and Robert Y. Shapiro. "The Rational Public and Democracy." In *Reconsidering the Democratic Public*, edited by George E. Marcus and Russell L. Hanson, 35-64. University Park: Pennsylvania State University Press, 1993.

Paul, Richard. *Critical Thinking*. Rohnert Park, Calif.: Center for Critical Thinking and Moral Critique, 1990a.

——. "McPeck's Mistakes." In *Teaching Critical Thinking*, edited by John E. McPeck, 102-11. New York: Routledge, 1990b.

Pennock, J. Roland, and John W. Chapman, eds. *Liberal Democracy*. (NOMOS 25). New York: New York University Press, 1983.

Peshkin, Alan. *God's Choice*. Chicago: University of Chicago Press, 1986.

Peters, R. S. *Essays on Educators*. London: George Allen & Unwin, 1981.

——. *Ethics and Education*. London: Allen & Unwin, 1966.

Phillips, Anne. "Must Feminists Give up on Liberal Democracy?" In *Prospects for Democracy: North, South, East, West*, edited by David Held, 93-111. Cambridge, U.K.: Polity Press, 1993.

Pierce v. Society of Sisters, 268 US 510 (1925).

Piven, Frances Fox, and Richard A. Cloward. *Why Americans Don't Vote*. New York: Pantheon Books, 1987.

Plato. *Theaetetus*. Translated by M. J. Levett and Myles Burnyeat. Indianapolis: Hackett, 1990.

Postman, Neil. *Amusing Ourselves to Death*. New York: Viking, 1985.

——. *Teaching as a Conserving Activity*. New York: Delacorte Press, 1979.

Pratte, Richard. *The Civic Imperative*. New York: Teachers College Press, 1988.

Ravitch, Diane. "Multiculturalism." *Reference Shelf* 63, no. 5. New York: H. W. Wilson (1991): 91-111.

——. "Multiculturalism Yes, Particularism, No." *Chronicle of Higher Education* 24 (October 1990): A44.

Rawls, John. *Political Liberalism*. New York: Columbia University Press, 1993.

——. "Justice as Fairness: Political Not Metaphysical." *Philosophy and Public Affairs* 14, no. 3 (1985): 223-51.

——. *A Theory of Justice*. Cambridge, Mass.: Harvard University Press, 1971.

Raz, Joseph. *The Morality of Freedom*. New York: Oxford University Press, 1986.

Raywid, Mary Ann. "The Democratic Classroom: Mistake or Misnomer?" *Theory into Practice* 15, no. 1 (1976): 37-46.

Resnick, Daniel P. "Historical Perspectives on Literacy and Schooling." *Daedalus* 119, no. 2 (1990): 15-32.

Resnick, Lauren B. "From Aptitude to Effort: A New Foundation for Our Schools." *Daedalus* 124, no. 4 (1995): 55-62.

Resnick, Philip. *"Isonomia, Isegoria, Isomoiria, and Democracy at the Global Level."* *Praxis International* 12, no. 1 (1992): 35-49.

Rice, Suzanne, and Nicholas C. Burbules. "Communicative Virtues and Educational Relations." *Philosophy of Education* 48 (1992): 34-44.

Rich, John Martin. "Autonomy and the Purpose of Schooling." *Educational Philosophy and Theory* 18, no. 2 (1986): 34-41.

Richardson, Henry S. "The Problem of Liberalism and the Good." In *Liberalism and the Good*, edited by R. Bruce Douglass, Gerald M. Mara, and Henry S. Richardson, 1-28. New York: Routledge, 1990.

Riesenberg, Peter. *Citizenship in the Western Tradition*. Chapel Hill: University of North Carolina Press, 1992.

Rose, Peter I. "American Ethnicity in the Year 2000." In *Multiculturalism and Intergroup Relations*, edited by James S. Frideres, 153-58. Westport, Conn.: Greenwood Press, 1989.

Rousseau, Jean Jacques. *The Social Contract*. New York: Penguin Putnam, 1968.

Ryn, Claes G. *Democracy and the Ethical Life.* Washington, D.C.: Catholic University of America Press, 1990.

Sabine, G., and T. L. Thorson. *A History of Political Theory.* Hinsdale, Ill.: Dryden Press, 1973.

Salkever, Stephen G. "'Lopp'd and Bound': How Liberal Theory Obscures the Goods of Liberal Practices." In *Liberalism and the Good,* edited by R. Bruce Douglass, Gerald M. Mara, and Henry S. Richardson, 167-202. New York: Routledge, 1990.

Sandel, Michael J. *Liberalism and the Limits of Justice.* Cambridge: Cambridge University Press, 1982.

Sanders, Barry. *A Is for Ox.* New York: Pantheon Books, 1994.

Sanders, Lynn M. "Against Deliberation." *Political Theory* 25, no. 3 (1997): 347-76.

Sartori, Giovanni. *The Theory of Democracy Revisited.* Chatham, N.J.: Chatham House, 1987.

Scardamalia, Marlene, and Carl Bereiter. "Development of Dialectical Processes in Composition." In *Literacy, Language, and Learning,*" edited by David Olson, Nancy Torrance, and Angela Hildyard, 307-32. Cambridge, U.K.: Cambridge University Press, 1985.

Scheffler, Israel. *Reason and Teaching.* New York: Bobbs-Merrill, 1973.

Schmidt, David. *Citizen Lawmakers.* Philadelphia: Temple University Press, 1989.

Schrag, Francis. *Thinking in School and Society.* New York: Routledge, 1988.

Schumpeter, J. *Capitalism, Socialism, and Democracy.* New York: Harper & Row, 1975.

Shanker, Albert. "Raising the Bar." *New York Times,* 14 May 1995.

Shapiro, Ian. *Democracy's Place.* Ithaca, N.Y.: Cornell University Press, 1996.

Sheridan, James J. "Skipping on the Brink of the Abyss." *New Directions for Community Colleges* 77 (spring 1992): 51-62.

Shotter, John. *Social Accountability and Selfhood.* Oxford, U.K.: Basil Blackwell, 1984.

Shuy, Roger W. "Analysis of Language Functions in Dialogue Journal Writing." In *Analysis of Dialogue Journal Writing as a Communicative Event,* edited by J. Staton, R. Shuy, J. Kreeft, and Mrs. R [Pseud.]. Washington, D.C.: Center for Applied Linguistics, 1982.

——. "Language as a Foundation for Education." *Theory into Practice* 26, Special Issue (1987): 388-95.

Siegel, Harvey. *Educating Reason.* New York: Routledge, 1988.

Sinopoli, Richard C. *The Foundations of American Citizenship.* New York: Oxford University Press, 1992.

Sizer, Theodore. "Silences." *Daedalus* 124, no. 4 (1995): 77-84.

——. *Horace's School: Redesigning the American High School.* Boston: Houghton Mifflin Co., 1992.

——. *Horace's Compromise: The Dilemma of the American High School.* Boston: Houghton Mifflin Co., 1984.

Skinner, Quentin. "The Italian City-Republics." In *Democracy,* edited by J. Dunn, 57-70. Oxford, U.K.: Oxford University Press, 1992a.

———. "On Justice, the Common Good and the Priority of Liberty." In *Dimensions of Radical Democracy,* edited by Chantal Mouffe. New York: Verso, 1992b.

Smith, Rogers. "The 'American Creed' and American Identity." *Western Political Quarterly* 41, no. 2 (June 1988): 225-52.

Snauwaert, Dale T. *Democracy, Education, and Governance.* Albany: State University Press of New York, 1993.

Spitz, Elaine. "Citizenship and Liberal Institutions." In *Liberals on Liberalism,* edited by Alfonso J. Damico, 185-200. Totowa, N. J.: Rowman & Littlefield, 1986.

Splitter, Laurence J. "Critical Thinking: What, Why, When, and How." *Educational Philosophy and Theory* 23, no. 1 (1991): 89-109.

Stephens, Otis H., and John M. Scheb, eds. *American Constitutional Law.* New York: Harcourt Brace Jovanovich, 1988.

Stotsky, Sandra. "On Developing Independent Critical Thinking." *Written Communication* 8, no. 2 (1991a): 193-212.

———. *Connecting Civic Education and Language Education.* New York: Teachers College Press, 1991b.

Strike, Kenneth. "On the Construction of Public Speech: Pluralism and Public Reason." *Educational Theory* 44, no. 1 (1994): 1-25.

Sullivan, William M. "Bringing the Good Back In." In *Liberalism and the Good,* edited by R. Bruce Douglass, Gerald M. Mara, and Henry S. Richardson, 148-66. New York: Routledge, 1990.

———. *Reconstructing Public Philosophy.* Berkeley: University of California Press, 1982.

Takaki, Ronald. *A Different Mirror.* Boston: Little, Brown, 1993.

Tallian, Laura. *Direct Democracy: A Historical Analysis of the Initiative, Referendum, and Recall Process.* Los Angeles: People's Lobby, 1977.

Tarrant, James. *Democracy and Education.* Brookfield, Vt.: Avebury, 1989.

Taylor, Charles. "The Politics of Recognition." In *Multiculturalism: Examining the Politics of Recognition,* edited by Amy Gutmann, 25-74. Princeton, N.J.: Princeton University Press, 1994.

———. "Shared and Divergent Values." In *Options for a New Canada,* edited by Ronald L. Watts and Douglas M. Brown, 53-76. Toronto: University of Toronto Press, 1991.

———. *Sources of the Self.* Cambridge, Mass.: Harvard University Press, 1989.

———. "Overcoming Epistemology." In *After Philosophy,* edited by K. Baynes, et al., 464-88. Cambridge, Mass.: MIT Press, 1985.

———. *Philosophy and the Human Sciences.* Philosophical Papers, Vol. 2, Cambridge, U.K.: Cambridge University Press, 1985.

Thompson, Dennis. *The Democratic Citizen.* New York: Cambridge University Press, 1970.

Tocqueville, Alexis de. *Democracy in America.* Translated by George Lawrence and edited by J. P. Mayer. Garden City, N.Y.: Doubleday, 1969.

Turner, Bryan. "Outline of a Theory of Citizenship." In *Dimensions of Radical Democracy: Pluralism, Citizenship, Community,* edited by Chantal Mouffe. New York: Verso, 1992.

Vincent, Andrew, and Raymond Plant. *Philosophy, Politics, and Citizenship.* Oxford, U.K.: Blackwell, 1984.

Vogel, Ursula, and Michael Moran, eds. *The Frontiers of Citizenship.* London: Macmillan, 1991.

Vygotsky, L. S. *Thought and Language.* Cambridge, Mass.: MIT Press, 1962.

Waldron, Jeremy. "Rights and Majorities: Rousseau Revisited." In *NOMOS* 32, *Majorities and Minorities,* edited by John W. Chapman and Alan Wertheimer, 44-78. New York: New York University Press, 1990.

Walzer, Michael. "The Civil Society Argument. In *Dimensions of Radical Democracy: Pluralism, Citizenship, Community,* edited by Chantal Mouffe. New York: Verso, 1992.

——. "What Does It Mean to Be an 'American'?" *Social Research* 57, no. 3 (1990): 591-614.

——. "Citizenship." In *Political Innovation and Conceptual Change,* edited by Terence Ball, James Farr, and Russell L. Hanson, 211-19. New York: Cambridge University Press, 1989.

——. "Civility and Civic Virtue." *Social Research* 41, no. 4 (1974): 593-611.

Warehime, Nancy. *To Be One of Us: Cultural Conflict, Creative Democracy, and Education.* Albany: State University of New York Press, 1993.

Waters, Mary C. *Ethnic Options: Choosing Identities in America.* Berkeley: University of California Press, 1990.

Weber, Max. "Science as a Vocation." In *Max Weber's "Science as a Vocation,"* edited by P. Lassman and I. Velody, 3-32. London: Unwin Hyman, 1988.

Werne, Leif. "Political Liberalism: An Internal Critique." *Ethics* 106, no. 1 (1995): 32-62.

White, John. *Education and the Good Life.* New York: Teachers College Press, 1991.

White, Pat. "Education, Democracy, and the Public Interest." In *The Philosophy of Education,* edited by R. S. Peters, 217-38. London: Oxford University Press, 1973.

Whitman, Walt. *Two Rivulets.* Camden, N.J.: [Walt Whitman] 1876.

Wiebe, Robert H. *Self-Rule.* Chicago: University of Chicago Press, 1995.

Wilcox, Delos F. *Government by All the People: The Initiative, the Referenda, and the Recall as Instruments of Democracy.* New York: Macmillan, 1912.

Will, George. *Restoration.* New York: Free Press, 1992.

Williams, Melissa. "Justice toward Groups." *Political Theory* 23, no. 1 (1995): 67-91.

Williamson, Janet L. *The Greensboro Plan.* Santa Rosa, Calif.: Foundation for Critical Thinking, 1991.

Wisconsin v. Yoder, 406 U. S. 205 (1971).

Wolff, Robert Paul. *In Defense of Anarchism.* New York: Harper and Row, 1970.

Wolin, Sheldon. "The Liberal/Democratic Divide." *Political Theory* 24, no. 1 (1996): 97-119.

———. "Democracy in the Discourse of Postmodernism." *Social Research* 57, no. 1 (1990): 5-30.

———. *The Presence of the Past*. Baltimore: Johns Hopkins University Press, 1989.

———. "Why Democracy?" *democracy* 1, no. 1 (January 1981): 3-5.

Wood, Gordon S. "Inventing American Capitalism." *New York Review of Books* 41, no. 11 (9 June 1994).

———. *The Radicalism of the American Revolution*. New York: Alfred A. Knopf, 1992a.

———. "Democracy and the American Revolution." In *Democracy*, edited by J. Dunn, 91-106. Oxford, U.K.: Oxford University Press, 1992b.

———. "Democracy and the Constitution." In *How Democratic Is the Constitution?* edited by Robert A. Goldwin and William A. Schambra, 1-17. Washington, D.C.: American Enterprise Institute, 1980.

———. *The Creation of the American Republic, 1776-1787*. New York: W. W. Norton, 1972.

Wooton, David. "The Levellers." In *Democracy*, edited by John Dunn, 71-90. Oxford, U.K.: Oxford University Press, 1992.

Young, Iris Marion. "Justice and Communicative Democracy." In *Radical Philosophy: Tradition, Counter-Tradition, Politics*, edited by Roger S. Gottlieb, 123-43. Philadelphia: Temple University Press, 1993.

———. *Justice and the Politics of Difference*. Princeton, N.J.: Princeton University Press, 1990.

———. "Polity and Group Difference: A Critique of the Ideal of Universal Citizenship." *Ethics* 99, no. 2 (1989): 250-74.

Young, Robert. "Autonomy and the Inner Self." In *The Inner Citadel: Essays on Individual Autonomy*, edited by John Christman, 77-90. Oxford, U.K.: Oxford University Press, 1989.

Zapf, Rosalind M. *Democratic Processes in the Secondary Classroom*. Englewood Cliffs, N.J.: Prentice Hall, 1959.

Zinsser, William. *Writing to Learn*. New York: Harper & Row, 1988.

Zuboff, Shoshana. *Living in the Age of the Smart Machine*. New York: Basic Books, 1988.

Index

accountability, 3–4, 42, 58, 70
active thinking, 119
Adams, John, 31n2, 32n28
Adams, Samuel, 19
Adler, Mortimer, 134, 169, 178, 214
age-appropriate thinking, 183–88, 200n3
America 2000, 214–15
American Revolution, 17, 18
Amish, 43, 44–45, 47, 54n19, 92–93, 115n14
analogy, 154n27
Anti-Federalist, 18, 31n9
Appleby, Joyce, 31n7, 139
Arendt, Hannah, 142, 154n29, 168
argument network, 125–26
Aristotle, 1, 52n14, 65, 84, 108, 110, 195, 208
Aronson, Sidney, 18
artificial learning v. authentic learning, 160
assessment, 160–63
asymmetrical intensity, 197
Athenian citizenship, 110
Athenian democracy, 62, 64, 65, 76, 108, 117n27
Austin, Benjamin, 17
authentic learning v. artificial learning, 160
autonomous choosing, 45
autonomy. *See also* critical thinking; dialogue: collective, 76–78; conditions of, 73; definition of, 1; and democratic deliberation in school, 196–97; difference from freedom, 49, 55n22; education as fostering, 96; full, 74–75; and language, 40–41; meaning of, 36–40; as process, 2; relationship to

democracy, 2; as self-governing, 2–3, 4; social nature of, 6, 40–42

Bacon, Francis, 167
ballot, multichoice, 193, 197
Barber, Benjamin, 66, 68, 116n18, 193
Barfield, Owen, 143–44
Barton, J. H., 141
Battistoni, Richard, 113
Beiner, Ronald, 26, 190
Benn, Stanley, 38–39
Berthoff, Ann, 8, 135, 142, 143, 149, 159, 167, 172, 201nn5
Beyer, Landon E., 179
bigotry, 98–99
book banning, 101
Boyer, Ernest, 167
Brann, Eva, 75, 110
Braybrooke, David, 63
Brighouse, Harry, 7, 81n28, 104, 105
Brown, Harold, 52n14
Bryan, Frank, 198–99
Burke, Edmund, 65
Burnheim, John, 28
Burtt, Shelley, 93

Callan, Eamonn, 7, 9, 103, 104–5, 106, 117n21
call-in hearing, 67
candidate: choosing, 27–28; importance of money to, 28–29
careful reader, 152n11
Carter, Landon, 30n2
Chamberlin, Rosemary, 185
character, personal: formation of, 107, 108–9; relationship to critical thinking, 123–24
charter school, 174

Chipman, Nathan, 20
The Challenge of Connecting Learning,
    197
citizenship, 35, 97; Athenian, 110;
    education needed for, 83–84; as
    intellectually undemanding, 95,
    114n5; liberalism's version of,
    114n4; requirement for, 26
civic education, 90, 106–8. *See also*
    education; aim of, 103–4, 108;
    present state of, 85
civic virtue, 98
civility, 75
Civil War, 80n23
classical liberal, 74
classical republicanism, 15, 19, 31n8
classroom: democratic, 185–88; lack of
    challenge in, 125–26; number of
    students in, 215–16, 221n16;
    participation in, 75; reflective
    discussion in, 168, 170–73
class size, 215–16, 221n16
collaborative learning, 171
collective autonomy, 76–78
collective self-direction, 76
commitment, difference from devotion,
    48–49, 54n20
Committee for Economic Development,
    215
compulsory schooling, 96–97, 116n15,
    198
conflict resolution, and young children,
    204
Constant, Benjamin, 35
context-free, 40
continual v. continuous involvement, 3–4
Copenhagen, Denmark, school in, 188
counterpublics, 81n25
Countryman, Joan, 139–40
Crabtree, Charlotte, 116n14
critical reflection: and critical self-
    reflection, 83, 94; v. self-
    reflection, 102–6
critical self-reflection, 83, 94, 106
critical thinking, 1–2, 4, 39; age-
    appropriate, 183–88, 200n3; and
    character, 123–24; failure of
    school to teach, 120–21, 198,
    207; as field-specific (*See*
    McPeck, John); as generalizable

skill, 130, 134, 135, 136 (*See also*
    Paul, Richard; Siegel, Harvey);
    at post secondary level, 127–28;
    purpose of, 142; teaching (*See*
    teaching critical thinking);
    teaching across the curriculum, 7;
    through writing, 136–40; weak v.
    strong, 126, 128, 129
Cronin, Thomas, 27, 68
cultural imperialism, 43
curriculum: for deliberation, 4–5; issue-
    analysis, 114n8

Dagger, Richard, 78n5, 203n22
Dahl, Robert, 16, 62, 63
Darling-Hammond, 221n16
debate, as different from reflective
    discussion, 172
deliberation, 60–65, 95; elements of, 4;
    relationship to democracy, 95
deliberative decision making, lack of
    opportunity for, 1–2, 4, 6, 13
deliberative democracy, 5, 11n2, 61, 83,
    88, 192–200
democracy. *See also* deliberative
    democracy; liberal democracy:
    Athenian, 62, 64, 65, 76, 108,
    117n27; basis of, 91; as collective
    autonomy, 76–78; definition of,
    3; Madisonian, 63, 64, 79n12; as
    process, 2; relationship to
    autonomy, 2; relationship to
    deliberation, 95
democratic classroom, 185–88
democratic dialogue, 172–73
democratic discussion, 184–85
democratic education, 81n28, 86–90, 89,
    93, 109
democratic school, 7, 109–10, 179–84;
    classroom in, 185–88; democratic
    assembly/ward in, 188–89;
    discussion in, 184–85; pooling
    perspectives in, 189–90; school
    newspaper in, 205n39; scrutiny of
    perspectives in, 190–91; small
    group conference in, 191; voting
    in, 191–92
democratic standard, 47, 173–79
democratic state of education, 86
democratization, 25

devotion, difference from commitment, 48–49, 54n20

Dewey, John, 5, 110; on active thinking, 119; and classroom questioning method, 168; on conflict, 197; on full education, 183; on reflective thinking, 136, 152n12 & 14, 177; on student interest, 159–60, 178–79; on student participation in democracy, 181–82

diagramming sentence, 160

dialectical reasoning, 124–25

dialectic of social inquiry, 59

dialogic democracy, 59

dialogue, 4–5, 58, 119, 149, 168, 172–73

dialogue journal, 158, 168, 200n1

Diamond, Martin, 16

Dietze, Gottfried, 24–25

direct democracy, 35

direct primary, 28, 32n32

discretion, derivation of, 32n23

discursive writing, 138, 145, 153n20

"The Disharmony of Democracy" (Gutmann), 3

diversity, 35–36, 43, 46, 47, 89–90, 103, 104, 210. *See also* multiculturalism

domestic tranquillity, 36

Dworkin, Gerald, 51n8

Easley, Jack, 171–72

education. *See also* civic education; compulsory schooling; education in deliberation; education standard; school; student: adequate, 92–97; aim of, 86; authority in, 87, 92; for citizenship, 83–84; democratic, 81n28, 86–90, 89, 93, 109; as fostering autonomy, 96; government role in, 89–90; in inform discretion, 22–23; in Japan, 151n4; liberal, 89, 119; and literacy, 95–96, 97; and nondiscrimination, 87; and parents, 85, 86, 87, 89, 90–91, 94, 100; philosophical, 106–7, 108; primary, 107; voucher program in, 87

education for autonomy, 1, 102

education in autonomy, 1, 102

education in deliberation, 1, 4, 88–89, 97; compulsory participation in, 194–95; as democracy's midwife, 5; as encouraging activism, 5

education standard, 199, 200; minimum, 91–92, 94, 95, 97, 115n13

education theory/practice, relationship to political theory/practice, 8

egalitarianism, 35, 100

Eichmann, Adolph, 154n29

electoral system, 59

elementary student: deliberative education of, 197; and democratic discussion, 184–87, 188

elitism, 10, 62

Elster, Jon, 52n14

Emerson, Ralph W., 194

Engle, 102, 106, 116n20

enlightened understanding, 62–63

essay writing, 138–39, 140–43

essential interest, 50–51n6

ethical servility, 9, 103, 104, 105

faction, political, 16

family state, and education, 85

Federalists, 14–15, 17, 18–19, 24, 31n9, 32n28

Ferguson, Thomas, 28

Fishkin, James, 7, 60, 62–64, 79n12

Forbes, Steve, 32n31

formal operational thought, 37

Founding Fathers, 2, 14, 25. *See also* Hamiltion, Alexander; Jefferson, Thomas; Madison, James

Framers, of U.S. Constitution, 6, 25–26, 28, 29–30, 88

Fraser, Nancy, 72, 81n25

freedom, difference from autonomy, 49, 55n22

full autonomy, 74–75

full literacy, 203n22

fundamentalist Christian, 94

fundamentalist parent, 103

fundamentalist school, 176, 177

fundraising, political, 29

Gadamer, 59

Galston, William, 7, 59, 90–91, 93, 98, 102, 106–8

Gardner, Howard, 159, 173, 174, 175
generative procedure, 78n6, 204n36
Glickman, Carl, 179–81
Goodlad, John, 120
good life, 209; Amish view of, 45; liberal
    values for, 36; limited range of,
    98–101; and self-reflection, 58–
    59, 209
good reason, 122–23
grammar, 144–50, 174, 175
Gray, John, 50–51n6
Greene, Nathanael, 30–31n2
Greensboro Plan. *See* Reasoning and
    Writing Project
group identity, 54n20
guardian democracy, 24
Gutmann, Amy, 7, 93, 176; on
    accountability, 3–4; on aim of
    primary education, 107; on
    autonomy, 3; on bigotry and
    children, 98–99; on character
    formation, 108–9; on
    deliberation, 60, 94, 95, 106, 120;
    on deliberative democracy, 3, 5;
    on democratic education, 81n28,
    86–90, 109; on dialogue and
    reason, 119; on education in
    deliberation, 88–89; on
    egalitarianism/sexism, 100; on
    family state, 86; on good life, 98;
    on government role in education,
    89–90; on minimum standard of
    education, 94, 95; on mutual
    respect, 53–54n18, 81n26; on
    nonrepression, 87, 89, 101; on
    right reason, 99–100; on self-
    government, 3; on self-reflection,
    102; on self v. critical reflection,
    76; on state of families, 86, 100;
    on state of individuals, 86; on
    value of liberty, 3; on values for
    democratic state, 94

Habermas, 40, 53n18, 63, 81n25, 81n29
Hacker, Andrew, 209–10
Hamilton, Alexander, 18, 57, 60–61, 83
Hawkins, David, 159
Head Start, 215
Heidegger, Martin, 54n20
Henn, T. R., 135–36

Henrion, Claudia, 153n23
hermeneutical judgment, 190
home school, 91, 94, 97, 200
Horton, Susan R., 142
House of Representatives, incumbent in,
    29–30, 33n34
Howard, V. A., 141

ideal speech situation, 63
identity, 39–40, 54n20
illiteracy, 85, 96, 116n18
incumbent, 29–30, 33n34
independence, 39–40
individualism, 97
individual rights, 36
indoctrination, 108, 175–76, 200
information superhighway, 150n2
inherited life, 91, 92, 93–94. *See also*
    Amish; effect of scrutinizing on,
    89, 98, 115n14
initiative, politics of, 66–68
inner-city school, 178. *See also* public
    school, unequal funding of;
    teacher, disparity in salary for
intersubjective validation, 42

Japan, education in, 151n4
Jefferson, Thomas, 25, 30, 32n22, 60, 64,
    77–78, 81n30, 200; democratic
    vision of, 6, 20–23, 59, 64, 65–66
judgment, 52n14, 106–13

Kasulis, Thomas, 186
Kateb, George, 40, 59
Kornfeld, John, 181
Kozol, Jonathan, 210–11
Krauthammer, Charles, 26
Kraybill, Donald, 44
Kuhn, Thomas, 52n14

Langer, 139
language: and autonomy, 40–41; mode of,
    167–68
language of disciplines, 133–34
Lawson, Anton, 158–59, 200
learning: artificial/authentic, 160;
    collaborative, 171
liberal democracy, 13–14, 23–30, 36
liberal education, 89, 119
liberal idealism, 8–9

liberalism, 35
"liberalism with spine," 9, 53n15
liberal neutrality, 86
liberal state, as softly neutral, 9
liberal values/rights, 36–37
liberty, 36
linguistic intelligence, 174
listening-point circle, 186
literacy, 95–96, 97, 203n22
living standard, 220–21n10
Locke, John, 151n8
logic, 130, 131, 134
logically completed debate, 63
loyalty, 108
Lucas, J. R., 187
Lukes, Steven, 41

Macedo, Stephen, 7, 8, 46, 53n15, 53n17, 58, 76, 103–4
Madison, James, 6, 24, 60–61; view on representative government, 14–16, 18, 19
Madison, Wisconsin, school at, 187
Madisonian democracy, 63, 64, 79n12
Maimon, Elaine, 141
Mansbridge, Jane, 66, 205n37
Manville, Philip Brook, 110, 117n27
mathematics, 139–40, 153n23
McDonald, Forrest, 24
McGinley, 201n7
McLean, Iain, 66
McPeck, John, 7; on critical thinking, 122, 129–36; on critical thinking as field-/subject-dependent, 129–30, 134–35; on language of disciplines, 133–34; on logic, 130, 131; on philosophy, 132; on reading, 132–33; on reflective skepticism, 130–31; on teaching critical thinking, 134; on thinking/discussion, 169–70; on writing, 132–33, 135; on writing/reading, 132–33
Meier, Deborah, 215–16
Mendus, Susan, 43, 44, 47, 48, 53n15
metacognition, 177
Meyers, Diana, 51n10
middle school student, and democratic discussion, 187–88

Mill, John Stuart, 5–6, 23, 37–38, 50–51n6, 53n17, 72
minimum standard, in education, 91–92, 94, 95, 97, 115n13
minority student, 213
mission, of public education, 8
Mitchell, Richard, 137, 144–45, 146, 147–48, 163
Morris, Gouverneur, 33n33
Morse, Jedidiah, 31n3
Moses, Robert, 178–79
Mouffe, Chantel, 84
Mozert v. Hawkins, 103
multichoice ballot, 68, 193, 197
multiculturalism, 72, 136, 173, 175, 209
mutual respect, 36, 53–54n18, 73, 89, 95, 185

National Caucus, 79n10
national initiative, 68, 69, 80n17
neutrality, 52n15
Newell, 138–39
nomos, 38, 39, 40
nondiscrimination, and education, 87
nonrepression, principle of, 87, 89, 101
Norman, Richard, 74–75

Oakeshott, Michael, 193
Ochoa, Anna S., 102, 106, 116n20
openness, 36, 46, 48, 50n3, 53–54n18, 74

parent: and education, 85, 86, 87, 89, 90–91, 94, 100; fundamentalist, 103; religious, 115n13
parental choice, in education, 87
parental education, 92
participation, 9, 109, 111, 205n37; duty to/not to, 112; limiting, 14–15, 16, 17, 18, 31n8; and politics of initiative, 68–70, 72–74
Paul, Richard, 7, 121; on critical thinking, 124–29; on teachers, 168; on writing, 133
personal intelligences, 175
Peters, R. S., 183
philosophical education, 106–7, 108
philosophy, 132
phronesis. See judgment
Piaget, Jean, 37, 115–16n14, 183, 200n3, 201n4

Pierce v. Society of Sisters, 92
Plato, 110, 184
plebiscite, difference from politics of
    initiative, 68
pluralism, 9–10, 36, 39, 58, 70, 86, 209
political conflict, 71–73
political education, 92
political equality, 216–17
political faction, 16
political party, candidate selection by, 28,
    29
political theory/practice, relationship to
    education theory/practice, 8
politics, indifference to, 26–27
politics of initiative, 7, 67–74, 77;
    difference from plebiscite, 68;
    and political conflict, 71–73; and
    political leadership, 68; and
    political participation, 68–70, 72–
    74
populism, 5
portfolio, 161
Postman, Neil, 152n11
Pratte, Richard, 204n31
primary, 28–29, 32–33n32
principles, and reason, 122–23
prison budget, 221n10
private deliberation, 88
private school, 91, 94, 200
public education, mission of, 8. *See also*
    education
public opinion, 68
public/private separation, 36, 71–72, 77,
    89
public school. *See also* education
    standard; school: class
    segregation in, 209, 210; class
    size in, 215–16; compulsory
    attendance for, 96–97, 116n15,
    198; deliberative curriculum for,
    4–5; readiness measures for, 214–
    15; resources for, 8, 216; safety
    in, 8, 213–14; unequal funding of,
    210–13, 216, 222n20
punctuation, and meaning, 146, 148

questioning, in critical thinking, 125
Quincy, Josiah, 18

rational inquiry, 106–7, 108

rationality, 38, 39, 40, 41, 42, 52–53n14,
    52n12, 60, 176–77
Rawls, John, 8–9, 53n15, 53n17, 54n17
Raywid, Mary Ann, 194
reading, 132–33; importance of, 146; self-
    directed, 201n7
reasonableness, 36
Reasoning and Writing Project, 165–67
reflective discussion, in classroom, 170–
    73
reflective skepticism, 130–31, 151–52n10
reflective thinking, 152n12
reflective thought, 152n14
religious cult, 49
religious diversity, 103
religious fundamentalist, 46, 54n18
religious parent, 199
religious zealot, 49
Renewing America's Schools (Glickman),
    179–80
representative democracy, 4, 5, 13, 24, 35,
    59, 64, 180; decision making in,
    1–2; necessity of affective ties to,
    113
Resnick, Daniel, 121, 178
Resnick, Lauren, 214
rights/responsibilities, 111–12
Rogers, Joel, 28
Roosevelt, Franklin D., 83
Rousseau, Jean-Jacques, 23, 32n25, 57

safety, in public school, 8, 213–14
Salkever, Stephen, 110
Sandel, Michael, 49, 54n20
Sanders, Barry, 149, 202n19, 203n22
Sanders, Lynn, 11n2
Savage Inequalities (Kozol), 210–11
scholarly writing, 135
school. *See also* public school: difference
    from political community, 194;
    differences among, 220n7;
    fundamentalist, 176, 177; home,
    91, 94, 97, 200; private, 91, 94,
    200
school choice, 174
schooling, compulsory, 96–97, 116n15,
    198
school safety, 8, 213–14
Schrag, Francis, 134, 151n10
Scriven, Michael, 132, 134

secondary school student, deliberative education of, 197–98
self-criticism, 53n17
self-definition, 37
self-directed reading, 201n7
self-direction, collective, 76
self-examination, 91
self-governing, and self-ruling, 208–9
self-reflection, 37–39, 40, 41, 42; and commitment, 48; and critical thinking, 126–27; effect of socialization on, 51–52n10; as hallmark of autonomy, 1, 4; v. critical reflection, 102–6
self-reflective choice, 86
self-ruling. *See* autonomy
Senate, incumbent in, 33n34
separation of church/state, 46–47
sexism, 100
Shanker, Albert, 212
Shapiro, Ian, 44
Shuy, Roger, 157–58, 200n1
Siegel, Harvey, 7, 122–24, 128
Sizer, Theodore, 109, 186, 204n29, 209
slavery, 80n23
Smaller Schools of Smaller Classes, 202–3n20
social inquiry, 59
social studies, 116n20
Socrates, 168, 202n18
soft liberal neutrality, 9, 45–50
South Africa, open election in, 85
speaking, and grammar, 144–45
standardized test, 120–21, 131, 160
state, and imposing autonomy on students, 1, 6, 77
state education, 92
state of families, and education, 86
state of individuals, and education, 86
Stosky, Sandra, 150
student, performance of, 213, 221n15
student-teacher ratio, 202n20
student/teacher relationship, 170–71, 185, 187, 200n2
subject-neutral principle, 122–23
subject-specific principle, 122, 123
suffrage, 26

Taylor, Charles, 36, 41, 42, 51n6

teacher, disparity in salary for, 216, 221n18
teaching critical thinking, 157–60; assessment in, 160–63; Greensboro Plan, 165–67; reading/speaking/listening, 167–73; teacher training for, 163–65
Teaching Critical Thinking (McPeck), 132
teaching to the test, 151n4
theory, derivation of, 154n26
thick promotion, of values, 46, 47
thin promotion, of values, 46–47
Thompson, Dennis; on deliberation, 60; on dialogue and reason, 119; on mutual respect, 81n26
thoughtfulness, 106–13
throwness, 54n20
Tierney, 201n7
Tocqueville, Alexis de, 17, 31n7, 77, 81n30, 96, 205n37, 218, 219
tolerance, 36, 43, 46, 47–48, 50n3, 53n18, 90, 103
Toleration and the Limits of Liberalism (Mendus), 43
town meeting, 62, 64, 67, 198
township, 22
traditionalist, 48, 49
trivium, 152–53n15
"two hooks of the government," 6, 20

unexamined life, as worth living, 90–91
U.S. Constitution, 16, 17–18

values, 3, 36, 46–47, 94, 110–11
virtue, classical, 19, 31n7
vote, value of, 2, 10n1, 88, 114n6
voting, 26, 88
voucher program, in education, 87
Vygotsky, L. S., 200n2

ward, 20
ward democracy, 20–23, 59, 66, 67
Washington, George, 30n2
Weber, Max, 58
Webster, Noah, 65
welfare state, 36
Whigs, 32n27
Whitehead, Alfred North, 138
Whitman, Walt, 30

WIC, 215
Wiebe, Robert H., 17
Wilcox, Delos, 68–69
Wilde, Oscar, 69
Will, George, 7, 60–61, 63, 65
Williamson, Janet, 166–67
Wisconsin v. Yoder, 54n19, 92–93
Wittgenstein, 132, 133, 136, 147
Wolff, Robert Paul, 78n5, 79n12
Wolin, Sheldon, 24, 27, 83, 88, 208, 209
Wood, Gordon, 16, 17–18, 19, 31n8
Wooten, David, 28
writing, 135–36; across curriculum, 139–
        40; as communication, 136, 141–
        42; composing, 142–43; critical
        thinking through, 4, 7, 136–40;
        difference from lecturing, 138,
        202n19; essay writing, 138–39,
        140–43; and grammar, 144–50;
        importance of practicing, 138–39,
        148, 157; and mathematics, 139–
        40; permanence of, 137; pre-
        seventh century, 202n19; in
        testing, 161
Writing across the Curriculum, 139
WuDunn, Sheryl, 151n4

Young, Iris Marion, 54n20

Zinsser, William, 135, 139
Zuboff, Shoshana, 116n15

About the Author

Jack Crittenden is Associate Professor of Political Science at Arizona State University, where he teaches political theory. He is also a member of the Board of Directors of the Integral Institute of Boulder, Colorado, as well as a member of its Politics Branch and Chief Facilitator of its Education Branch. The author of *Beyond Individualism* (1992), he is currently working on a book on cosmopolitan politics.